# LET THE WISDOM
# OF YOUR SOUL TRANSFORM
# YOUR BODY AND YOUR LIFE

Illness, unresolved emotional issues, and patterns of thinking are actually coded messages from your own soul. *The Energy Body Connection* teaches you the truth about these major soul imprints and shows you how to fully embody your own spirit essence.

This embodiment process acknowledges emotions and physical problems as signposts of transformation. Instead of denying them, you can restructure their energy patterns, awakening your body's cells and tissues through the infusion of a loving spiritual presence.

*The Energy Body Connection* presents many new insights into the human energy field, including:

- How archetypal soul patterns influence your personal growth and the process of disease

- How planetary fields affect the human energy system

- How to reclaim energetically lost parts of yourself

Let *The Energy Body Connection* be your guide to spiritual expansion as you explore different dimensions of transformation and healing.

# ABOUT THE AUTHOR

Pamela Welch, M.A., is a psychotherapist, counseling astrologer, and healer who specializes in working with adult children of dysfunctional families and issues of spiritual awakening. She holds a Master's degree in Humanistic Psychology and is a certified Gestalt therapist, a trained hypnotherapist, and certified massage therapist, as well. In addition, Pamela has training in numerous other body-mind healing modalities and vibrational healing systems, including homeopathy, cranial-sacral therapy, and various forms of energy healing.

Pamela's interest in spiritual development and the hermetic sciences began over twenty-five years ago during ten years of intensive study with an esoteric teaching order. She has been teaching others about meditation, healing, and spiritual growth since that time, and her published articles have appeared in national astrology magazines. Pamela maintains a private psychotherapy, energy healing, and counseling astrology practice in Denver, Colorado.

# TO WRITE THE AUTHOR

If you wish to contact the author or would like more information about this book, please write to the author in care of Llewellyn Worldwide and we will forward your request. Both the author and publisher appreciate hearing from you and learning of your enjoyment of this book and how it has helped you. Llewellyn Worldwide cannot guarantee that every letter written to the author can be answered, but all will be forwarded. Please write to:

Pamela Welch
℅ Llewellyn Worldwide
P.O. Box 64383, Dept. K-819
St. Paul, MN 55164-0383, U.S.A.

Please enclose a self-addressed stamped envelope for reply, or $1.00 to cover costs. If outside U.S.A., enclose international postal reply coupon.

PAMELA WELCH, M.A.

# THE
# ENERGY BODY
# CONNECTION

## THE HEALING EXPERIENCE
## OF SELF-EMBODIMENT

2000
Llewellyn Worldwide
St. Paul, Minnesota 55164-0383, U.S.A.

FIRST EDITION
First Printing, 1999

Cover design by William Merlin Cannon
Editing and book design by Astrid Sandell
Excerpt on page 289 reprinted by permission of Jeremy P. Tarcher, Inc., a division of Penguin Putnam Inc. from *Joy's Way* by Brugh Joy. Copyright ©1979 by W. Brugh Joy, M.D.
Excerpt on page 56 copyright ©1992 by Percy Seymour. From *The Scientific Basis of Astrology: Tuning to the Music of the Planets* by Percy Seymour. Reprinted by permission of St. Martin's Press, Incorporated.
Excerpt on page 4 reprinted by permission of the author, Fred Alan Wolf from his book *The Body Quantum: The New Physics of Body, Mind, and Health.*
Excerpt on page 44 from *Psyche and Substance,* by Edward C. Whitmont. Copyright ©1980. Used with permission of North Atlantic Books, Berkeley, CA.
Excerpt on page 152 reprinted by permission of the author and publisher. Fritz Perls, *Gestalt Approach and Eyewitness to Therapy.* Science and Behavior Books, Inc., Palo Alto, CA.

**Library of Congress Cataloging-in-Publication Data**
Welch, Pamela, 1950–
   The energy body connection : the healing experience of self embodiment /
Pamela Welch. — 1st ed.
      p. cm.
   Includes bibliographical references and index.
   ISBN 1-56718-819-2
      1. Mental healing. 2. Chakras. 3. Mind and body—Health aspects. I. Title.

RZZ401 .W44 2000
615.8'9—dc21                                                                99-045445

Llewellyn Publications
A Division of Llewellyn Worldwide, Ltd.
P.O. Box 64383, Dept. K819
St. Paul, MN 55164-0383, U.S.A.
www.llewellyn.com

Printed in the United States of America

# DEDICATION

This book is dedicated to my daughter, Lisa,
and the divine love of the One Heart within each of us.

# AUTHOR'S NOTE

The intention of this book is to give you information that can assist you in your process of personal growth and self-discovery. The skills contained here, which reflect the personal experience of the author and many individuals with whom she has worked, are not a substitute for good medical care or psychotherapy. The author of this book does not dispense medical or psychiatric advice nor prescribe any technique as a form of treatment for medical or psychological problems without the advice of a physician or other healthcare professional. All names of clients used in this text have been changed to protect their privacy and maintain anonymity.

# CONTENTS

# ACKNOWLEDGMENTS

I would like to acknowledge all the teachers and healers who have, through the years, been joint midwives in my own process of healing and growth. A special thanks to Anne DeChenne for both her ideas on weekly meditations and several great affirmations. Her consciousness and spiritual gifts have had a deep impact on both my personal spiritual awakening and my work with others. Many blessings to Tirzah Firestone who, during my dark night of the soul, helped me to believe in myself again, and to Ray McCall whose bodywork has been an essential part of my personal growth. Thanks also go out to Dr. Nicholas Nossaman, Lightsong Wolters, and Dr. Robert Jaffe for their wonderful healing skills, and to Grandfather Peter Koyote for his encouraging words. I also want to acknowledge Cher and Charles Bebeau, the teachers who first helped me see the archetypes through the planetary lens. I deeply appreciate all of the clients who, through their work with me, have contributed to this book.

# INTRODUCTION

**WELCOME TO *THE ENERGY BODY CONNECTION*,** a guide to your process of personal growth, healing, and spiritual awakening. If you currently have physical problems, unresolved emotional issues, mental patterns that no longer serve you, or if you seek a sense of purpose and meaning to your life, this book can help you on your journey of healing and self-improvement. In addition, if you are seeking to develop a connection with the Creative Source and to more fully realize your own spirit essence, this work can assist you in your process of unfolding consciousness.

In my view, there is really no separation between these two things, between healing and the evolution of consciousness. In order to know the truth of your own being, all that is not of that true Self, everything that separates you from your divine essence within must be revealed. Much of what we think about ourselves is distorted information that we've internalized from culture, society, and our families of origin. These misconceptions with regard to our essential nature, and the wounds to the self relating to them, must be healed before we can experience true spiritual awakening. For this reason, the process of emotional healing will enhance and ground your spiritual practice. At the same time, I find that when the spiritual dimension is incorporated into the work of personal growth and healing, the process becomes much more effective and efficient as a result.

The information presented in this book will address the whole person that you are—the spiritual, mental, emotional, physical, and energetic dimensions of your being. One of my intentions with this book is to help heal the split that has existed within individuals and within our culture between body and spirit. In the past, obtaining spiritual enlightenment has often involved a path of denying the body, the emotions, and the instinctual desires. In striving toward a spiritual ideal, many people have left a consciousness of their bodies behind. However, true self-development and spiritual awareness is not found through excluding whole parts of our being in this way. After all, how can one possibly succeed in a process of self-discovery through hiding away parts of the self that one is seeking to know!

Instead of denying emotions and physical problems, this embodiment process acknowledges them as signposts of transformation. The body, mind, and emotions can then be transformed as part of a more unified spiritual consciousness. In this way, the very cells and tissues of the body can be awakened through the infusion of a spiritual presence. What is then gained is the wisdom born of spirit fully penetrating matter, the God Self radiantly embodied. This is what embodiment means, realizing the divine Self within and fully manifesting it in physical form.

Embodiment is, by its nature, a spiritual path. However, I have used the processes and teachings in this book with individuals who were either unaware of any spiritual reality or who had no specific intention for spiritual growth. They then became interested in consciously developing a greater connection to Spirit after opening to a more expansive and creative place within themselves through these processes.

I was inspired to write this book both because my clients desired information on working with their process independently, and because I saw that people had some confusion with regard to spiritual growth. Some individuals were using meditation techniques and metaphysical principles in order to avoid their problems and escape from physical reality. Others were being misled by spiritual leaders who seemed more interested in gaining power for themselves. As more metaphysical ideas entered the main stream of thought, I also heard terms such as *karma* or *ego* being misused and misunderstood. I felt that what was needed was a commonsense, practical approach to healing, personal growth, and spiritual development that would empower people in their experience of the Creative Source and their own essence Self. In addition to my work with clients, my own personal healing journey and spiritual quest has led me to believe in the importance of the body as part of this process.

I was scarcely aware that I had a body for a good part of my life. I now know that this type of separation from the body—or dissociation as it's called—is common to people who have experienced some type of abuse or physical trauma. I remember at the age of eight, my mother started me ice skating in the hope that it would somewhat ground me, help my concentration, and bring me some physical integration. It helped me somewhat, at least my school grades improved. I was intelligent and athletic, but things felt strangely disconnected. My boundless energy was fragmented and erratic, much like electrical energy with no place to ground.

As a young woman, I spent the '70s dedicated to my spiritual enlightenment. It is no great surprise that I chose to work with a spiritual group that paid little attention to the physical or emotional realms. I meditated, prayed, studied the great universal

*[handwritten margin note: Object from a place of consciousness or awareness]*

truths, and tried desperately to transcend the body and the emotions. I thought that I had transformed many of my problems. In reality, I was in a state of deep denial and had no idea what my true emotional issues were.

As part of my participation in this spiritual organization, I facilitated a healing group. I discovered how the mind can affect the physical body through prayer and affirmations, and also became interested in the process of inner healing, the healing of past emotional wounds. I began to realize the importance of the emotional component in healing and wanted to know more. I wanted to explore the body-mind connection further.

Then in 1979, I made a move which would change my life. I enrolled in massage school. As part of my training, I had body massages all the time and a whole new world opened up to me. I began to experience more conscious awareness of bodily sensations and feelings. However, although I loved the touch and the sensuality of massage, I also found that it was difficult for me to relax and let go of control. There were many uncomfortable feelings locked inside and held in my body. As bodywork went deeper into my tissues, releasing armored muscles, a door leading deep into my own psyche opened up. A lifetime of stored emotions came flooding forth like a tidal wave. I found that my experiences also had a spiritual component. The type of expansive sensations and visions that I was having were similar to what I had experienced in meditation. Only they now had depth and power that I had never felt before.

One such experience happened one day after a bodywork session that involved work on my legs and lower body. I got up and started to get dressed when I began feeling very peculiar, as if I had crossed over into another world. I was very self-conscious, not knowing if I looked as weird as I felt. I don't know what I was mumbling, but David, my bodyworker said, "It's all right to be yourself. I like who you are." This statement touched a deep place within me and I started to cry, a full-body sobbing.

As I settled in and allowed myself to feel this, something else began to happen. A rush of energy like a thundering waterfall began moving through my whole body, all along my spine. The sensation focused in my lower abdomen, like a huge column consisting of some unseen vibrating force. It got heavier and heavier, pulling me downward, down into my core and into the very guts of my being. The words that I heard inside me said that my freedom was buried in the consciousness of this place, deep within my abdomen. The cost of that freedom was surrender to the realm of the body, feelings, and instinctual wisdom. I felt enfolded in what I can only describe as a wonderful feminine presence, like the nature of creation itself. This feminine energy seemed to be calling me home to a place deep inside me in a powerful way. Suddenly, I had a grounded presence in my body that I had never felt before. Luckily, I was lying down when all this started happening, the experience was so intense and physically overwhelming that for some time I could hardly move.

I had studied a bit about the chakras—the energy centers of the body—and knew that the bodywork that day had facilitated a powerful release affecting the second chakra. However, this intellectual understanding couldn't compare to the illuminating presence that I felt within me that day. I realized that the path of my own healing had been shown to me. Freedom and spiritual awakening could only be obtained by delving deeper into the body and the subconscious mind. This and subsequent experiences showed me that the body was more than just a temple or vehicle for the Spirit. Spirit and matter were integrally connected like strands of a woven fabric.

As my journey of self-discovery continued, I sought to heal the emotional wounds of my past through the process of psychotherapy. As I experimented with different approaches, I sometimes became frustrated. I enjoyed the body-centered therapies, but found that some were causally based and often centered on a disease model, which saw things in terms of what needed to be "fixed." I knew that certain life events could create a particular psychological state and somatic patterns of armored muscular tension. Yet, I saw a greater process going on. My experiences had shown me that the body provided an opportunity for transformation, for spiritual as well as personal growth. I felt that there was a whole dimension that many of these therapies were missing.

I was also drawn to Jungian and Transpersonal approaches.[1] These therapies validated my spiritual experiences and gave me a greater depth of understanding about them. However, I missed the emotional release of body-centered approaches.[2] In my process of healing and growth, I ended up going to several different types of therapists to get the pieces that I needed. Today, through the work of Arnold Mindell, a greater understanding and utilization of the symbolic processes of the body has enhanced the Jungian perspective.[3] Likewise, many body-centered therapies have also now expanded to incorporate a Transpersonal view.

First in my work as a massage therapist, and later as a psychotherapist, I found that each person's multidimensionality has to be acknowledged and engaged. There is a healing intelligence within us that expresses itself through our spiritual, mental, emotional, and physical levels of being. By acknowledging each of these aspects and consciously inviting them to participate in your process, a powerful synergistic force is made available for your healing and growth. Mental beliefs, developmental issues and emotional expression, somatic information, dreams, and expansive spiritual experiences are all important and provide you with information leading you to a deeper realization of your own being.

I was able to directly experience the transformational power of such a multidimensional approach during my own personal healing crisis. At a time in my life when I was open to a greater influx of spiritual energies, I was also in the midst of severe emotional trauma and depression. My own healing journey taught me what I needed to know in order to help others heal, grow personally, and expand spiritually. This book introduces the methods that I use to assist people in this process. It is an eclectic approach, since I have gained from many different modalities in my own process of healing and spiritual growth. Throughout this book, I also refer to various other techniques or books that you may find helpful on your own journey.

# HOW TO USE THIS BOOK

The first two chapters of this book will define the body-mind, explain the dynamics of the human energy system, and provide a framework for your process of personal growth and spiritual discovery. You will also identify essential soul qualities that you can experience more deeply as you proceed through the book. The information presented in this section lays a foundation by giving you some idea of the psychospiritual territory you will be covering on your journey. It can be likened to having an accurate map with you on a hike. It can't tell you what trails to take or what specific experiences you will have, but it does act as a guide you can refer to when you need to orient yourself to your surroundings.

The ideas contained here provide you with a useful perspective from which to work. They are meant to inform you and act as a helpful starting point in your own process of self-discovery. If there are things you don't agree with or that don't fit into your personal system of beliefs, please keep what is useful for you in the material and leave the rest. The exercises provided throughout this book will help you to discover the truth for yourself, based on your own experiences.

The book continues by guiding you through the various facets of your journey to Self, providing tools that will assist you on your path. Each section of the text emphasizes a particular aspect of this process by focusing on a different dimension of your spiritual, mental, emotional, and physical experience. Chapters 3 and 4 address the mental level, helping you to discipline your thinking mind and direct your consciousness through affirmations, journal writing, and meditation. Quieting the thinking mind through the techniques presented here allows you to connect with the deeper dimensions of your being, which are further utilized in subsequent chapters.

Chapters 5 and 6 focus on the body and emotions, helping you to listen the messages of your sensate-feeling self in order to transform physical problems and related emotional issues. You will also be learning how to reclaim lost parts of yourself, emotionally and energetically, in order to become the whole radiant being that you truly are. Chapter 7 provides an additional tool for exploring your subconscious feelings by aiding you in discovering the meaning of your dreams. Chapters 8 and 9 further your spiritual development by helping you learn how to work with healing light, spirit helpers, sacred ceremony, and expansive initiatory experiences. Chapter 9 concludes with the Light Embodiment process, enabling you to more fully embody your own spirit essence by seeding in the soul qualities that you discovered earlier in the book.

The various segments of this book are designed to be used together in order to provide a multidimensional approach to your process of self-discovery. The affirmations, meditations, and guided visualizations contained herein will be more effective if they are used along with the core emotional healing processes found in chapters 5 and 6. Clearing emotional content from the body-mind in this way will enable you to realize more of your spiritual nature. Using the many spiritual resources presented here will then, in turn, provide a support for your experience of emotional growth and healing.

The processes in this book are also meant to be used over a period of time for the various aspects of your personal growth. For example, chapter 4, Awareness and Meditation, contains meditation exercises designed to be experienced over a two-month period. During that time, you might also choose to use the information in chapter 7 to explore several of your dreams, receive information on a physical symptom through the exercises contained in chapter 5, or resolve an inner conflict with the healing processes found in chapter 6. You may want to do many of the exercises when initially reading the whole book through, and then refer back to various sections of the text for the specific processes that you want to continue to use. As you proceed with this, be sure to go at your own pace. There is an abundance of information contained here, and it will take time to integrate it.

As you get a sense of how your own process of healing and growth is unfolding, pay attention to what your specific needs are spiritually, mentally, emotionally, and physically. Most individuals will find it helpful or even necessary at some point in their lives to obtain the assistance of a professional therapist in working with aspects of their emotional growth. Others will benefit from a support group or a meditation circle to assist them on their journey. Remember, however, that in working with others or with the processes in this book, you are always the one responsible for your own healing. If it feels like there is something more that you need for yourself, follow that guidance.

We are now living in a time of great change and accelerated transformation. It will be continually important, in the days to come, to have ways of addressing the issues of our spiritual awakening in order to assist our personal evolution. My intention is that each one of you reading this book and working with the processes contained within it will, in some way, experience a deeper realization of your own creative essence and carry that awakened consciousness into the world.

## Notes

1.  Transpersonal is a word used to define therapeutic approaches that acknowledge the spiritual dimension and recognize the potential for experiencing states of consciousness that extend beyond the usual limits of ego and personality. See Frances Vaughan, Ph.D., *The*

*Inward Arc: Healing in Psychotherapy and Spirituality*, 2nd ed. (Nevada City, CA: Blue Dolphin Publishing, Inc., 1995). Also see, Roger Walsh, M.D., Ph.D. and Frances Vaughan, Ph.D. (ed.), *Paths Beyond Ego: The Transpersonal Vision*. (New York: Jeremy P. Tarcher/Putnam, 1993). Jungian psychology also addresses such numinous experiences.

2. There were some exceptions to my experiences that blended Transpersonal and body-centered perspectives such as certain types of Transpersonal breathwork.

3. Arnold Mindell, *Dreambody: The Body's Role in Revealing the Self* (Portland, OR: Lao Tse Press, 1997). Arnold Mindell, *Working with the Dreaming Body*. New York: Viking Penguin, 1989.

# PART I

## The Map

# 1

# BODY, MIND, SPIRIT

### *The Human Energy System*

**MANY PEOPLE ARE EITHER NOT AWARE** or not convinced that a relationship exists between mental-emotional states and physical experience. However, in light of the discoveries made in the fields of neuroscience and quantum physics, the existence of a body-mind connection can no longer be denied.[1] It is now known, for instance, that information-transmitting substances in the body, called neuropeptides, are the biochemical links to our mental and emotional experience. These chemical messengers, which are secreted from nerve and immune cells and released to receptor sites found on the surface of cells throughout the body, both influence and respond to our psychological states. In essence, these substances transform mind into matter as our emotions trigger certain cellular signals that are then translated into physiological changes.[2]

The quantum theory of physics, on the other hand, has created a dramatic shift in the way we think of all matter. For example, it has been found that, at the subatomic level, recognizable phenomena are influenced by and dependent on the presence of a human observer. The conscious decision of this human observer determines whether subatomic substance (an electron) appears as a particle or occurs in the form of a wave phenomenon. This means that, out of the possibilities, it is our consciousness that determines what will be seen, experienced, or made manifest. In the words of physicist Fred Alan Wolf, "the physical world of hard matter, light, and energy simply does not and cannot exist independent of human consciousness."[3]

The clear and concrete boundaries that we once had between matter and mind, between form and energy, no longer exist. Instead, we are part of a quantum field, a continuous medium present everywhere in space with the potential to manifest as particles or waves, as material substance or its surrounding field. Particles of matter exist where there is a local condensation in this field.[4] Thus, solid material substance, including the physical body, is merely a denser concentration of this energy field. From this perspective, the processes of the body can no longer be considered as separate from what we think, feel, or know.

In fact, physicist Dr. David Bohm suggests that the manifest world of the physical universe, or what he refers to as the "explicate order," is actually less fundamental than the primary reality of the unmanifest, unseen realm or "implicate order" out of which the physical unfolds.[5] In his work, Bohm addresses the apparent dual particle-wave nature of the electron and proposes that at the same time an electron is manifesting as a particle, it is being informed about the other parts of the physical universe through a wave-like information field surrounding it. This informing wave field interpenetrates all space and time, providing a network of awareness which Bohm called "quantum potential." Even though an electron is behaving like a particle, it is also interactively aware of the rest of the universe and perhaps potentially guided in some way through this wave-like information field.[6] Bohm thus felt that all of reality is in continuous flux and part of a whole interconnected flow of movement, which he named *holomovement.* This means that all things are connected, are dynamically affecting and affected by one another, and that the whole of this universal flow is holographically contained within each of its unified parts. So, according to this theory, not only are we an interconnected part of the vast universe all around us, but the essential pulsing pattern of all creation is also, in some way, contained within each of us.

We are, then, essentially enveloped in an ocean of energy, a universal energy field which is intelligent, alive, and carries information in the form of light waves. Our bodies are composed of this energy substance and our individual consciousness interacts with it continually. This energy has been described by my spiritual teacher as a "living, conscious substance," the nature of which is love, and this can be tangibly felt with the necessary receptive sensitivity. What I see when I look at this universal energy field are minute colored streamers of light bouncing around at phenomenal speeds. What I feel emotionally when I sense it is pure love. Its qualities, then, are simply light, life, and love.

## THE ENERGY BODIES

The matrix of energy that surrounds and connects all matter, and of which all matter is composed, surrounds the physical body in the form of energy planes or bodies. These concentric planes exist as interpenetrating fields of energy[7] with each successive layer being less dense and of an increasingly higher harmonic frequency or vibration.[8] Although these energy fields are in the ultraviolet frequencies, beyond what we know as the visible spectrum, they only remain invisible until one becomes sensitive to their presence. These fields can be seen, for example, by those who have clairvoyant vision and by healers who have been trained to see, sense, or feel the human energy system.

Each energy plane also serves a particular function and is indicative of a particular state of consciousness. Just as we develop mentally, emotionally, and physically from childhood, we also continue to evolve in consciousness and expand our awareness. The energy bodies represent different aspects of this expansion in consciousness. Becoming familiar with the specific function of each energy plane and the dynamics of the whole human energy system will not only assist you in your own process of personal growth, but will also help you better understand the connection between body, mind, and spirit. Various schools of metaphysics, philosophy, and healing have different systems that explain these functions. The following description provides a framework that I have found helpful in understanding their nature. For our purposes, we will be dealing with the first seven primary energy bodies.

## The First Plane: The Etheric Field

The first layer, the etheric, has to do with the functioning of the physical body. The etheric body acts as a type of pre-physical blueprint that organizes and maintains the dense physical form. It appears as tiny bluish-white to violet-gray luminous energy lines in constant motion, extending just slightly beyond the physical body. This web-like energy matrix contains the same structure and anatomical parts as the physical body and serves as a pattern for it.[9]

*[handwritten margin notes: my gift is sense or feeling the human energy system]*

*[handwritten bottom notes: how do disorientations or faults in one field effect the other? how are the symptoms manifested? what is their interrelationship and dependency?]*

The research of people such as Dr. Harold Saxton Burr has confirmed scientifically what clairvoyants have known for ages regarding the etheric field. Burr measured electrical potential by developing an electrode, which he first inserted into living tissue and later put near the surface of organisms he studied. For more than thirty years, he studied organisms from single cells to plants to humans. He found that every living system had an electrical field that served certain functions with regard to growth, morphogenesis, and the maintenance and repair of living things. Burr felt that this field affected and was affected by its atomic physio-chemical components, and thus helped to maintain organic equilibrium and act as a type of electronic matrix giving shape to the corporeal form.[10]

The electromagnetic force that emanates from and surrounds the body has more recently been measured by a very sensitive instrument known as the Super Conducting Quantum Interference Device (SQUID). In addition, research by Soviet scientist Alexander Dubrov found that in the process of mitosis, or cell splitting, there is a photon radiation (light) and high frequency sound given off from the cells.[11] This bioluminescent energy, although beyond the visible spectrum, is being produced and emanated from our bodies all the time.

Visual confirmation of the etheric field of the body was provided through the technique of Kirlian photography. Through this method developed by Semyon and Valentia Kirlian in the 1940s, the electrodynamic field of the body can be visualized photographically by exposing film to an object in the midst of a high-intensity electromagnetic field. Since then, further research has demonstrated correlations between fluctuations in the photographed field and an individual's physiological and psychological state. Variations in the observable corona have also been found when acupuncture and other healing treatments were administered.[12] Clearly, the etheric body registers our dynamic level of health and vitality and responds to changes in the environment to maintain homeostasis. In addition to our physical vitality, the etheric body also affects our ability to enjoy physical sensations and the pleasures of the physical world around us.

## The Second Plane: The Emotional Body

The second energy plane, known as the emotional body, relates to your feelings and emotions. This level of the field corresponds to the feelings we have about ourselves and our ability to accept and emotionally nourish ourselves. It also relates to expressing emotions in a healthy way that is in harmony with your spirit nature and the other aspects of your being.

## The Third Plane: The Mental Body

The third energy plane is the mental body and it corresponds to our intelligence, both concrete and abstract thought. Your sense of mental clarity is associated with this energy body as well as with your ability to use the mental faculties in a way that is in balance with the intuitive and feeling functions. Without this balance, the analytical thinking processes can dominate your consciousness and judgmental or critical thought patterns can also be experienced.

## The Fourth Plane: The Astral-Intuitive

The fourth level, the astral-intuitive, is sometimes referred to as the Buddhic plane. It is associated with intuition and the individualized expression of love. This body acts as a bridge to the subsequent spiritual planes, and it is on this level that we begin to experience the expression of our higher nature through the qualities of intuitive wisdom and love. Your ability to love and feel a connection with others, as well as your intuitive understanding of things, are therefore related to this energy body.

### The Fifth Plane: The Divine Will

The fifth, or divine will plane, relates to the conscious alignment of your own personal will with the higher will and perfect pattern of the Divine. It can thus affect the patterns that you create and respond to in your life. Your sense of order, level of integrity, and ability to live in harmony with the divine truth of your own being are also associated with this energy body.

### The Sixth Plane: The Soul Body

The sixth plane, which I refer to as the soul body, is associated with expansive states of spiritual ecstasy. You may have experienced such feelings during sacred ceremony, in meditation, or while appreciating uplifting music or the beauty of nature. We feel our connection with all things and experience ourselves as part of a greater body of divine love through the consciousness of this plane.

This energy field relates to your connection with your own soul and your individualized spiritual essence or God Self. If you are disconnected from your spiritual nature and the directive patterns of your own soul, it will affect your ability to experience the expansion that this energy plane represents.

What do I mean by soul and spiritual essence? Each of us has an individualized spiritual essence which is the spark of the Divine Presence within us. This God Self is the limitless, timeless core of our spiritual being. It is an enlivened cell in the body of God. If you thought of God as the Sun, then each divine Self can be thought of as an individualized flame in that solar body. The God Self, sometimes referred to as the Higher Self to distinguish it from the outer personality of the ego self, is the center of our highest spiritual consciousness, wisdom, creativity, peace, joy, and love.

The soul surrounds the God Self and can be likened to a type of sheath or covering that acts as a protection for it. The soul contains the patterns and memory of all our experience, and its impulses provide direction so that we gain the necessary life experiences for our own evolution. It is this soul memory and intelligence that keeps the physical body and human energy system functioning. This is because the soul provides the specific necessary pattern of information that nature uses to supply our bodies with the material substance required for physical functioning.

As we come into physical existence on Earth, we also develop an ego personality and a false image of ourselves. The ego is the conscious thinking, feeling, and acting part of the psyche that develops through contact with the external world. It provides the basic framework of self-identity by which we experience and interact with the world around us. It is thus through the ego that you recognize yourself as a separate individual. The ego serves an important function by retrieving and processing information that enables us to maintain physical existence here. For instance, it lets us know how to protect and sustain a material body. However, the information it gives us is based on what it has learned from the world in the past. Its interpretations of life are therefore limited in comparison with the expansive knowledge of the Divine Self.

The perspective of the ego self can be very distorted because its information is often based on painful life experiences or false ideas learned from society and the particular dynamics present within our own families. A false concept of one's self or false persona is then created and dominates the soul personality, rather than allowing the true expression of the Higher Self to guide one's life. The false persona is a type of mask we create, an outer cloak we wear in order to get approval and protect the vulnerable parts of ourselves that we feel are unacceptable to others. It is the part of us that identifies with the concepts of the thinking mind; that is, what we "think" about ourselves rather than who we actually *are* as magnificent divine beings. For example, an individual may think of himself as worthless and undeserving of love when in actuality he is merely disconnected from his true essence and the divine love that is always available to him. To compensate, this person might have an obsessive need to do things perfectly and please others. This perfectionism would be an expression of the individual's false persona.

The fact that the ego personality presents a false and distorted self-image has led to many misconceptions about how it relates to spiritual growth. The ego is not meant to be eliminated as part of spiritual development. A positive sense of self is a necessary element for a healthy psyche. Rather, the ego personality and thinking mind must be transformed or purified in service to the Divine Self. In other words, instead of running the show based on erroneous information, the ego self surrenders to the wisdom of the Higher Self and makes choices based on its guidance. To achieve this, you must first choose to acknowledge and express your spiritual nature, as opposed to identifying solely with the physical body or the separateness of the ego and its distorted interpretations of reality. As you allow yourself to experience more of your spirit essence in this way, the ego and its accompanying false patterns are transformed. You then, in turn, are able to more fully realize and embody the presence of your true God Self.

## The Seventh Plane: The Universal Mind

The seventh energy body, universal mind, relates to your connection to the unmanifest Source of all, the Cosmic Intelligence which enfolds and connects all things, providing the perfect pattern for all creation. At this level of consciousness, you know and experience yourself as one with the Creator and gain an understanding of your part in the perfect plan of a loving

For each of these energy fields there must be sharpen and process to energize and integrate them

universe. Through this knowledge and understanding, you gain a sense of fulfillment and peace. Just as the Divine Intelligence enfolds all things, the seventh energy body also encompasses all the other fields and forms a protective golden egg of light that holds them together.

## Energy Bodies in Balance

When all the energy bodies are aligned and functioning according to their highest expression, we are able to know our connection to the Creative Source (universal mind); experience the peace, joy, creativity, and love of our own essence Self (soul body); align our will with the perfect pattern of a loving universe (divine will); express this love through our connection with others (astral-intuitive); use our conscious intelligence in a way that is in harmony with our feeling nature and the Higher Self (mental body); lovingly accept and express feelings in a balanced way (emotional body); and experience health, vitality, and an awareness of bodily sensations and feelings in a way that brings a sense of joy and pleasure (etheric body). When energy flows harmoniously through the energy bodies in this way, the physical vehicle is naturally nourished and healthy with all the physical systems in balance.

Each level of the human energy system is, therefore, related to a different aspect of our experience. Our spiritual consciousness, mental processes, emotional feelings, and somatic sensations are all related to various locations in our energy field. All the energy planes are connected and work together to maintain balance and optimum health throughout the whole body-mind. If there is an imbalance or blockage of energy in one layer of the field, it can in turn affect the flow of energy to the other bodies. Mental body issues such as critical thoughts about yourself can thus influence your emotional state—for example, create depression—which then affects the functioning of your physical body.

The energy bodies are not only responsive to one another, but are also sensitive to the frequencies conveyed by other fields. Remember, each of the energy bodies has a particular harmonic frequency. We are constantly sending out a certain pattern of energy from our energy fields depending on our spiritual, mental, emotional, and physical state of being. You may have experienced a response to another person's energy emanation if you've ever had a strong reaction to another person for no apparent reason. If there is a resonance or harmony between your energy field and another's, a positive feeling will be produced. If there is a dissonant quality between the two fields, you will most likely have a negative response of some kind. Often this response will be felt as a sensation in a particular area of your body, such as a sense of anxiety in your solar plexus, a knot in your stomach, or a pain in your heart.

Sometimes individuals even have a particular way they try to manipulate energy. You may have felt this as a type of energetic sucking, withdrawal, or even attack from people at times. People who are energy suckers are often very needy people who want something from you or need you to do something for them. Of course, we all have times when we feel more in need. However, when you are around these people it will feel as though they have a big bottomless hole inside of them that is impossible to fill. Often such individuals are expecting others to fill them up emotionally and energetically, instead of taking responsibility for themselves.

With people who withdraw, you feel as though they vacate the premises and recede into a shell or back away energetically from interacting with you. You wonder, "Where did they go?" I have actually seen people lift up out of their physical body energetically into the higher energy planes as a form of retreat. Usually energetic withdrawal is a defense mechanism, a learned response to fear. Individuals will often do this if a situation reminds them of a painful past experience or if they are afraid of such things as criticism, external control, or even intimacy. Energetic attack is often accompanied by verbal aggressiveness and a body stance that suggests the person has power over you. It may feel invasive or as though an energetic bulldozer is in your face.

Perhaps you can think of other ways that you feel people energetically, such as when you're in the presence of a person who emanates love and vitality, or when someone is being seductive with you in a charming manner in order to get his or her own way. You can become more consciously aware of these dynamics by beginning to notice how the things people are saying or doing feel energetically in your body and how it feels to be around them. Is it pleasurable and nourishing to be with this person, or is it draining and uncomfortable? Begin to notice what your energetic response is to these types of interactions and also to other situations and behaviors that you might be involved in. Use the information that you receive as guidance in order to determine which activities are life enhancing for you and which activities are no longer useful for your continued well-being.

In the morning before going to work or during the day—particularly if you feel drained, irritated, or ill—bring your conscious awareness to the space surrounding your physical body and intuitively sense or imagine the boundaries of your energy field. Does your auric field seem constricted and defensively held too close to your physical body, or is it overexpanded and dissipated, leaving you susceptible to everyone else's energy? If so, lovingly breathe into the energy around your body. Through sensing, intuitive knowing, creative visualization, or simply affirming intention, adjust your auric boundaries to what feels appropriate for you—usually this is an oval-shaped egg of energy all around your physical form, within two or three feet of your body.

In private or more expansive situations such as meditation sessions, your energy field may extend much farther than this. However, if your aura expands a great distance at other times, especially in public, you need to have the spiritual consciousness necessary to have complete mastery of your energetic presence at that distance. To further enhance and strengthen your aura, visualize the edge of your field as the golden color of the seventh energy body.

Other energy frequencies, such as those produced by electrical fields, can also affect us. Energy from electrical sources (EM fields) is constantly bombarding our physical nervous system and energy bodies. On a physiological level, this is because the axon, or message transmitter of the nervous system, is not only stimulated by electrical activity generated from within the neuron itself, but from external stimulus as well. Stress is also created because the vibrational frequency emitted by the electrical source is not in resonance with the human energy field. This dissonance creates a condition where the etheric body is constantly expending energy trying to adjust and maintain balance, thus lowering the overall vitality of the individual. This is why continually working at computer terminals can be stressful. If you use a computer, get a filtering screen that blocks out much of this EM radiation.

Television can also affect your energy fields. I began to feel more and more drained or even agitated when watching television, and decided to do a meditation on its effects. The information that I received was that the energy frequency emitted by the television was interfering with my own energy field. This is what was creating the physical and emotional agitation. In addition to being constantly bombarded, my etheric body was being pulled into resonance with the field of the television. This lowered the vibration of my own energy field, which left me drained. I was particularly sensitive at the time because I was in the midst of a healing process. The television watching was actually interfering with the healing that was trying to take place within me. Needless to say, I reduced my television viewing time considerably.

The energy fields are therefore not only emitting energy, but always responding to other energy frequencies to maintain homeostasis. Whether we are aware of it or not, we are constantly transmitting and receiving energy through our energy bodies. How consciously we work with these energies will determine how affected we are by them. Being aware of your body and how it feels in your body when you're in a particular place, when you're with another person in their energy field, or while you're involved in a certain activity or behavior, will help you become more conscious of what is happening energetically.

## THE CHAKRAS

The energy bodies are actually part of a whole system, which includes the chakras. These whirling vortices of energy are dynamic centers that distribute energy throughout your whole body. Their main function is to take in the energy from the universal field surrounding us and break it down to be used by the body. In this way, the chakras help sustain human life through the conversion of energy into matter. The seven major chakras, which I will discuss here, are located along the spine. However, there is also a chakra located below the feet, which I address later in the book, as well as minor ones in areas such as the knees, feet, and hands.[13]

Each chakra actually exists on every level of the energy field. The energy bodies are bound together at these chakra points, creating a passageway of communication between them. This is part of the mechanism by which, for example, a mental body issue can affect the emotional or etheric level. Like the energy planes, every chakra resonates at a certain vibratory frequency and emanates a particular color. In addition, each of the seven major chakras is related to a specific area of the body and is associated with and affects a major nerve plexus and endocrine gland. In this way, the chakras influence biochemical and hormonal responses, which affect both our physiological and our psychological well-being. The chakras act as the interface, the link between subtle energy and actual psychosomatic changes in the body-mind.

The chakras also interact with another force within the body called the kundalini. In Eastern spiritual teachings and Yogic philosophy, the kundalini is known as the creative life force, the primordial life-giving substance and essence of Mother Earth. Although this life force energy is constantly interacting with the chakras, there is also a fuller awakening and rising of the kundalini that coincides with spiritual awakening and the process of evolving consciousness.

According to Yogic traditions, the dormant kundalini lies coiled up like a snake at the base of the spine until it is awakened either spontaneously, through meditation, or as part of a specific spiritual practice. The kundalini energy then begins to uncoil and ascend the spine, energizing the chakra centers as it does. As the chakra centers are activated by the kundalini, they are vivified and more fully awakened to inflowing Cosmic energies. This process signifies the transformation of the false persona, and the baser desire nature—the self-absorbed expression of emotions and instinctual drives in a way that is not conscious or life enhancing—being spiritually purified so that consciousness can be raised to a more expansive level.

The chakras, therefore, interact with two main energies. First, the Cosmic energy from the universal field enters through the crown at the top of the head, becoming denser as it filters down through the chakras along the spine. Secondly, the kundalini enters the human body through the base of the spine, where it is stored. The kundalini rises up through the spinal cord, meeting the flowing Cosmic energies as it does. As the two forces meet, they generate a spinning wheel-like activity. This is where the name *chakra*, the Sanskrit word for *wheel*, originates. This dynamic is significant of Cosmic energy or Spirit seeking to penetrate physical matter and be embodied and physical matter seeking to raise in energy level or vibration and merge with Spirit.

Both of these functions are important and necessary in our evolution and process of expanding consciousness. These two essential energies, the Cosmic and the creative life force, are continually at work within the body and both are equally important for our total health and well-being. We thus draw energy from both our spiritual beingness and our life force or earth essence. Truly, Heaven and Earth are joined as one within us. Let's take a closer look now at each chakra center to see how it specifically relates to our physical and psychological well-being.

### The Root Chakra

The first, or root, chakra is located at the base of the spine at the sacral-coccyx joint. It appears red in color and is associated with the functioning of the physical body. As the place where the kundalini resides, this chakra relates to the creative life force and the will to live. It promotes the vitality of the physical presence and energy. Dysfunction of this chakra can affect one's overall physical energy, health, and awareness of proprioceptive, kinesthetic, and tactile senses.

The root chakra influences the adrenals, which affect many functions of the body. The adrenals, along with the sympathetic division of the autonomic nervous system, are responsible for the "fight or flight" response, preserving the life and energy of the organism. Survival issues, the desire to live, and one's sense of wanting to be here on Earth are related to this chakra center.

When there is an imbalance in the root chakra, it is difficult for individuals to feel comfortable in the world. They may not feel welcomed here on the planet or may feel alienated without a sense that the world can be a safe place. This is especially true if there have been early childhood experiences regarding emotional or physical survival. In these cases, there are often deep feelings of rage and terror associated with this chakra concerning these childhood issues. People with dysfunction of this chakra can also be ungrounded and disconnected to some degree from material reality.

## The Sacral Chakra

The second, or sacral, chakra is located just above the pubic bone. It appears orange in color and has to do with the regenerative function and sexual energy. It relates to both a basic trust in life and the capacity for satisfying intimate relationships with the ability to give and receive pleasure through sexual union. We receive emotional nourishment through this union and our bodies are nourished with life force energy through orgasm as well. Problems with the sexual organs or unsatisfactory sexual experience can develop if there is a malfunction in this chakra. The urinary system, colon, and lower back can also be affected.

Developmental dynamics involving this chakra concern issues of nurturing and security versus abandonment. If you didn't have a sense of being secure and nurtured as a child, it can continue to affect your ability to trust and experience emotionally nourishing relationships. Any type of physical, emotional, or sexual abuse will create this kind of dynamic.

## The Solar Plexus Chakra

The third chakra, the solar plexus center of emotions and power, emanates the color yellow and is located in the upper abdomen just under the diaphragm. The pancreas is related to this chakra, and the spleen, stomach, small intestine, gall bladder, liver, and nervous system are supplied with energy through it.[14] This chakra has to do with emotional power, a sense of self-acceptance, and personal will.

Often in childhood our sense of power is taken away by over-controlling or dysfunctional caretakers. Our basic instinctual sense of things may be denied and the desires of our instinctual nature controlled. Our connection with our personal power and innate wisdom then shuts down and feelings of fear, anger, and sadness develop. For this reason, imbalance of the solar plexus center is common. This can affect how well individuals take care of themselves, their sense of personal power, and emotional expression. A repression of emotions or hysterical extremes can result from malfunction of this chakra, and a need for restrictive control of one's self or others can occur. When individuals feel a lack of power within themselves, they will sometimes try to find it outside of themselves by manipulating or having power over others. Obsessive or controlling people usually have an imbalance in the solar plexus center.

When people are in a state of fear, they often experience physical sensations in the solar plexus area. Many times, people are actually apprehensive about the powerful and instinctual emotions that reside here, and are fearful that they will be unable to control them. If there is also an imbalance in the first chakra, and a sense of grounded security is lacking, this sense of anxiety will be greatly amplified.

Individuals may also protect themselves from any uncomfortable feelings held in the solar plexus area by breathing in a shallow manner, thus keeping life and breath from animating the feelings that reside there. Breathing fully into your abdomen can reverse this process, helping you to connect more deeply with your body and instinctual feelings.

Although the kundalini interacts with all the chakra centers, it is associated in a specific way with the first three. These chakras reflect the cycles seen in all of nature, the process of birth, preservation, death, and rebirth. The root chakra is the home or womb where the primordial life-giving substance of the kundalini lies coiled at the base of the spine. It represents our connection with the Earth, the Mother from which this vital creative life force springs forth. The second chakra relates to the regenerative nature of this feminine Earth presence and the capacity for preservation, growth, and nurturing. The third chakra is associated with the powerful and destructuring aspect of nature, the destroying and explosive aspect that we often see expressed in volcanic and earthquake activity.

When your instinctual nature is denied or expressions of the life force such as sexuality, emotions, or power are repressed because they are considered unacceptable, problems can arise in these chakras. I'm reminded of a line from an old margarine commercial that said, "It's not nice to fool Mother Nature." When we don't listen to our instincts and deny or repress innate feelings, then we may arouse the powerful and destructive aspect of nature and have to deal with the consequences. In other words, when feelings are denied and needs are repressed, deeper psychological and physiological problems can result. This is true in our individual psyches as well as collectively, and our society reflects this.

In this culture, we have been taught to deny the instinctual functions in favor of cognitive knowledge and mental control. The civilized mind has ignored animal wisdom or gut-level knowledge and has nicely domesticated emotional passion. The ability of the mind to discriminate is a necessary function. It is what separates us from the animals. However, when the mind has total control, we become little more than mechanized robots. The denial of the instinctual-feeling nature in this culture is sometimes subtle, often blatant, and always pervasive. This feeling aspect in both men and women has been hurt, denied, and neglected. I've worked with many people who had to learn that having feelings, especially sad or angry ones, is a natural part of being human. I've also found that many individuals feel disconnected from their sensuality or are uncomfortable with their bodies. The painful feelings that we haven't dealt with inside, as individuals, then pour out into society, manifesting as the violence all around us. The healing of our collective emotional pain needs to take place in order to bring balance within and without.

Another manifestation of the denial of our instinctual earth nature is found in the collective abuse of the planet through pollution. In response, nature seems to cry out desperately to find balance through earthquakes, storms, volcanic activity, famine, and other natural disasters.

Instinctual drives for survival, procreation, and power often emerge from a place below the level of conscious awareness. Thus, the domain of the first three chakras also represents the realm of the subconscious mind and the emotionally charged contents that reside there. In order to express our emotional power, will, and instinctual nature in a clear and balanced way, the unresolved issues of the past must be healed. This requires that we bring the light of consciousness into the shadow world of the subconscious mind to confront the distorted elements of denial, pain, and fear that are held there. As these wounds to the self are healed, you are then able to truly feel a secure and grounded presence on Earth (first chakra), trust in yourself (second chakra), and fulfill your emotional needs (third chakra). Only then can you evolve beyond the power and control issues and fear-based consciousness associated with the third chakra.

### The Heart Chakra

The fourth, or heart, chakra is located in the center of the chest and radiates the color green. We love ourselves and feel our connection and love for others through this chakra. Imbalances

What is manifested in a deficient or open chakra — and how do the channels affect their temperament on a plane?

in the heart chakra relate to the inability to give or receive love and acknowledge heartfelt feelings. There can also be a sense of isolation and a lack of loving connection with others.

The love that flows from the heart center also brings in a new consciousness, a compassionate, more spirit-centered understanding. The heart chakra represents a turning point, a transition out of the instinctual consciousness of the first three chakras into an experience of the emerging Self. It signifies individuation, the process by which one becomes a psychologically separate and autonomous individual expressing the essential Self. Just as a child must leave the womb at birth in order to continue to develop and grow as a separate entity, we must eventually move beyond the purely instinctive emotional womb represented by the first three chakras to realize who we are as unique individuals and spiritual beings. For this reason, the developmental dynamics of the lower chakras concerning survival, emotional needs, and the right to basic instincts must be dealt with before one can experience the individuation represented by the heart chakra.

As part of this process, I often find that people return in their memory to certain childhood stages of development that relate to individuation. The theme of becoming an autonomous individual, for example, can be seen in the experience of a two-year-old who says, "No," and feels herself as separate from her mother for the first time, or in the teenager's struggle to find out who he is by rebelling against his parents. Once we feel a grounded connection with the life force, trust our own instincts, and feel empowered to fulfill our own needs, we can then open more fully to the experience of unconditional love and the discovery of our spiritual nature.

At the heart chakra, the kundalini energy is refined and transmuted into a purer substance through the consciousness of love. Just as the ancient alchemists sought to transmute baser

! Heart Energy

energy field developmental dynamics

What is the pattern is there a pattern of development among those who are energy practitioners?

*it is the self that converts/transitions one from the 3rd curm to the 4—?*

.!?

metals into gold, it is here in the heart center where the baser desire nature is transformed through the quality of love. This alchemical process opens the way for an individual to move beyond the unconscious reactions of the emotional realm into an experience of spiritual consciousness. It is the energy of the heart chakra that enables us to integrate our spiritual essence and our instinctual nature into a divine humanness. The heart chakra thus acts as a mediator between the mind and emotions, and can help us to understand and resolve the conflicts that arise between instinctual desires and spiritual values. Often it is the stress of this type of conflict that results in heart problems.

In the process of becoming adults, many of us have "lost heart," because the creative, loving child part of us has been lost and hidden away. In order to truly know ourselves, that inner Child of Light must be rediscovered, loved, and healed. People involved in this process of individuation and healing often have irregular heart palpitations, strange chest pains, or burning sensations in the chest area. The pain of their childhood seems to temporarily manifest as this physical heartache. More serious body phenomena involving actual structural changes such as blocked arteries, various forms of heart disease, and circulation problems can also result from dysfunction of the heart chakra.

I have also found that people involved in the process of individuation can have dreams, images, and past-life experiences involving the heart, such as images of the heart being cut out. This is often symbolic of the sense of self that was taken away during childhood and that now has to be reclaimed. Whether you believe in the possibility of reincarnation and the authenticity of past-life experience, or simply view it as symbolic metaphor similar to dream content, it emerges as an important aspect of personal growth and spiritual development.

The heart chakra relates to the thymus gland, which plays an important role in the immune system. According to traditional medical science, the lymphocyte-rich tissue of the thymus is replaced by fat after the age of puberty, and the gland then atrophies by maturity. Interestingly, it is also at puberty that a person's open, childlike nature gives over to more adult pursuits and concerns. The individual, at this time, can become more interested in the ways of the world than in the still, small voice from within the heart. In the process of individuation and realizing our true essence, we come home once again to this place within our heart.

## The Throat Chakra

The fifth chakra, located in the middle of the throat, appears sky blue in color and is associated with the thyroid gland. The thyroid regulates the body's metabolic response. Similarly, the throat chakra relates to how individuals respond and express themselves. It is here in the throat chakra that one's life force is expressed and communicated. This includes not only verbal skills, but writing and the creative arts as well. This chakra relates to having a voice and taking responsibility for expressing one's needs, will, and creativity. People with a dysfunction of this chakra may be unable to speak the truth of their own being and bring it forth into manifestation. They may have trouble expressing their needs and creativity or be excessively talkative, lacking any self-regulation. Their ability to hear well or listen receptively may also be affected. Physical symptoms such as thyroid imbalance, laryngitis, or other throat problems can accompany these types of issues involving the throat chakra.

As children, many individuals are taught to shut up and listen, especially in denial-filled families where they may be prevented from talking about the things that they see, feel, and know. In abusive homes, the consequences of speaking up for one's self are often life threatening. Such childhood patterns often create a passivity that continues into adulthood, making it difficult for individuals to express themselves. For this reason, many people have an imbalance in this chakra. In addition, our society often criticizes those who have unconventional things to say that threaten the status quo. This makes it difficult for such individuals to bring forth their often unique and creative ideas. The throat center also acts as a bridge between head and heart, between thoughts and feelings. Consequently, the conflicts between what our logical mind thinks and what our heart feels is often experienced in the throat chakra.

The transmutation process that takes place in the heart center is a necessary one affecting throat chakra dynamics. The heart enables us to use the double-edged sword of our creative word in a conscious and compassionate way for healing, rather than for harm. When the middle three chakras are operating together in a balanced way, we are able to express the creative word (fifth chakra) with power (third chakra) and compassion (fourth chakra). Reciprocally, it is also by giving voice to the power of the third chakra through the throat center that the individuation process of the heart chakra becomes more complete. I find that it is usually when people begin to speak out about their feelings, beliefs, and personal truth, that they solidify their own psychological boundaries and have a fuller sense of themselves as unique individuals.

There is also a specific valve-like link to the electromagnetic matrix of the energy bodies in the throat center that transduces and controls the flow of higher vibrational energy and information for the physical vehicle. To help things move more smoothly, if you feel you are having difficulty assimilating this expanded, accelerated energy, it can be helpful to breathe love into the throat area while visualizing light there. Then call on Spirit and your own Higher Self to assist you by making any adjustments that may be necessary in your throat center or other parts of your energy system.

## The Brow/Third Eye Chakra

The sixth, or brow, chakra is located in the middle of the forehead between the eyebrows. It emanates a deep blue indigo violet color and relates to the pituitary gland. The pituitary as master gland controls many bodily functions and regulates the other glands through its hormonal secretions. The brow chakra has a similar regulatory function by breaking down and distributing the Cosmic energy, which enters at the crown.

The brow or third eye center is associated with creative ideas and the ability to visualize and perceive mental concepts and bring these ideas into form. People with an imbalance in this chakra may have strong negative images or judgmental views, may have trouble forming ideas, or be unable to follow through on the creative ideas that they have. Mental strain, anxiety, worry, confusion, headaches, and other symptoms involving the head can also result.

The sixth chakra also has to do with opening up to spiritual wisdom, intuition, or what's often called the "sixth sense" of extrasensory perception. We all have the ability to open up our psychic eyes to the nonphysical world. In fact, children do it quite naturally before they are taught otherwise. I'll never forget one day when my then three-year-old daughter, Lisa, pointed up into the air in front of us and said, "Teacher, mommy, teacher!" She continued to gaze in the spot she was pointing to, acknowledging and interacting with someone I couldn't see. I did very much feel a presence with us, however, and was very in awe of my daughter's experience.

Intuitive ability is a spiritual tool and, like any tool, it can be developed through understanding and practice. There is actually a constant influx of intuitive perception flowing through us all the time. However, this more subtle energy is usually drowned out by the constant blaring noise of our rational thinking minds and limiting beliefs. By beginning to discipline and still the thinking mind, you can learn to tune into this intuitive inner guidance.

Many times, people who refuse to acknowledge the higher wisdom and spiritual sight of the brow chakra experience eye or vision problems. I have also witnessed individuals with a dominant sixth chakra who were very psychic, yet were blocked in the heart chakra. When this dynamic is present, what the person psychically sees will be spoken forth in a judgmental way without compassion or understanding for other people's experience.

The pituitary gland, which is associated with this center, is situated in a groove of the sphenoid bone, which is composed of two wing-like structures. This is symbolic of the ultimate expansive flight that our consciousness will take as it is illuminated with the spiritual wisdom of the sixth chakra. Here, as we expand in consciousness and increase in the light of spiritual wisdom, we prepare to experience union with the Divine Source of all things.

## The Crown Chakra

The crown chakra is located at the top of the head and relates to the pineal gland. This chakra, light violet to white in hue, is the center of spiritual presence, knowing, and authority, which represents our connection with the Divine Source of all being. It signifies that place of consciousness where we experience self-mastery and have full realization of the God Self as our dominant reality. Eventually, a state of Cosmic consciousness is reached where the aspects of the false persona completely fall away and one merges with Absolute Spirit in enlightened transcendent oneness. As the crown chakra is stimulated and more fully activated by the rising kundalini energy, it results in expansive mystical experiences of this nature.

The operation of the seventh chakra affects a person's experience of the spiritual realm and their sense of themselves as a spiritual being. In this culture, we are spiritually malnourished and have become very estranged from the states of divine bliss that the crown chakra represents. As a poor substitute, we see people addicted to other means of experiencing this spiritual elation by using drugs, alcohol, gambling, sex, and the like. Perhaps part of the problem is that some of our religions have led us to believe that we must wait until we die and actually leave the body to experience union with Spirit. Yet, this is not the case. In fact, this type of limiting belief actually keeps us from receiving the spiritual energy that we all need to nourish our being. People with an imbalance in this chakra may experience a lack of meaning in their lives or feel cut off from a spiritual source. Physical symptoms of the head, similar to those involving the sixth chakra, can also result.

The physiology of the pineal gland is still somewhat obscure. However, I find it interesting that the pineal is sensitive to light since it is here, at the crown chakra, that the light of Cosmic consciousness enters and where we, in turn, commune with it. The pineal also degenerates in most people between the ages of seven and thirteen, appearing in adults to be largely fibrous tissue. Similarly, by the age of puberty, most people have lost their childhood connection with the collective oneness of all being, and oneness with their mothers, to develop as individuals. From this experience of the individuated Self, represented by the heart chakra, we evolve once again to know ourselves as part of an infinite oneness and experience union with the Divine.

If the individuation process of the heart chakra has not been accomplished, however, an experience of oneness can often seem very overwhelming. One of my clients, Mara, is an excellent example of this dynamic. Mara had begun to have experiences of a spiritual nature. She became very anxious one night in a group meditation where she was guided in connecting with others in an enfolding light. Mara realized that she feared this merging and was afraid of being engulfed; that is, controlled and overpowered by an energy or by other people to such an extent that she would lose her sense of self-identity. As a child, this is what happened to her in her family, and group situations recreated those enmeshed family dynamics for her. This experience came at a time when she was opening to the spiritual reality, as well as emerging as a psychologically separate individual. In order to experience the spiritual union she ultimately desired, Mara had to heal the wounds of her childhood past and complete the individuation process that had been initiated in the heart chakra.

This illustrates how important the psychodynamic development of each chakra is in our process of spiritual growth. Problems often arise if the sixth and seventh chakras are not operating in a balanced way that is aligned with the other chakra centers. In such a case, an individual can have psychic experiences that are overwhelming, including visions, extrasensory perception, and out-of-body experiences. It is important for individuals to have a vital root chakra connection to ground this influx of spiritual energy and knowledge, or else a detached spaciness can result. Imbalances also occur when the psychological issues of the lower chakras are not addressed before the higher centers develop. In these cases, individuals can become overidentified with the psychic opening and phenomena that occur, using it for their own personal power and control. The influx of spiritual energies may then have the effect of inflating the ego and feeding psychic energy into the person's dysfunctional patterns, rather than transforming them.

You may have noticed a general correlation between the role of the various energy bodies and the psychodynamic function of the chakras. Remember, both the energy bodies and chakras work together to maintain physical, emotional, mental, and spiritual health. There is a danger in viewing either the energy bodies or the chakras in a hierarchical way, seeing the lower chakras, for example, as inferior. It is important to remember that the chakras are all equally important and function together as one whole system. It may be more useful to view the chakras, and the psychospiritual development they represent, as functioning in a continual spiral fashion. As we grow personally and evolve spiritually, we may cycle through the developmental process represented by the chakras many times, each time at a deeper and more conscious level of being. At one level of heart chakra development, for example, a person may work with issues concerning a basic sense of self-esteem and self-love. Then at another stage, relationship issues may emerge, enabling the individual to develop healthy and loving connections with others. A third cycle of heart chakra activation might bring the same individual an expansive and deeper understanding of her ability to connect with Spirit through intuitive heart knowing.

 As we cycle through the different stages of our healing, growth, and spiritual development, we realize more of our whole self and the different dimensions of our being that the chakras represent. In this process, our spirit and mental intelligence must listen to our feeling-instinctual nature, allowing any denied feelings to be expressed. The physical and instinctual parts of us must, in turn, open to receive the illumination and guidance from our spirit essence. The heart brings compassion and balance to the process. In this way, emotional clearing allows for deeper spiritual understanding and all aspects of self, body, mind, emotions, and spirit are brought into harmony and alignment. All of these different aspects then work together in a balanced way as part of our total functioning.

# CHAKRA MEDITATION

Now that you've been given an intellectual understanding of the human energy system, I'd like to help you experience the different dimensions of your own being through the chakra centers. The following guided visualization process will help you connect with these different aspects of yourself for your own healing and spiritual growth. Read through the exercise fully first and familiarize yourself with it. This will enable you to go through each step of the process in a relaxed state. You can also record this meditation for yourself on audio tape. If you do this, be sure that, as you record it, you allow enough quiet time to complete each part. Allow yourself approximately twenty to twenty-five minutes to do the whole exercise, taking about three minutes for each chakra. You may find, however, that your perception of time shifts during the exercise, so feel free to spend more time with it if you like.

People experience this exercise in various ways. You may visualize or see the chakras with your "inner eyes," experience certain sensations in your body such as warmth or tingling, or have certain emotional feelings emerge as you go through the exercise. The important thing is to observe your experience and notice what you feel. You may even want to keep a record of these experiences in a journal, in order to see how the process evolves for you over time. To gain the most benefit from this exercise, do it every day for seven continuous days. This guided visualization can also be used as a daily meditation practice, or whenever you feel a need to center in and connect with all the parts of your being. (See chapter 4, Awareness and Meditation, for more information on meditation techniques.)

## *A Guided Meditation: The Chakras*

Take a relaxed, comfortable position, adjusting your body so that your spine is straight.

Close your eyes and take a few cleansing breaths, allowing any thoughts or tensions to be released and just drain right out of your body with each exhalation. It may help you to make a soft sighing sound as you exhale each breath. Then, just breathe naturally, letting your breath be soft and easy. Have a sense that with each exhalation, now, you can sink a little deeper inside, a little deeper into your body. Ask that the protective presence of white light enfold you for this meditation experience.

Bring your consciousness to the base of your spine and the root chakra. Breathe deeply into this area, sensing or visualizing the color red as you do. Imagine that just as the trees have roots that extend deep into the ground, you have a red tail-like root extending out of the coccyx bone at the base of your spine, into the Earth. Have a sense of your own root connection with the Earth and your physical earth body through this base chakra. Feel it ground you deep within yourself, helping you feel present and centered in your own body.

As you breathe into this area at the base of your spine, feel the creative life force from the Earth that is available to you through this chakra. Allow this life force energy to fill you completely. Feel, sense, or imagine it flow up into every part of you from this chakra, nourishing every muscle, bone, organ system, and cell of your body with gentle, loving kindness. Experience your own physical vitality enhanced with each breath. Acknowledge your body for the way it has served you and be receptive to anything the wisdom of your body has to share with you at this time, anything that your body wants you to know.

Now that you've connected with the life force in some way, allow your consciousness to move up the spine to the area of your abdomen. Imagine the orange color of a sunrise infusing the sky at dawn. Breathe this orange color into the area just above your pubic bone. Feel this orange color enfold you like a warm, comfortable blanket, like a mother lovingly holding her child. Allow yourself to simply rest and be nurtured by this energy of the second chakra.

Bring your consciousness, now, to the solar plexus area just above your navel. As you breathe into this area, imagine a warm yellow sun here emanating vibrant light and energy. Feel your connection with this part of you, your instinctual feelings, personal power, and will. Notice what you sense from this place. Because of things that have happened in the past, you may have lost a sense of this part of you at times. Affirm your desire, now, to heal and listen to this aspect of your being. Notice if there is anything you feel, sense, or experience from this place now, or any guidance that your instinctual self has to share with you.

When you are ready, breathe into your heart area as you imagine the healing color of a deep, mossy green forest or the clear green light of a shining emerald. Feel this healing green energy and light radiate forth from your heart center and bathe your entire body. Feel the love that emanates from this part of you. If you have trouble with this, it may help you to remember a time when you felt a lot of love for someone or something.

Feel the compassionate understanding from your heart for where you are now in your life process. There may have been times in the past when you became disheartened, or gave your heart away to another. Lovingly invite this heart energy back to you now, welcoming this part of you home, for the heart can help you more clearly understand your true desires. Breathe this energy, deeply and completely, right back into your heart area and surround it with a soft, healing light. When you are ready, notice any intuitive feelings or guidance that your heart may have for you at this time.

Continuing, then, along your spine, imagine your throat chakra as a beautiful cup or chalice filled with clear blue liquid light. Feel, sense, or imagine yourself taking the cup to your lips. As you slowly inhale, drink in this clear blue liquid light of your divine truth and breathe in its healing vapors. Feel this substance circulate throughout your whole body. As you exhale, feel it assisting you in speaking forth the truth of your own being, and eliminating any blocks that you may have to expressing yourself.

Move now to the third eye center in the middle of your forehead and imagine a deep indigo violet color in this area. Have a sense of dropping into that place deep behind your eyes, in the middle of your brain. Imagine that a beam of light emerges, like a lighthouse beacon, radiating indigo light from this chakra center. As you breathe slowly, feel this light beam scanning your immediate environment, like a lighthouse lamp illuminating the seacoast, aiding you in seeing and perceiving yourself and the world around you more clearly.

As you continue, bring your awareness up to the crown of your head. Imagine a flower at the crown of your head slowly unfolding. It will open up just enough for you at this time to let just the right amount of spirit essence in. There may have been times in your life when you felt your spirit self had to recede from full presence with you. Welcome your spirit self home, now, as you see, feel, or imagine a radiant white light coming into your head through the flower at your crown. It will be just the right amount for you at this time.

Breathe in this radiant spirit light. Receive it in as it continues down into the brain and all along your spine. Feel it circulate throughout your whole body. Allow every part of your body, every cell, to be bathed and infused with this healing light. Feel the light awaken, energize, and enliven every part of your being. As you do, open to receive any guidance or wisdom that your spirit self has for you now.

Then bring your conscious awareness back to your heart area. Feel both the life force energy from your root chakra and the spirit light entering at your crown join and mingle in your heart center. Breathe these energies deeply and completely right into your heart and into the very core of your being. From this place, experience your connection with both Heaven and Earth within you. Have a sense of bringing all of the parts of yourself—spirit, intuitive heart feelings, instinctual will, and body, into balanced harmony and alignment. Allow yourself to just savor this experience of wholeness for a while. Notice how you feel in your body now.

Gently and easily, take a few moments to come back to external awareness. When you are ready, open your eyes.

Write down anything that you would like to about your experience, especially any guidance or intuitive feelings that you may have had. Were there any chakra centers that were more difficult for you to connect with and experience? Were there uncomfortable feelings associated with any of the chakras, or did any of the chakra colors appear murky or brownish gray in your mind's eye? If so, this may indicate areas where energy has been deficient or blocked. Spend extra time bringing energy into these areas with your breath. As you breathe into these areas, it will help you to inhale and exhale the colors related to the specific chakras involved—for example; root, red; abdomen, orange; solar plexus, yellow.

---

## Notes

1. The term *body-mind* in this text refers to the connection between the physical body and the conscious and subconscious elements of the psyche. This includes both personal subconscious forces and the deeper universal components of the mind, which all humans share, referred to as the collective unconscious.

2. Candace B. Pert, *Molecules of Emotion: Why You Feel The Way You Feel* (New York: Scribner, 1997).

3. Fred Alan Wolf, *The Body Quantum: The New Physics of Body, Mind, and Health* (New York: Macmillan, 1986), p. vii.

4. Fritjof Capra, *The Tao of Physics: An Exploration of the Parallels Between Modern Physics and Eastern Mysticism* 3rd ed., Rev. (Boston: Shambhala, 1991).

5. David Bohm, *Wholeness and the Implicate Order* (New York: Routledge, 1980).

6. Ibid.; also, William Keepin, Ph.D., "Astrology and the New Physics: Integrating Sacred and Secular Sciences." *The Mountain Astrologer*, August/September, 1995.

7. Virginia MacIvor and Sandra LaForest, *Vibrations: Healing Through Color, Homeopathy, and Radionics.* (New York: Samuel Weiser, 1979).

8. Itzhak Bentov, *Stalking the Wild Pendulum: On the Mechanics of Consciousness* (Rochester, VT: Destiny Books, 1988).

9. Barbara Brennan, *Hands of Light* (New York: Bantam Books, 1988). Virginia MacIvor and Sandra LaForest, *Vibrations: Healing Through Color, Homeopathy, and Radionics* (New York: Samuel Weiser, 1979).

10. Harold S. Burr, *The Fields of Life: Our Links With the Universe* (New York: Ballentine, 1972).

11. Jack Schwartz, *Human Energy Systems* (New York: NAL/Dutton, 1979).

12. Ann Hill, *A Visual Encyclopedia of Unconventional Medicine* (New York: Crown Publishers, 1979).

13. There are reportedly twenty-one minor chakras located at various points in the body. See Barbara Brennan, *Hands of Light* (New York: Bantam Books, 1988).

14. Barbara Brennan, *Light Emerging* (New York: Bantam Books, 1993).

do all individuals
who pursue transpersonal
healing as a profession go
through the same stages
in the evolution of their
consciousness?

# 2

# THE PSYCHODYNAMICS OF HEALING

## *Archetypal Patterns of Energy*

**LET'S LOOK MORE SPECIFICALLY NOW AT** how psychosomatic changes occur in the body-mind. Within the body itself, there is a physiological reflection of the universal matrix of energy that surrounds and connects all matter. This organizational substance of the body is the translucent connective tissue called fascia. These sturdy yet elastic fascial sheaths are interwoven throughout the whole body. They surround every muscle, bone, nerve, blood vessel, and visceral organ.

The web-like fascia connects and defines, enwraps and also supports all the parts of the body, integrating them into a functional whole. If one part of this body system is acted upon, the other parts are affected and respond in much the same way that pulling lightly on a section of a spider's web will result in the whole web stretching and moving in response to the pulling.

This fascial matrix is the material substance that carries much of the energy from the similarly web-like etheric body to every part of our physical vehicle. If there are places of tension or blockage in the fascia, energy is unable to flow as effectively into the various systems of the physical body.

How does this type of blockage develop? Through contact and communication with the nervous system, muscles and surrounding fascia respond to physical injury, emotional trauma, and habitual patterns of thought and action. For example, imagine that you are experiencing the emotion of sadness, perhaps due to a painful situation in your life. You might feel vulnerable and unprotected. In response to this sensory information, motor neurons would transmit impulses to the muscles signaling them to contract. Your shoulders might be brought forward and around shielding a concave chest. Myofascial layers thus respond to these sad, vulnerable feelings by providing protection. If the sad feelings are accompanied by a sense of having to be big and strong, the muscles might provide a compensated pretense of strength by pushing the chest up and out. This posture is often found in men, which is not surprising since men in our culture have been taught to never show any sign of weakness.

If this type of painful situation continues, such body patterns may become set. Muscles will shorten and thicken and/or become fused together by invading connective tissue. This prevents the natural independent movement of the muscles. A structure of fixed muscle tension or "armor" is formed. The wisdom and efficiency of this process is that the body can function without constantly having to be activated for emergency defense. The protection is set automatically so that the body-mind system can attend to other things. However, the dynamic moves from a conscious external level to an unconscious one. At this point, you may no longer be consciously aware of rounded shoulders or even feelings of vulnerability.

Long after the painful experience is past, the body may still hold this armored pattern, unable to relax. This character pattern can then continue to affect the way you perceive the world. Instead of a direct experience—a spontaneous feeling in the present—experience is restricted, filtered through patterns of the past held in the body-mind. This creates a tendency to be bound psychosomically—psychologically and physically—to a particular character formation such as the protective pattern of the concave chest. Several body-mind approaches have systems of character typology based on such somatic patterns.[1]

This dynamic of mental-emotional states creating an effect on the physical body is also seen in certain somatoform disorders. In these cases, people with a pattern of anxiety exhibit complaints of bodily symptoms for which no organic basis can be found. What may not be realized in traditional psychology is that the body is responding to what is happening emotionally. Remember, the etheric body, which serves as the energetic pattern for the physical form, is sensitive to impressions from the mental and emotional planes via the chakras. Even though no actual physical changes have occurred, people with somatoform disorders may indeed be feeling sensations on the etheric body level. If the emotional disturbance continues and is not dealt with, then organic physiological changes could indeed take place. What we don't heal on the emotional level is held in the physical body as the pattern becomes more somatically formed.

The reverse can also be true. If there is a physical disturbance, it can sometimes affect the mental-emotional state. The trauma of a physical injury itself can affect our emotional and mental outlook. The fascia also reacts to physical injury in the same way that it does to emotional trauma. Connective tissue surrounds the injured muscle or part, bracing the area and providing protective reinforcement. Other muscle groups may have to compensate and overwork because the injured part cannot function normally. A set body pattern or armor can also result from this, and in turn affect the mental and emotional state. For example, let's say you injure your back in a fall. You may learn to walk carefully to protect yourself from pain and further injury. If the recovery process is long, this pattern may continue for a while. This required carefulness in walking could bring forth anxious feelings that might even develop into an emotional inflexibility that continues long after the body heals.

This illustrates quite clearly that there is a linear causal dynamic; that is, mental-emotional disease can cause somatic disturbance, or physical pathology can cause psychological disturbance. However, with physiological information feeding back to the mental-emotional sphere and vice versa, it becomes hard to distinguish which came first, the mental or physical disturbance. This is somewhat like trying to figure out which came first, the chicken or the egg. In the case of the back injury just mentioned, for example, was emotional inflexibility caused by the injury or did the mental and emotional rigidity cause the inflexible body stance and result in physical injury? This leads to a whole different dynamic operating in the body-mind, the principle of synchronicity.

# SYNCHRONICITY

Carl Jung used the word *synchronicity* to describe the relationship between two or more events that are linked in a meaningful way, yet have no apparent causal connection. These seemingly coincidental events are connected by an identical theme or similar meaning that is being expressed. For instance, the identical theme in the previous example of the back injury is rigidity and inflexibility. The individual's injury left the back inflexible.

Emotional rigidity is also a type of inflexibility. From this perspective, the individual's injured back would be seen as a synchronistic occurrence to the rigid mental-emotional state.

The back injury could, in fact, be bringing the individual's attention to the rigid behaviors, thus providing an opportunity to heal on a much deeper emotional level.

Physical symptoms are often synchronistic with other themes or events taking place in our lives. I had an experience once when I was thinking of separating from my husband that illustrates this point. I kept beehives and one day was stung on my wedding band finger. This was unusual in itself, because I rarely got stung. What was even more unusual is that I had a bad reaction and my finger swelled up like a balloon. Soon the wedding ring was preventing the circulation of blood in my finger, and the wedding band had to be cut off with wire cutters. As the band was being separated from my finger, I was aware of all my feelings about separating from my husband and ending the marriage. My finger quickly returned to normal after the ring was removed. The bee sting and ensuing events were synchronistic to my desire to separate. The marriage was constricting and confining me just as the wedding band was preventing the flow of blood to my finger so it could heal. I could no longer deny what I knew in my heart to be true. I had to end the marriage. In this way, the synchronistic body disturbance acted as a guiding message for my life.

Sometimes extraordinary external synchronistic events can occur that are related to our internal state. For example, a client of mine was awakened at 1:30 in the morning by a house fire alarm and could find no physical reason why the alarm had been triggered. However, when he was a senior in high school more than thirty years previous, at that exact time and on that same date, his father had suffered a heart attack. It was a traumatic event, and he had thought about it every year since then around that time. The fire alarm incident acted as a synchronistic "wake-up call," bringing his conscious attention to this unresolved emotional issue that still existed relating to his father.

Edward Whitmont describes synchronistic forces as fields of
energy that exert a certain tension or stress. The only way the
field can be observed is through the objects that enter it and
respond in certain ways:

> (for instance, a magnet needle responds mechanically
> with deflection, a neon tube with a light phenomenon
> to the same electric field. A piece of wood will not
> respond at all.) Thus, the field is a kind of transcenden-
> tal entity never directly observable which we know only
> through the particular behavior of the objects which it
> affects and through which it manifests itself.
>
> Similarly, the transcendental "meaning" underlying the
> synchronistic occurrences manifests itself to us only
> through the objects which it affects and which, each in
> their own and characteristic way, give it expression.
> Thus, whenever . . . one's course of life passes through
> a "field of meaning" this field manifests itself through
> events on various levels (for instance, psyche, soma), all
> of them in their own different fashion giving expression
> to that same formative factor.[2]

This illustrates that there is a type of synchronistic energy
field connection between psychological and physiological
states. In the case of my synchronistic experience, the energetic
field of meaning manifested in the form of a bee sting along
with the physical symptom of the swollen finger and the
accompanying emotional feelings and realizations surrounding
my marriage.

So now we know that the energy bodies and chakras relate to
our mental, emotional, and physical states of being and that
there is a synchronistic principle involved when symptoms
occur. What might be the underlying purpose and core
dynamic operating in this process that affects changes in the

body-mind system? For the answer, let's take a look at the role of the archetypes.

# ARCHETYPES

Jung recognized that there are certain fundamental guiding themes of life that occur as part of the human experience. He believed that just as the human species has a common anatomy regardless of race or culture, so too does the human psyche have a prototypical pattern or blueprint of experience stored in the collective ancestral memory. Jung called these primordial patterns *archetypes* and found that they are the central factors around which elements of our life are organized. Archetypal themes such as Masculine, Feminine, Self, Child, Ruler, Hero, Warrior, Birth, and Death are principles that all people experience in their lives in some form or another. All humans experience a childhood, are faced with a particular ruling power, and see the heroes of the day rise and fall. We also deal with these themes internally in our own psyches. For instance, it's possible to experience an internal death as old patterns and self-perceptions die. Similarly, there is a Warrior within all of us that can call us forth to moments of great courage and strength.

Jung viewed an archetype as a dynamic pattern that carried a real force and embodied a specific energy.[3] He felt that the archetypes act as the core focus around which the experiences and contents of our psyche are formed. Emotionally charged groups of ideas, memories, and feelings, known as complexes, constellate around these central archetypal themes. As guiding mechanisms, the archetypes focus our attention on certain issues and dynamics to aid us in giving expression to an essential quality within us. They operate as the guiding factors behind synchronistic events and the meaningful connection between them. For example, the guiding mechanism behind my client's fire alarm experience was archetypal Father. It brought his conscious attention to the emotionally charged memories and feelings surrounding his own father's death. Only through resolving these issues from the past could he come into the true inner authority and wisdom that archetypal Father represents.

Through the archetypal lens, we are able to experience the different dimensions of our own being. In this way, we come to realize more of our true nature, our essential Self. This was certainly true in the case of my bee sting. The experience brought my conscious attention to feelings that I was trying to ignore. This old pattern of denying my real feelings in the marriage was falling away so that I could begin to know and express myself more authentically. Like the bee sting, ending the marriage was painful. However, it was also a doorway that brought me into a deeper realization of my true Self and my power as a woman.

Although the archetypes represent experiences that we all share as human beings, certain specific archetypal qualities will be more dominant or significant in each individual's life. In this sense, they represent aspects of our essential soul nature guiding us on our path in this lifetime. Archetypal Teacher, Healer, Artist, or Mystic may represent an important essential part of your soul path and purpose. I have included an exercise at the end of this chapter, along with a list of the main archetypes, to assist you in discovering your own essential soul energies.

## Fragmentation

The archetypes help us give expression to an essential quality within us and represent a part of ourselves that we need to integrate, usually a part that has been denied. Through wounding experiences in this lifetime (or past lives), these parts of us become unacceptable and actually split off in an energetic sense. I had a client give a wonderful example of this in describing an experience that she had with her father. As a young woman, her father had called her worthless and said that she was a "waste." She remembered the feeling this way: "It was as if time stood still and there was a blast, and everything shattered."

Her father's message was strong. His comment was so shocking and damaging that this individual lost a part of herself and her womanhood that day. The part of her that knew she was a worthwhile woman split off. She carried this sense of worthlessness and low self-esteem into adulthood. It took a series of relationships with abusive men for her to see that she was repeating this pattern set by her father.

When archetypes first emerge carrying the energy of these split off parts of ourselves, they often take the form of internal guides or spirit helpers. Some people see or imagine guides visually. Others sense a presence or hear them as an inner voice. For still others, they appear in dreams or meditation. They bring direction, guidance, and understanding, and have a specific character related to the archetypal energy they embody. In the case of the woman just mentioned, two archetypal energies in the form of internal guides came forth to help in her healing process. One of the guides who emerged was an old Wise Woman who helped her reclaim her feminine spirit and self-esteem. The other, a male Indian Warrior, brought empowerment and provided a positive masculine aspect. By communicating with these two archetypal guides through a type of internal dialogue, she was able to heal and change the self-abusive pattern that she had been in.

The energetically fragmented parts of ourselves are like pieces of a broken vessel trying to come back to become one whole piece again. When these denied parts originally split off, they retreat from full presence with us. This usually involves a difficult emotional experience or physical trauma. People are usually not conscious of it when it happens. However, they often describe such a traumatic experience as "I felt like a part of me died," "I lost a piece of me that day," or "I locked a part of me away." They may lose a certain vitality or connection with life. This can be likened to a partial death of sorts. At death, the soul leaves the body. When denied parts split off, it's as if some aspect of the soul leaves and temporarily retreats from full presence with us. Sometimes this happens as a matter of survival. If a part of us is unacceptable to an abusive parent, for example, that part must recede in order to assure our continued physical and emotional well-being.

When an essential archetypal soul energy is denied, distorted, or fragmented in this way, subpersonalities develop. Subpersonalities are semi-autonomous parts of the personality that are expressions of complexes. They embody these emotionally charged contents of the psyche. As parts split off because of traumatic or difficult experiences, these subpersonalities form, creating a distortion in the way the essential archetypal energy expresses itself. The positive qualities of the archetypal energy then deteriorate and are expressed in a negative way.

The work done by psychologists Hal Stone and Sidra Winkelman has greatly increased the understanding of subpersonality dynamics.[4] They demonstrate that each person's psyche contains many different subpersonalities, including the Critic, the Protector or Controller, the Child, and the Perfectionist or Pusher. The Critic is an embodiment of all internalized negative messages such as "You're so stupid. You can't do anything right." The Protector/Controller subpersonality is an inner big boss who exerts control to make sure that the false persona stays in place, both for protection and to gain acceptance and approval from others. The Child within contains the memories and feelings of all our childhood experiences. Although it can express itself in creative and playful ways, this subpersonality is often an immature part of us that can be the source of angry, vulnerable, or needy feelings. The Perfectionist/Pusher, on the other hand, pushes one to achieve more, and do it either bigger, faster, or more perfectly.

If you've ever heard a critical voice inside of you dominating your consciousness, or experienced feeling like a scared little child, you've been dealing with a subpersonality. You might even have felt, at times, as if there were two parts inside of you fighting for control regarding a particular issue. For example, the Child in you may want to go to the movies, but your Perfectionist subpersonality wants you to go over that business proposal for your boss one more time. By becoming aware of their presence and consciously communicating with your subpersonalities, such conflicts within the psyche can be resolved and disowned parts of your personality can be reintegrated.

To illustrate, imagine that you incarnate with the archetype of the Artist and are ridiculed by your father who wants his child to be an athlete. The Artist aspect would recede as you tried to please your father, avoid embarrassment, and get the love you needed. As a result of this experience, a vulnerable Child subpersonality might develop along with a Critic like the father and perhaps a Rebel subpersonality fighting against the control. As an adult, you might experience being uncontrollably self-critical or act inappropriately rebellious and argumentative at times. If the Artist soul quality was severely repressed, you might be unaware of any creative or artistic talents, or possibly have put these interests aside long ago. In order to fully realize and express the creativity of the Artist, you would need to heal these childhood injuries to self. As contaminating past experiences are cleared from the body and psyche, the subpersonalities and accompanying complexes are transformed and lost or disowned parts of the self are reclaimed. The true soul intention of the archetypal essence can then be expressed.

In extreme cases, when fragmentation happens frequently in childhood before the ego is strongly developed, a severe splitting of the ego personality can result and distinct autonomous independent personalities develop. This is known as Multiple Personality Disorder. Sometimes, people fear they have such a disorder when they first consciously experience their subpersonalities. However, this is usually not the case. Most people have a whole central ego operating with the subpersonalities merely exerting an influence on it. The key is strengthening the often weak and wounded ego and interacting with the subpersonalities in a consciously aware way so that the they no longer dominate the personality. Dialogue and journaling processes central to this type of healing work will be explained later in this book.

If you find at any time that you are hearing internal dialogue or voices that are making you fearful or telling you to do bad things, please seek the guidance of a professional therapist.

## Archetypes and Energy

I feel it is useful to think of the archetypes in energetic as well as psychological terms. The archetypal forces that help us reintegrate split-off parts of ourselves emit a specific, purposeful pattern of energy. In my view, these archetypal forces operate as meaningful energetic fields with a particular harmonic frequency, and thus interact with the body's own system of energy. The archetypes represent principles being expressed through us as certain essential soul qualities and patterns. They therefore carry higher vibratory frequencies. As these soul energies seek to be expressed and embodied, they bring this accelerated energy with them into the body-mind system.

 When an archetypal field of meaning, with its particular vibratory frequency, interacts with the chakras and energy bodies, it produces changes in the equilibrium leading to synchronistic phenomena in the body-mind. Remember, the chakras act as centers through which energy is transformed into matter. Likewise, the archetypal energy is also transformed and made manifest in some way through certain mental, emotional, or physical phenomena. In this way, that which is unseen and unknown can be brought to conscious awareness, enabling us to remember who we really are and manifest our true essence. These soul aspects of a higher and finer vibration are continually seeking to be more fully embodied through this process. As we grow in consciousness, we are also able to incorporate and maintain a greater level of this energy.

Whether or not the equilibrium of the body-mind is disturbed by an archetypal presence depends largely on the resonant quality of the fields involved. As an essential archetypal energy resonates with an aspect of our own soul and seeks expression through us, it will amplify and exert pressure on anything that is not in alignment with it. If one is totally aligned, without blockages to a particular archetypal soul quality, the body's energy field is in harmony with the vibration of the archetypal force and probably no psychophysical phenomena will occur. In such a case, the archetypal field meets no resistance and we can give full expression to an essential aspect of our own being. In most cases, however, because of core beliefs from childhood, cultural restrictions, or even past-life experience, we are unable or unwilling to acknowledge these aspects of ourselves. In these cases, the chakras are not aligned with the archetypal energy and this dissonance would show up in the specific chakras involved as a blockage or imbalance of some type. As these chakras come in contact with the archetypal field, they are stimulated to align with the vibration of the essential soul energy. In the process, the blocks or distortions of the energy at these chakra points manifest as various mental, emotional, and/or physical disturbances.

This view is similar to that of Samuel Hahnemann, the founder of homeopathic medicine, who believed that disease entered the body on mental, emotional, and physical levels in the form of subtle, undetectable forces called *miasms*. These energetic miasms impact the vital force, thereby creating certain symptoms and conditions. Hahnemann felt that an individual could be predisposed to certain diseases because of miasms passed down from generation to generation. Jung believed that archetypal themes ran through generations of families, as well. This would support the belief that perhaps, on a soul level, we choose certain family patterns or conditions in order to further our development as a being.

 As it stimulates the various chakra centers, the archetypal soul energy can manifest as past-life or mystical experiences, dreams and visions, mental patterns, emotional dynamics, or physical symptoms, depending on the particular centers that are affected. The resulting manifest symptoms act as symbolic messages, pointing the way to our essential Self as all that separates us from our true soul intention is revealed. By bringing conscious awareness to these symbolic phenomena, healing can take place, lost parts of ourselves can be reclaimed, and the essential soul message of the archetypal energy can be discovered.

My client Karen gives an example of how these archetypal energies can manifest in our lives. When I asked her if she had any particular dream in life or thing that she thought she might have a talent for, she replied that she'd always wanted to be a writer (Communicator archetype), but feared expressing her own power and truth. This theme of communication was expressed throughout her life in many ways. Karen felt self-conscious about her very long and slender neck, the area of the throat chakra and the center of communication and self-expression. In addition, when starting to talk, she sometimes felt a physically constricting sensation in her throat. She had been sexually abused as a child and forced to keep it a secret. Karen was again raped later in life and threatened with harm if she cried out in any way. It is no wonder that she also suffered through a codependent marriage to an alcoholic for many years while saying nothing to friends and church members. In a session where she remembered her birth experience, Karen realized that her mother had to get married because she was pregnant with her. She felt that her mother hadn't loved or wanted her when she was born. Karen had come into the world feeling like it wasn't OK to be here and express who she was. In the process of our work together, Karen also experienced a past-life session in which she had her head severed from her body at the neck as punishment for expressing her feminine power in some way.

The Communicator archetype expressed itself through Karen's somatic structure and bodily sensations, her current issue regarding self-expression, the birth and developmental childhood dynamics, and the past-life experience. Although this aspect of her essential Self was repressed through the dynamics of Karen's childhood, it continued to seek expression, thus activating the bodily sensations in the throat area and presenting emotional issues. It was only through the process of resolving the emotional issues from her past that Karen could begin to express her essential Self and allow the writer in her to come forth.

If several different synchronistic phenomena are possible, what determines the exact way in which an archetypal energy will manifest at any given time? One aspect involves the particular path a being chooses and the intention that is present before incarnating. Our soul essence is composed of certain archetypal patterns. We choose to give expression to a particular archetypal energy because we are seeking to reinforce, balance, or develop certain qualities in this life for our own soul growth. As part of this soul development here on Earth, each spirit is drawn toward certain conditions, situations, or experiences in order to come to know this essential soul quality more fully. For example, a being may incarnate with the soul mission of becoming a teacher, healer, or leader and have certain life experiences surrounding those archetypal themes. On a soul level, Karen may have chosen certain life experiences in order to develop her ability to express her truth. It is important to remember that within the chosen experience, there is always free will and various avenues that can provide the needed soul growth. In this regard, many people misunderstand karma as a type of punishment and judgment when in actuality, it is concerned with learning, gaining new soul experience, and evolving as a spiritual being.

 It is also true that when we incarnate into physical form, our pure essence and archetypal energies are often repressed or denied their true expression, especially if there is no accepting environment for those aspects. Karen's childhood experiences are an example of this. Even birth, our first experience here on Earth, is often a traumatic process that does not support our essential nature. This type of damaging life experience creates imbalances in certain chakra centers. Phenomena specific to these chakras will arise as the archetypal energy stimulates them, again seeking full embodiment in us and through us.

Another dynamic that may be at work is illustrated by a fundamental principle of homeopathy, which states that the defense mechanism of the human organism will respond to disease and adjust to stress in a way that is the least detrimental to the system given the current state of health.[5] The spiritual/mental dimension is seen as the most significant to the total functioning and expression of the organism, then the emotional sphere, and the physical, which is the least crucial. For example, a migraine headache is a less serious threat to health than suicidal depression. However, a severe physical ailment such as a brain tumor will override this general hierarchy and be seen as a greater threat to functioning than a mild case of anxiety. Based on this principle, the body-mind system will respond to archetypal influence in a way that expresses the symbolic meaning of the archetype and allows for the greatest integrity of the whole system. Intuitive insights, benign synchronistic events, and dreams emerge as some of the most harmless responses, with severe physical and psychological disorders being at the other end of the spectrum.

If the initial symbolic message of the archetype is not acknowledged and the energy is denied, it may lead to more serious disorders. This is a similar process to repression on the emotional plane and suppression on the physical plane. Just as repression of basic feelings, such as sadness or anger, can lead to deeper and more serious psychological issues, so too can repression of an archetypal soul energy lead to more serious problems. This kind of repression has its correlation on the physical level with suppression of certain symptoms that are a healing or balancing factor. Masking or suppressing signs of an illness can cause symptoms to intensify and manifest on a deeper, more vital level of the organism. For example, suppressing cold symptoms such as a cough or sinus congestion with certain medication may cause the symptoms to go deeper into the lungs and bronchus.[6] Physiologically, certain antihistamines may cause the mucus in your head and sinus to thicken, making it a better trap for virus particles that are then passed along to the ears and throat.[7] Of course, we need medicine sometimes and must do what is needed to bring healing. There is nothing wrong with this. Whenever possible, however, it is preferable to use healing systems, such as homeopathy, that work with the whole person rather than just fixing symptoms.

Yet another dimension of the way archetypal energy influences the body-mind is found in the relationship between planetary cycles and events on Earth. The planetary configurations at the time and place of an individual's birth relate to the expression of specific archetypal soul energies operating in that person's life. Much like our own human energy system, planetary bodies also have emanating fields of energy that radiate into space. These planetary magnetic fields affect the Earth's magnetic field, as well as our own energy bodies. I highly recommend Dr. Percy Seymour's book, *The Scientific Basis of Astrology*, to anyone interested in investigating the ways the Sun, Moon, and other planetary bodies affect the Earth's magnetic field and how species behavior responds to those fluctuations. Dr. Seymour, who is the principal lecturer in astronomy at the University of Plymouth in England states:

> The whole Solar System is playing a symphony on the magnetic field of the Earth . . . we are all genetically "tuned" to receive a different set of melodies from the symphony.[8]

As Dr. Seymour describes, the planets create a gravitational tidal tug on the hot gases held within the magnetosphere surrounding the Earth, causing the vibrations of the Earth's field to come into resonance with planetary movements. In addition, the magnetic field of the Sun is disrupted by the position and motion of the planets. These planetary magnetic patterns are in turn transmitted to the Earth by means of the solar winds, creating fluctuations in the geomagnetic field. According to Dr. Seymour, these changes in the Earth's magnetic field create an electrical stimulation to the human nervous system. In the womb, the fetus' developing nervous system is constantly picking up these messages from the planets via the ever fluctuating magnetic field of the Earth. The planetary configurations then become synchronized with the internal biological clock of the fetus, which controls the moment of birth. We thus come into the world with our own unique planetary imprint encoded in our nervous system and are "phase-locked" to resonate with certain planetary emanations.[9]

Although Seymour's work provides a scientific basis for celestial influence based on the effect of planetary magnetic fields, from the standpoint of David Bohm's concept of holomovement, there can be no question that since all things are connected and are effecting and affected by one another, that planetary resonance exists.

Dr. Seymour also refers to the research done by Michel Gauquelin, the former director of the Paris Laboratory of Relations Between Cosmic Cycles and Psychophysiology. Gauquelin repeatedly performed stringently controlled experiments, which revealed that noteworthy individuals in various professions tend to be born at times when certain specific planets are close to the horizon or the upper and lower culmination points (Zenith and Nadir).[10] For example, military men, entrepreneurs, and athletes tend to be born with Mars located near one of these points, while scientists have Saturn positioned there. This demonstrates that there is a relationship between the planets and specific archetypal qualities. Mars, for instance, relates to the Warrior archetype and Saturn relates to the archetypal Elder authority. In fact, Gauquelin's experiments showed that the individuals in each field were seen to have similar personality characteristics consistent with the energy attributed to their prominent planet. Those with Mars dominant were dynamic, brave, energetic, daring, and strong-willed fighters, whereas those with a strong Saturn influence were reserved, methodical, somber, wise, and observant. Those with Venus in prominence, were beloved, charming, agreeable, seductive, and considerate. Likewise, my client, Karen, had the planet Mercury, which embodies the archetype of communication and self-expression at the Zenith or Midheaven at the time of her birth.

As mentioned earlier, each being is drawn to the conditions, situations, and experiences that are needed to fulfill the specific tasks and evolutionary process in each lifetime. Those conditions include the particular planetary configurations that will support the soul's journey on Earth. Each being chooses to incarnate at a time when the planetary dynamics are most conducive to the completion of its soul purpose. Although the nervous system of the developing physical form is affected by the planetary emanations during the whole gestation period, the major imprint happens at the time of actual birth.[11] Up to this point, the soul has been protected from outer influences by an etheric womb, which was formed at conception.[12] At the time the soul incarnates, this protective etheric womb is removed and the being is very open and impressionable to all outer influences, including the planetary energies and the Earth's magnetic field. At the moment of birth, planetary emanations stream forth and imprint a specific pattern on the individual's nervous system and auric field. This planetary imprint is encoded in the being's physical nervous system and energetic chakra centers.

The natal planetary imprints continue to be activated by the current position of the planets throughout each individual's lifetime. The emanating rays of the planets resonate with our natal archetypal soul patterns urging us to express our true essence and complete our soul task. This is especially true at periods of one's life when the planetary energies make certain challenging aspects—such as 90-degree square angles or 180-degree oppositions—to the celestial birth patterns, or when natal planetary configurations are repeated—like the yearly return of the Sun to its position at the time of your birth (your birthday), or when Saturn returns to its natal position around age twenty-nine. At such times, the impact of the archetypal energies on the body-mind may be amplified, creating certain synchronistic psychophysical phenomena.

In her book, *Liquid Light of Sex*, Barbara Hand Clow correlates key life passages to the cycles of certain celestial bodies. The return of Saturn, for example, to the position it had at birth relates to the time for achieving maturity and the discipline to accomplish our life task. Clow associates the period when the planet Uranus directly opposes its natal position, which occurs around the age of forty, to the process of midlife crisis and kundalini awakening.

If it seems difficult to imagine that a planet from so far away can have this kind of impact, consider the principle of resonant amplification. Just as the dynamic of resonance increases the amplification of one musical note to the point it can break a glass of equal frequency (Ella Fitzgerald-style), so too can the planetary archetypes affect the human energy system through resonating with an aspect of our own soul and the celestial imprint encoded in our nervous systems. Ella's shattering glass demonstrates what a powerful and impactful process this can sometimes be.

As a psychotherapist and counseling astrologer, I have continually had an opportunity to observe the way planetary cycles are reflected in the lives of my clients through the issues they are currently experiencing. For example, my client Joan, who had suffered intestinal difficulties in the past, had recently been sick with a cold that affected her throat. Joan is a herbalist who often felt like she had to appease people. She would overburden herself, trying to heal the pain of others while unaware that she was ignoring her own. Joan was born with the small planetary body Chiron (Healer archetype) descending or setting on the horizon with Saturn (Elder power and authority) at the point directly opposite the Midheaven known as the Nadir. In addition to the Midheaven and the East (Ascendant, rising) and West (Descendant, setting) horizon points, the Nadir position can also be significant. As the point located farthest below the local horizon and outside of the view of an observer, it can represent those things that are more hidden within and below the surface, those elements of which we are not as consciously aware. For Joan, it meant that there were possibly subconscious issues preventing her from expressing her true power and authority as a healer.

Joan came in for a session one day when Pluto's current position was at the same point as her Midheaven at birth, directly opposite her natal Saturn, and in a challenging ninety-degree square aspect to her natal Chiron. Pluto's transformative theme of death and rebirth seemed evident as Joan expressed feelings of grief and sadness for which there was no immediate cause. While exploring the roots of these feelings, she began having a sensation of heaviness in her chest that was making it hard for her to breathe. As I had her deepen into this sensation with her intention and breath, she experienced memories and feelings of being in a past life during which a catastrophic event took place that she had contributed to in some way. She felt that the time and culture which she was experiencing was that of Atlantis.

I asked Joan what her heart sensations seemed to be telling her about this past life. Joan reported that her heart was communicating that, during this lifetime, she had been in a position of leadership and power. However, she had allowed her mind to dominate her decisions rather than listening to her intuition (heart) and gut-level feelings (intestines). She let her intellect and scientific mind rule what she said instead of expressing (throat) her doubts and intuitive feelings to others. The eventual consequence of this decision making process was part of a whole series of events that led to other people's pain and death. Joan had carried forward into her present life the resulting guilt for causing this damage and death (Pluto) by feeling responsible for fixing everyone's pain and problems, a distorted expression of the Healer archetype. However, as a result of this session, she realized that the best way for her to make amends now for what had happened then was to be grounded in her body, listen to her heart, and speak forth her truth from this intuitive place.

Joan's heart and throat chakras were stimulated by the Healer archetype seeking expression through her. Joan was also learning to take care of her own needs, listen to her gut-level feelings, and express her personal power without fear—all aspects of the solar plexus chakra, which relates to the digestive organs and her intestinal difficulties. Pluto's current position activated the wounded healer issues, represented by Joan's natal Chiron, which had kept her from her true authority (Saturn) as an intuitive herbalist. The transformative power of Pluto, resonating with Chiron and Saturn's planetary imprints, brought on the emotional grieving, the heart sensations, and the memories of the past-life experience that were blocking Joan's ability to bring through the intuitive heart-wisdom of her archetypal Healer. By clearing this past-life issue, Joan was able to reclaim her psychic healing gifts, which she had denied because of her residual fear of misusing them, enabling her to more fully embody her essence Self. As part of this, she also established a pattern of listening to her heart and instincts, rather than going into her thinking mind and denying her body and feelings.

Becoming aware, through personal study or a professional consultation, of your own natal planetary energies and the current planetary patterns influencing them, will help you work more consciously with the issues that emerge for you relating to your personal growth and spiritual development.[13]

Although, as the previous session shows, disorders sometimes emerge as a result of an archetypal presence, that same presence is available as an ally in the healing process. In a sense, the archetype is the source of both the sickness and the cure. Rather than resisting this healing force, we can better understand the nature of the archetypal energy and consciously participate with it by being aware of what is happening in the body-mind. Instead of denying qualities in us that are unpleasant or by being embarrassed about physical problems, we need to openly accept the teachings they bring. For many people, especially those raised in emotionally unhealthy homes, this kind of openness is difficult. Denial and perfectionist attitudes make it easy to label these characteristics as undesirable elements that need to be suppressed or avoided. There may even be feelings of shame concerning certain things. Although these

qualities may seem negative, ultimately there is a positive healing intention behind them. In order for transformation to take
place, we must take responsibility for bringing conscious awareness to them.

Becoming aware is like tuning in a radio. Going through the
dial settings, we test back and forth the areas of static to tune in
to the clearest transmission of sound. However, even when the
tuning is a little off, the basic force of the radio wave is still
transmitting clearly and trying to get through. This is similar to
the archetypal energy trying to express itself through us. The
static of our body-mind issue tells us that we need the finer tuning of healing and transformation in order to more clearly manifest our true being. Of course, as humans, we prefer to be seen
in a good light without static or problems, and avoid looking at
this "shadow" side, as Jung called it. However this kind of denial
leads to further unhealthy repercussions in our body and psyche.

Conversely, by identifying the purpose of these physical,
mental, and emotional disturbances, the positive true intent of
the archetypal influence can be discovered. That true intent is
the realization and expression of our essential Self. Through the
energetic presence, support, and guidance of the archetypal soul
essence, lost parts of the self can be reintegrated. As part of this
process, repressed qualities, talents, and abilities that we previously might not have been aware of, become available to us.
Also, by listening to these synchronistic messages, these stirrings
of our own soul, we can feel and know our connection with the
meaningful purpose of a loving universe.

# ARCHETYPAL SOUL QUALITIES

To more fully understand the different essential soul qualities that you embody, I'd like to give you an understanding of the major archetypes. Working with the archetypal energies in a conscious way will help you to activate these dynamic soul patterns and more fully embody your essential Self. The following descriptions are brief definitions of the archetypes meant to provide a basic understanding that will facilitate your process of personal growth and spiritual development. Also included are the "shadow" expressions and subpersonalities that can emerge when the archetypal energy is distorted. In addition, I have included the planetary associations to the archetypes where applicable. Although I mention most of the major archetypes and subpersonalities here, this is by no means a complete list. You may also have different names that you prefer to use for the subpersonalities that I do mention. For further information and expansion on these and other archetypal themes, please refer to the writings of Carl Jung and the many fine Jungian authors who elaborate on these subjects through the use of symbolism, dreams, myths, and fairy tales.

Although I have previously discussed the Self, I will mention it again here with regard to the archetypal energies. The archetypal Self, also referred to in this text as the God Self, Higher Self, and essence Self, is that limitless, timeless core which is the spark of the Divine within us. Initially, we exist as the Self experiencing the unity of all being, and then the ego develops as we come into physical existence here and begin to interact with the external world. Although the ego operates as the center of the conscious personality, the Self is the unifying center of the entire psyche, the central ordering principle encompassing both the conscious and subconscious mind. The Self, therefore, is at once both the core center as well as the wholeness of our entire being, in the same way that God can be expressed as both the essence and the totality of all things.

Personal growth and spiritual development involve fully realizing and expressing the Self, which acts as the essential guiding mechanism in this process of individuation. Just as a plant emerges from its nourishing seed center into full growth, so do we awaken spiritually guided by the Higher Self to manifest our true essence. The ability to differentiate and express one's individual needs, desires, and dreams is an important part of this process.

The Self represents the unity of all things and that oneness that unites all opposites (male and female, human and divine, light and dark) into one whole. To realize the wholeness of the Self, the splits within us must be healed and the denied parts of us reclaimed. Symbolic images of unity and wholeness such as the circle, mandala, and the ouroborous snake eating its tail are representative of the Self. The Sun, for example, which is symbolized by a circle (wholeness and union) with a dot in the center (essential core) represents the light of the God Self. In the same way the Sun is the radiating source of life and light in our solar system, the Self is also our center of life and energy. This inner part of our being is the guiding force in our lives and is our connection to the Creative Source of light, love, and consciousness in the universe. We receive this guidance through inspiration, dreams, visions, intuition, and meaningful events in our lives.

The initiatory process of individuation and self-realization is an archetypal journey. This quest, this adventure, this life path we travel, may involve a test of some sort, or require us to accomplish specific tasks. For example, a healing journey, which can lead us to a deeper realization of our Self, requires us to accomplish all the tasks involved in recovering from a certain illness. The journey experience is sometimes solitary in nature, as demonstrated by the vision quest of the Native American tradition in which an individual goes to a sacred wilderness place, alone, to wait for guidance and a vision or realization of his purpose.

One's journey of self-discovery requires a descent into the dark underworld of the subconscious mind so that we can heal the denied and hidden shadow elements residing there and discover the light of life within us. This is the process of bringing that which is unconscious or in darkness into the light of conscious awareness so that it may be healed and transformed. On this journey we confront different forms of an adversary, which is the block, limitation, or resistance that must be transformed or defeated. This can take the form, for example, of a disease, a negative emotional pattern, or an actual person who opposes us. The adversary may be perceived as a wall or great abyss, a dark or evil force seeking to wound or destroy us in some way.

In our personal process of growth, it is important to take responsibility for our own issues and the dynamics at work within us rather than continually blaming our experiences on others or outer circumstances. Often, our greatest adversary to transformation is the ego persona, which may resist change that would unseat its power and upset the false image it projects to the world. For this reason, it is important to resolve the emotional issues that hold our core misbeliefs about ourselves and the world in place. In this way, the ego consciousness can be assisted in aligning with the true intentions of the Self.

Dealing with the adversary on our journey involves the archetypal struggle between Good and Evil. This process provides grist for the mill. We gain strength and grow through these experiences as we come to a deeper realization of our own being.

Sometimes an adversary comes in the form of a Trickster. This cunning or deceptive energy tricks you into confronting your own issues, so that you obtain the life lessons and growth that are necessary in order to trust in Spirit and rely on your inner guidance from Self, rather than the logic of your rational mind. For example, Sarah found herself with automobile problems while on a major highway. She was initially scared when the car motor stopped running. However, she soon found herself on an off-ramp, coasting toward a gas station into which she was able to easily maneuver her car. She felt literally pushed into the station and the mechanics there were easily able to fix the problem. This woman, who had been dealing with the issue of trust, felt very protected and realized that she could trust in a universal power greater than herself. As a result of this experience, she was able to feel her connection to Spirit and trust the way in which it was operating in her life at a much deeper level.

## God or Goddess Archetype

Archetypal God/Goddess is the embodiment of a universal creative power and spiritual presence that we can look to for help, guidance, and inspiration. The expressions of this archetype are as varied as the diverse spiritual beliefs and religions, both past and present, that we see manifest throughout the world along with the creation myths that accompany them. The biblical Judeo-Christian God, masculine in its expression, is in contrast to the more ancient manifestation of divinity referred to as the Magna Mater or Great Mother Goddess. Jehovah is a fiery Father God and heavenly power while the Goddess, the womb of creation, is deeply connected with the processes of life and the forces of nature.

Mythically, however, both of these divine aspects share a dual expression, one light or compassionate and the other wrathful or devouring. For example, the Old Testament God sent a devastating flood as a purifying punishment to humankind, yet He also freed the Hebrew people from slavery by providing safe passage out of Egypt and, in the New Testament, lovingly sent his only Son, the Lord Christ, to bring light to the world. The Great Mother, whose nurturing and comforting expression is illustrated by the gentle and merciful Chinese goddess, Kwan Yin, also has her Terrible Mother expression as is seen in the Indian triple goddess Kali Ma, the powerful Dark Mother of creation, preservation, and destruction. Kali is both womb and tomb, the giver of life and the devouring destroyer of individuals, the Earth, and ultimately even the universe as she spirals into the formless space from which she will bring forth her creation once again.

These dual expressions of God/Goddess are reflected in the way people experience the Divinity. Some people experience God as a judgmental, wrathful, and punishing power to be feared. Others know the Supreme Being as a compassionate and loving presence who nurtures and sustains them. I have also found that people's perception of a spiritual authority can be affected by their childhood relationship with father and mother, their first and primary experience of all powerful "creators" and providers who are responsible for them. A child, for example, who grew up with an austere and strict father who constantly punished him may have a hard time perceiving a God who is compassionate and merciful. These types of beliefs can affect your experience of the God or Goddess archetype. Now, more than at any other time, I believe we all have the opportunity to look beyond our personal and collective myths about the God or Goddess and expand to experience the truth about this creative consciousness in the universe.

Connection with the God or Goddess can be a very expansive, elating, and highly elevating experience. However, when this energy is distorted by the false persona, it can lead to ego inflation and a delusional overidentification with the deity. This results in self-centered behavior and a belief that one is a god, above the rules and norms that apply to mere mortals. Another distortion of this archetype is seen in the obsessed follower who projects the deity on to others. This type of individual will give all her power away to the projection of God she has created in another and then blindly obey everything that other person says. Many self-proclaimed "Guru" types feed off of this dysfunctional behavior in their followers. If the expression of the God/Goddess is unbalanced, it can also lead to religious obsession or an overly ascetic life devoid of sensuality and the pleasures of the earth. A Nun or Monk subpersonality can embody such rigidly pious or repressive qualities as this.

In meditation, guided visualization, journal writing, and various healing processes, individuals often experience some aspect of the God or Goddess. It may appear as a being of light or in a form similar to one of the various gods and goddesses of Greek, Roman, or Eastern mythology. (The gods and goddesses of mythology may also have specific attributes that may relate to other archetypes. Aphrodite/Venus has to do with Love, Aries/Mars with the Warrior, etc.).

My client, Mara, had an internal guide emerge in the form of a goddess during a session with her massage therapist. She described this internal figure as a very large and empowering Grecian-looking woman. Because this goddess figure emanated a feminine presence that was both powerful and spiritual, she was able to assist Mara in her process of self-empowerment in a way that was deeply connected to her essence Self. Mara's Greek goddess was both a source of inspiration to her and an internalized positive expression of the empowered feminine.

## Child Archetype

The purest expression of the Child archetype is the Golden Child or Child of Light, which represents the essential Self. It also is associated with the shining light of our own Sun. The qualities this archetype embodies are love, joy, creativity, self-awareness, feeling, intuitiveness, spontaneity, playfulness, and curiosity. Initially, as children, all we know is what we feel, and that is what we spontaneously express. We are instinctively in touch with our core spirit and the archetypal attributes that are a part of it. For this reason, the Child archetype can help us heal, bring us to a deeper realization of our whole being, and act as a doorway to other archetypal energies as well. Dreams or images involving newborn babies are often symbolic of the innocence and purity of this Child archetype, and are significant of being reborn once again into your true divine nature. Dreams involving children needing assistance or babies who need to be nourished are also common to those working with the Child archetype.

In the process of realizing the Divine Self within us, the Child archetype often emerges because there are usually still unresolved issues from childhood that have affected one's sense of self-worth. In order to experience the deeper reality of the essence Self, it is necessary to transform the distorted core beliefs and childhood patterns that may be blocking its true expression. The hurts and unfulfilled needs of childhood must be addressed so that the love, joy, and creativity of this archetypal Child of Light can come forth.

Distortions of the Child archetype manifest when individuals who have unresolved issues from childhood remain emotionally immature. This happens because painful childhood events can interfere with normal development, leaving an emotional part of a person frozen in time without the resources that are usually gained through a natural maturation process. Such individuals will continue to try to get past needs met in unconscious ways. For example, a woman may continue to get involved with men who have addictions, unconsciously trying to get the love that she never got from her alcoholic father. A man may childishly need to constantly be the center of everyone's attention.

By working consciously with your Child subpersonality, the adult that you are now can nurture, protect, and reparent this part of you and change such patterns. Authors such as John Bradshaw, who have emphasized the importance of this "Inner Child" in the process of personal growth, are an excellent resource for working with this aspect of your personality.[14]

The other subpersonality expressions that can emerge with the Child archetype are the self-centered Brat, needing to have his or her own way; the Rebel, often a teenage stage; the Vulnerable Child, a sometimes hurt, needy, shy, or dependent aspect that may be sad or fearful; and the Clown, a mischievous and immature prankster.

## Masculine and Feminine Archetypes

Two other very important archetypes are Masculine and Feminine. All of us, whether man or woman, have a masculine and feminine element within us. These aspects are usually expressed according to patterns learned from our parents—for better or worse! Archetypal Masculine is an initiating, assertive, thrusting forth, and electric energy that has the ability to *do*. It is decisive, analyzing, discriminating, and provides structure. It is associated with the conscious mind and provides an objective, rational outlook. Because the Sun radiates light and energy, it is associated with this assertive Masculine quality and the conscious mind. Related to the male aspect is Archetypal Father. It embodies the aforementioned masculine attributes, gives guidance in the ways of the world, sets healthy limits or boundaries, and gives encouragement to accomplish a task. Archetypal Father relates to the planet Saturn, which is named after the Roman father god of the same name and represents an elder power and authority.

When the masculine is out of balance, its positive discerning and evaluating qualities can disintegrate into perfectionistic, rigid, strict, austere, stoic, critical, skeptical, and cynical behaviors. With this kind of imbalance, an individual can also be dominated by the logical mind and intellect while denying his feelings and emotions. The inner subpersonalities that can emerge when the masculine is distorted are the Critic; Pusher/Perfectionist; Protector/Controller; Judge, a judgmental aspect who decides what life's rules are and makes judgments about whether you or others are right or wrong; the Know It All, constantly proving how much he knows; and the Cynic, Pessimist, or Skeptic who doesn't trust subjective reality or the unseen world, doubts that anything can improve or change, and must have objective proof in order to believe.

Archetypal Feminine is a receptive, feeling, intuitive, nurturing, nourishing, and magnetic energy that represents the instinctual nature and the womb or fertile space from which things manifest. Unlike the Masculine, which is concerned with results and accomplishing things, the Feminine is interested in process. It has the ability to flow, allow, and just *be* instead of *do*. The Feminine aspect is also associated with the physical body, subconscious mind, and one's inner or subjective experience. Archetypal Feminine encompasses the young maiden or Virgin quality; the Mother aspect; and the Crone (see Wise Elder), which represents old age, death, and wisdom. Archetypal Mother signifies love, understanding, nurturance, nourishment, and protection for those in her care. The Moon, which reflects the light from the Sun, is symbolic of the subconscious mind and the receptive, intuitive, and nurturing qualities of the Feminine.

When the Feminine is out of balance, it can result in overemotional or hysterical tendencies, introversion, passivity, a state of disorganized confusion, overprotectiveness, and an inability to be objective or establish personal boundaries. This passivity and lack of boundaries can result in repeated victimization. A common distortion of the feminine energy is the tendency to be a perpetual caretaker, denying one's own personal needs, feelings, and life in order to take care of others. The Caretaker subpersonality is an expression of this dynamic as is the Super Mom, who neglects her own desires in order to be the perennially available perfect mother, and often wife, too.

The other subpersonalities that can emerge with this archetypal energy are the Rescuer, who is always needing to "fix" other people's problems; the Victim, continually in crisis without taking responsibility for making personal changes; the Drama Queen/King, an emotionally overdramatic or hysterical personality who is frequently in chaos; the passive Pessimist; and the Protector/Controller.

Jung called the feminine energy in a man his *anima* and the masculine energy in a woman, her *animus*. How a man or woman relate to these inner dimensions of their being will be reflected in the dynamics of their outer relationships. Archetypal Masculine and Feminine have various expressions, several faces, or ways they can manifest depending on your life experience and your resulting personal associations to them. For example, if your experience of mothering is cold and detached, archetypal Mother could manifest as a negative, frozen Mother or Witch. You might repeatedly find yourself in situations with women who manifest this type of cold, rigid, or nagging quality and perhaps find it is an aspect of your own personality as well. On the other hand, if your experience of motherly caretaking has been nurturing and loving, archetypal Feminine could present itself in more compassionate ways, such as through nurturing relationships with women or a positive connection to the Earth Mother and nature.

Psychodynamically, the internalized negative father and mother aspects within you must be transformed into positive healthy patterns that express your true nature. The healing of this original inner family dynamic is fundamental to the expression of a balanced masculine and feminine within and the realization of your essential Self. Archetypal Masculine, Feminine, and Child act as guides aiding you in this healing process.

## Artist Archetype

Archetypal Artist embodies the qualities of creative expression and the gifts of the creative arts (painting, music, acting, poetry, dance, sculpturing, etc.). The Self is our center of creativity, and as we realize and accept more of our essential nature, we are able to give expression to this spark of creativity within us. When we are disconnected from our own spirit, dreams, needs, or desires, we will most likely be cut off from our creative talents as well. It is especially important for artists to stay connected with this inner spiritual resource in order to keep their creativity flowing and alive.

People who express this archetypal energy have a wellspring of creative energy inside that can be accessed and expressed in various ways. However, when this energy is blocked, it can become self-destructive because the creative energies that seek expression or acceptance are turned back on one's self in a distorted way. We see these destructive tendencies in the lives of many famous artists and musicians.

The Artist archetype has a sensitive nature that allows individuals to receive impressions that they can then channel into a creative form. Artists are usually very receptive to the fertile, creative realms of the subconscious mind and the collective unconscious. This is the place from which many of their images and ideas spring forth. When this wonderful capacity is out of balance, however, they can be hypersensitive or self-absorbed and dominated by the dark underworld of their own subconscious mind. This dynamic creates a moody and introverted artist.

Artists can also be unconventional renegades who are acting as channels for new and innovative ideas. Sometimes they find their nonconformist ideas aren't immediately accepted, which leads to frustration and the suffering or starving artist syndrome. It can compound the problem when artists have a lack of discipline to their craft. I highly recommend Julia Cameron's book, *The Artist's Way*, to anyone who needs assistance in giving expression to the creativity of the Artist archetype.

The planet Venus, named for the Roman goddess of love who was known to the Greeks as Aphrodite, is associated with aesthetic beauty and artistic talents. This is because of the feminine nature of Venus, which is receptive to the inspiration and abundance of the creative forces.

The subpersonalities that can emerge with the Artist archetype are the Rebel, rebelling against society, tradition, or authority; the Starving Artist, often lazy, seldom successful, and always struggling financially; and, of course, the Critic.

### Birth-Death-Rebirth Archetype

This archetype represents the transitions, changes, and cycles of life. We are constantly experiencing transformation and rebirth as we grow and change. Death to old patterns, self-perceptions, and loved ones is a part of life. The grieving of such losses takes us deeper inside to birth more of our true Self. So, in addition to actually experiencing the death of loved ones in our lives, we also experience the Death archetype as we grow emotionally and spiritually. This is because we let go of concepts that are no longer useful and die to an old way of being as we open up to a new state of consciousness. The mythical phoenix, rising renewed out of its own fiery ashes, is symbolic of this transformational process. It requires a willingness to leave the confines of preconceived ideas and concepts and stand at the cliff's edge of the great unknown in order to step forth into new experiences. As we do this, it is important for us to fully grieve the losses of our lives. In this way, just as the snake sheds its skin, we can let go of what is old or past in order to move on to the new. Strange as it may seem, it is even possible to feel sadness over the loss of negative patterns and situations in our life if they have felt safe and familiar to us.

Often when we experience the Death archetype in our lives, it is indicative of a change that needs to take place. At a time when I needed to make some major changes in my life, the family pet rabbit died, two goldfish were attacked and eaten by another fish in the tank, and my daughter was writing poems about death. This was a very strong message regarding an emotionally abusive relationship that I was involved in that needed to end.

Sometimes individuals experience a great deal of intensity and crisis when they have the Birth/Death archetype predominant in their lives. Such people can remain stuck in the chaos of reoccurring negative patterns and never look within to discover the true purpose that it has in their lives. This type of individual usually has a Drama Queen/King or Victim subpersonality and is frequently in crisis or blaming others, without taking responsibility for making the personal changes that would bring about transformation. When life challenges are used as a means of personal growth and transformation, however, then the true gift of such situations can be discovered. Individuals who have experienced this type of transformational process, and the power it represents, are then able to assist others through the dark times of crisis. Such people often become therapists or other helping professionals in order to more directly share the wisdom and powerful insights they have gained.

Related to this transformational process of Death and Rebirth is the primordial life-giving energy of the kundalini. Different types of transformational death can occur as the kundalini energy rises up the spine and brings an experience of a more conscious state of being. Physical and emotional symptoms are one way in which this symbolic death is acted out. However, it is the old identity or persona falling away and dying through this process. This archetypal theme can also be experienced through past-life images of death at this time or may be experienced on a collective level, for example, through feeling intimately the death of Mother Nature through pollution. Elements from biological birth trauma, a life and death situation, can be part of this dynamic as well. For this reason, regression methods for working with past-life and birth experience can be useful during such times to facilitate the transition from psychological death into spiritual rebirth.

The snake or serpent, which represents the kundalini archetype as well as the sexual life force and instinctual processes of the body, is symbolic of this type of transformation. Sexuality, transformation, and death are, in fact, closely related. For in order to feel the ecstasy of sexual orgasm, we must let go and surrender to the experience. Death, whether physical or psychological, also requires that we move through the particular life transition by letting go.

When the Birth/Death archetype is out of balance, people can become very serious, self-absorbed, introspective, or depressed. It's as if the life force energy of the first chakra becomes shut down. Individuals can then lose a sense of their aliveness and become preoccupied with the dark or death aspect of the cycle, never completing the transformation into rebirth. This is the type of person who always looks for and dwells on the negative aspects of a situation. Such an individual may have a Pessimist or Grim Reaper subpersonality operating within with a morose, "doom and gloom" attitude. Another shadow expression is found in people who use the dark destructive forces to belittle or manipulate others and, like vultures, gain power for themselves through the emotional death of others. In addition to this Manipulator or Controller subpersonality, the Seducer/Seductress can also emerge, using sex to seductively manipulate others.

The planet Pluto is associated with the transformative process of the Birth/Death archetype. Its purpose is evolutionary change. In mythology, Pluto is associated with the underworld of death and is symbolic of that dark inner world or womb into which we must periodically descend in order to grow, heal, and be reborn.

## Communicator Archetype

The Communicator is the messenger who has the ability to impart information, express himself, and convey ideas through various forms including speaking and writing. The Communicator is mentally quick, inquisitive, logical, expressive, lighthearted, and loves to converse and interact with others. Archetypal Communicator knows the power of the spoken or written word when it is used with consciousness, and many people expressing this archetype are very powerful speakers. As an archetypal messenger, the Communicator conveys the truth and power of the word to others. The planet Mercury, named for the messenger of the gods of Roman mythology, represents this archetypal energy.

This archetype is related to issues of the fifth chakra. When the Communicator energy is distorted, it can manifest as the self-centered individual who is constantly dominating a conversation. It can also show itself in the tongue-wagging gossip or in the intellectual sparring partner who debates rather than communicates. Sometimes, the Communicator's quickness of mind can also result in a restlessness and an inability to just be quiet and relax. Another shadow expression is found in the superficial clown who puts on a smile to entertain others while denying her real feelings. An inability to express one's thoughts and ideas clearly is also common when this archetype is repressed. This issue can result in feelings of isolation and is often found in the shy and withdrawn person who becomes a social hermit.

There can be no denying the importance of good communication skills in the world today. Listening becomes as important as speaking as we seek to better understand one another's unique ideas and perspective. Many individuals never learned how to express ideas and feelings as children and then continue to carry these patterns into their adult life. Taking a basic communications skills class can be helpful in such cases.

In addition to the Clown, Gossip, Hermit, and Rambler—an aimless wanderer who is always on the move and constantly needing the stimulation of new surroundings, information, or other life changes—any of the subpersonalities which can exert an intellectual control such as the Critic, Judge, Cynic/Skeptic, Pusher/Perfectionist, Protector/Controller, or Know It All can emerge when the energy of archetypal Communicator is distorted or denied.

## *Healer Archetype*

This archetypal energy has the capacity to bring comfort, healing, and harmony to individuals and situations. The Healer embodies the qualities of compassion and empathy and is also sensitive psychically, emotionally, and physically. We all have a healing aspect within us as an inherent quality of our Higher Self. However, individuals with the Healer as a dominant soul essence will often have various healing gifts such as psychic intuition, hands-on or energy healing abilities, herbal wisdom, as well as the talents expressed through various health care professions. Often the Healer is the individual who it just feels good being around and talking with no matter what profession the person is in. Many times, the Healer archetype will manifest in the lives of individuals in the form of a wounded healer, presenting an illness that the person must first heal in themselves in order to truly express their healing gift. This healing journey provides the shift in consciousness that is necessary in order for them to serve as a healing guide for others. Many modern-day shamans have gone through this experience in some way.

One of the shadow expressions of this energy is the person who is so busy taking care of others that she neglects her own needs. Such people eventually get burned out or sucked dry by others because they are not able to nourish and revitalize their own energies. Another distortion of this energy is found in the hypochondriac who is preoccupied with his health and dwells on illness. This shadow expression can also be seen in people who go through life always expecting others to fix and solve their problems. The subpersonalities that can emerge with the Healer archetype are the Rescuer, the Caretaker, the Hypochondriac, and the Victim.

Chiron, a small celestial body with an extremely elliptical orbit usually traveling between Saturn and Uranus, is associated with healing and the wounded healer. Mythically, Chiron was the centaur, half-man and half-horse or unicorn, who founded the ancient Asclepian healing temple. His body, which unites human and animal in one form, is symbolic of the healing that needs to take place between the intellectual and instinctual nature within all people. Much physical illness in the body is a result of the split that has existed between our spiritual and animal natures.

Chiron was immortal. However he dropped a poisoned arrow on his foot and was forever wounded but could not die. He finally sacrificed himself so that the fire of Prometheus could be released from the Underworld. This myth expresses both the selfless service and wounded healer issues that can arise with the Healer archetype.

In my role as a counseling astrologer, I have found that healing issues emerge for individuals when Chiron's placement in the heavens forms a strong relationship to the planetary positions present at the time of their birth. The particular issue that an individual is seeking to heal—such as a relationship, a physical disorder, or an emotional problem—will surface at that time to be confronted in some way. This may come through directly experiencing the emotional wounding or illness, through objectively experiencing someone else dealing with it, or in actively healing it in one's self or in another.

## Hero/Heroine and Warrior Archetype

The archetypal Hero persistently and with great courage and strength brings resolution where there is conflict, crisis, or chaos. Individuals expressing this archetypal energy will impeccably uphold the highest principles and ideals, face difficult struggles, and emerge victorious. The Hero has self-confidence, takes initiative, and is steadfast in obtaining his goals and defending his principles. Like the mythical Jason who was given an impossible task by the King of Colchis in order to obtain the Golden Fleece, the treasured goal of his quest, a hero never gives up. The Hero is also adventurous and may be always setting off to explore some unknown territory or begin a new quest. Many adventure-seeking outdoor enthusiasts fit this description.

When the heroic energy is distorted, it can result in denying one's personal feelings and needs in a rigid, compulsive, or misplaced devotion to a cause. An example of this shadow expression is found in the person who, as a child, had the role of the "family hero" in an alcoholic or otherwise emotionally unhealthy family. In childhood, and later as an adult, this individual will be a high achiever who does what's right and is driven to obtain visible means of success (football hero, scholarship winner, prom queen, top sales executive, or successful law firm partner). This person may become a workaholic, feel responsible for everything, and have a need to always be right with no imperfections. Despite all the outer bravado and success, this type of person often feels quite inadequate inside.

Heroes can also be quite an independent and prideful lot, thinking they can do it all by themselves. This can lead to the inability to ask for help. Our mythic hero, Jason, set the right example, at least initially, when he asked the goddess Aphrodite for help and obtained the assistance of the sorceress, Medea. However, when one's heroic journey doesn't allow for this type of vulnerability or the sensitivity of feelings, it can become unbalanced. In the world of sports, we often see this dynamic. There is a constant denial of bodily pain and feelings in order to win the game. It is no wonder that some of our modern-day sports heroes have fallen off their pedestals of glory. It is symbolic of the fact that the glorification of such unhealthy patterns must end. I believe it also calls us to activate the courageous and impeccable hero qualities within all of us, rather than sitting passively, as couch potatoes, worshiping others who do it for us on television.

Another shadow expression of the Hero energy is the glory-seeking performer who needs to put on a show and save the day. This person can be more interested in getting attention for herself than upholding personal principles or helping others. Such individuals can also be addicted to crisis, always needing a situation to overcome or resolve. Distortion of the Hero archetype can also result in the reckless behavior of the daredevil who ignores his own safety for the addictive thrill of adventure and danger. The subpersonalities that can emerge when the heroic energy is distorted are the Pusher/Perfectionist; the Protector/Controller; the Rescuer; and the Daredevil, a reckless thrill seeker who is addicted to danger.

Related to the Hero archetype is the Warrior. The Warrior has the ability to assertively accomplish a given task and be aggressive when needed. This archetype embodies courage, bravery, personal power, decisiveness, vitality, and strength (both inner fortitude and physical strength). The knight, Indian warrior, Amazon woman, and soldier are expressions of the Warrior energy. The Warrior has the initiative, motivation, and ability to pave new paths and champion a cause. However, the need for action and excitement may sometimes result in the tendency to be impulsive and to act before thinking. Like the Hero, the Warrior has a strong will and can be very independent and self-reliant. When this energy is out of balance, it can result in the headstrong, insensitive, and egotistical person who is unaware of the needs or feelings of others. This independence can also prevent people from being able to take orders and be part of a group, unless, of course, they are the leader.

The same life force energy that gives the Warrior her assertive drive and power can be expressed negatively as belligerent aggression and a quick temper. This can result in the person who is continually opposing, attacking, or blaming others. The rageaholic, addicted to rage, is an example of this abusive pattern. Another shadow expression is the super competitive individual who is obsessed with competing or fighting with anyone. If the Warrior energy is repressed, on the other hand, it can result in the passive person who is unable to assert himself or take a stand.

The Warrior relates to issues of the third chakra and people expressing this archetypal energy may need to learn how to use their power in a conscious way. Powerful emotions such as anger or rage are often a part of this process. If we deny our anger, it can leak out unconsciously, usually affecting some innocent bystander around us. When we hold in our anger like this, it can merely simmer below the surface until we finally blow up, often getting inappropriately angry over some small issue that has triggered the erupting volcano of our repressed emotions. People working consciously with their anger are able to express their feelings and needs in a direct way, without such Mount Vesuvius blowups. It's important to confront our anger and deal with it appropriately, rather than suppressing it or acting out on others. This may mean self-care like writing the feelings in your journal, walking and exercising it out, or hitting a pillow to move it through your body. You can also wait and choose to talk to people when you are ready and capable of expressing feelings in a conscious way.

Subpersonalities that can emerge with the Warrior energy are the domineering and aggressive Bully; the Rageaholic, who is addicted to the release of anger; the Pusher/Perfectionist, who can be very competitive; and, when the protective element of the Warrior becomes distorted, the Protector/Controller, who can also seek revenge for any perceived wrong doing by blaming or persecuting others. The planetary energy related to the Hero and Warrior archetypes is Mars, named for the Roman god of war.

## *Lover and Community Archetypes*

The Lover is a loving, passionate, and compassionate energy that seeks connection, partnership, balanced cooperation, and harmony (including the harmony of nature and aesthetics). This archetype embodies the qualities of beauty, grace, sensuality, intimacy, tenderness, understanding, empathy, and loyalty. The Lover archetype, which relates to the dynamics of the second and fourth chakras, enables individuals to seek pleasure and feel the ecstasy of love. Through human relationship, individuals can experience the vibrational frequency of ecstasy and thus remember their true nature.

Archetypal Community expands this love and cooperation to encompass the collective group. It brings a consciousness of all people as equal brothers and sisters in the human family. As we love ourselves and open our own heart, we feel that love naturally spreading out to others. We realize our connection with all people and want to better the lives of others because, ultimately, it enhances our life also. People who express the Community archetype can thus be great humanitarians, future-oriented social reformers, and group visionaries.

The dynamic of love and relationship often provides us with a mirror that reflects back to us both our positive and negative disowned qualities. The angry nagging wife, for example, who is a reflection of her husband's inability to assert himself. His passivity, on the other hand, being an exaggerated reminder of the feminine-feeling quality lacking in his wife. We can also choose partners who have qualities which balance our own or stimulate us to bring forth undeveloped aspects of our being— the shy woman, for instance, who dates a self-assured man with many social contacts and, as a result, is gradually brought out of her shell of timidity. When this dynamic operates in a distorted way, however, we may project our best qualities on to another and love those aspects in them rather than developing or expressing those qualities in ourselves. Although relationships can evoke both the best and the worst in us, we often need the polarization that it can provide to activate our own self-growth.

The ecstasy of love also opens us to deeper dimensions of our own soul. It can lead us to union with our true beloved, the Self. Through outer relationship, we can more fully unite with our own positive anima or animus aspect within. In this way, we become whole and can experience the oneness of the Self.

Individuals who express the Lover archetype make good peacemakers, arbitrators, and diplomats. However, when this energy is unbalanced, it can result in the individual who keeps the peace no matter what the consequences are to themselves or others. This person may be uncomfortable with the expression of intense emotions, always wanting things to appear harmonious and be peaceful in a superficial way. This type of individual is often very nice and proper, avoiding or denying any feelings that seem negative or unpleasant. In such cases, a passive People Pleaser subpersonality is often present, always wanting to do those things that will make others happy and keep things pleasant.

When the Lover archetype is distorted, it can result in love addiction and the person who is more infatuated with the "high" of being in love than with any particular person. This individual may become a sex addict who uses relationship and sexual encounters like a drug for the euphoric feeling it can bring. In such cases, a Seducer/Seductress subpersonality may be operating. Sex is the most important thing in the world to this inner aspect of the Seducer/Seductress who can induce one to act inappropriately sexual or seductive at times.

Distortions of the archetypal Lover energy can also result in the person who is shut down sexually. Sometimes, this sexual dysfunction is accompanied by a Nun or Monk subpersonality, more interested in spiritual virtue than the enjoyment of life's sensual pleasures. Other shadow expressions of the Lover include the narcissist who is selfishly self-absorbed and in love with herself, and the codependent person who denies himself for the love of another, rather than loving himself by taking care of his own needs.

When love is denied, either on an individual basis or at the level of community, it is often accompanied by the Judge subpersonality. Judgment forms a barrier that prevents compassion and shuts down the ability to feel, express, or receive love. If we are judging something or someone, we are not in a place of loving acceptance and understanding. This doesn't mean that we shouldn't use discernment in deciding what is appropriate for us in our own lives. However, you will be more open to love and understanding if you avoid judging others. The Rescuer and Caretaker are two other subpersonalities that can emerge with the Lover archetype.

If the expression of archetypal Community is denied or distorted, individuals may have difficulty figuring out how they fit into society or everyone else's world. They can feel like a stranger in a strange land, lack friends, and be unconventional or eccentric in some way. An iconoclastic Rebel subpersonality is often present.

The goddess of love, embodied as the planet Venus, is naturally associated with the Lover archetype. The planet Uranus relates to archetypal Community and a humanitarian perspective that is concerned with the collective group. Mythically, these two planets are related, for it was Aphrodite/Venus who emerged from the foamy water after the god Saturn, the Greek Cronus, castrated his father, Uranus, and threw him and his phallus into the ocean. Venus sprang forth from the genitals, the sexual energy and creative force of her father, Uranus.

Much like this dismemberment experience of the god, Uranus, the energy of this planet can sometimes be quite fragmenting. Uranus often provides the shocking experience that awakens us to the pieces of our psyche that need to be integrated and synthesized in order for greater wholeness and freedom to take place. However, as the mythic Uranus and Venus demonstrate, from the initial jolt of these awakening insights, a more loving and humanitarian energy can come forth. Such mini-revolutions are occasionally necessary to evolve us toward the higher purpose of our lives.

## Magician Archetype

This is the wizard who is able to harness the tools of mind and consciousness to obtain the desired results. The Magician has the ability to focus, concentrate, and direct mental powers to manifest his intentions. By aligning his will with the Divine will, the alchemical Magician is able to refine the base metal of the old patterns of consciousness and manifest the gold of the essence Self. Someone expressing the Magician archetype believes in the magic of life and knows that everyday miracles do happen through the power of belief. The Magician is a co-creator who knows that words have power, that thoughts manifest, and that we create our own reality through these tools of consciousness. Many people attracted to metaphysics and the occult carry the Magician essence. The Magician believes in taking action to accomplish her goals through the power of mind rather than physical force.

When the Magician energy is distorted, individuals can use their mental will to manipulate others. Another shadow expression is found in the individual who constantly has to be taking action on situations by working, doing, and fixing, rather than patiently allowing things to unfold naturally. There can also be an inner imbalance with the intellectual or rational consciousness being dominant, so that the emotions are repressed. This person is often a positive thinker who is attempting to create certain circumstances through sheer will while denying underlying feelings. The true Magician, however, respects the subconscious realm because he knows it is part of the unseen world, the living creative substance with which he works. The conscious mind merely directs and forms this substance to bring things into manifestation.

This archetype relates to issues of the sixth chakra. When the Magician energy is out of balance, individuals can have difficulty bringing their thoughts into manifestation or may suffer

~~from magical thinking, always wishing upon a star but doing nothing concrete to bring their dreams into reality.~~

The planet associated with the Magician is Mercury. The Roman god, Mercury, with his magic staff or wand could put people to sleep or be a messenger of death. Mercury is also associated with the Egyptian god Thoth, the alchemist and magician who had the power to raise the dead.

Like the Communicator, which Mercury is also associated with, any of the subpersonalities that can exert an intellectual control such as the Critic, Judge, Cynic, Pusher/Perfectionist, or Protector/Controller can emerge when the Magician energy is distorted.

## Mystic Archetype

The Mystic embodies a compassionate spiritual energy that looks beyond the material realm to union with God and the cosmos. The Mystic seeks spiritual ecstasy and is sensitive, sympathetic, intuitive, psychic, and knows how to surrender the ego personality to the Divine Presence. Archetypal Mystic can guide individuals to the light of their own being and to psychic and mystical experiences as well. It thus brings expanded consciousness, a direct experience of God, and knowledge of the universe. The Mystic has the ability to be centered in quiet stillness and peace, to meditate, and take quiet time apart from the activity of life and the world to connect with the Self within.

The oneness that the Mystic embodies dissolves all limitations and boundaries to bring union with the Source of all things. When this sense of oneness is expressed in an unbalanced way, it can lead to a lack of personal boundaries. An individual may then tend to lose herself in others and be unable to separate her emotional identity from those with whom she energetically merges. This easily results in codependent behaviors in relationship. A person who expresses the Mystic energy can also be extremely sensitive to impressions from others, becoming a psychic sponge soaking up other people's feelings and negativity. For this reason, it is important for these individuals to be mindful of their environment and the type of people around them. It will also be helpful for such psychically sensitive people to remain consciously aware of the empathic impressions they are receiving from others, letting them energetically pass through, rather than internalizing them as their own.

The Mystic archetype relates to the seventh chakra and the expanded states of consciousness associated with it. Contact with such higher dimensional frequencies can result in the ungrounded space cadet who always seems to be in another world. He may tend to dissociate and leave his body, or be the continual dreamer who lacks the practical efforts needed to make those dreams a reality. In addition, the Mystic energy can be expressed in a distorted way as the martyr who seeks union with God through suffering, self-denial, and repression of the body. This can add to the ungrounded feeling and sense of discomfort with the physical realm. This type of individual often doesn't want to be here on Earth and is constantly seeking to leave through meditation or day-dreaming fantasies.

An example of the Mystic archetype is found in the woman who was sexually abused as a child and, like a martyr, took on the role of family savior, sacrificing herself to be abused by her mother's lovers in order to keep the family together. She hoped that someday Jesus would come and save her and take her away to be with Him. When she grew up, she joined a convent and became a nun, thus purifying herself by taking the Christ as her lover. Often the dynamics of mysticism and victimization are intertwined in this way with the Mystic archetype. In fact, this woman did have very mystical experiences involving a Native American spirit guide that came forth in her meditations and therapy sessions. The altruistic and self-sacrificing quality of

the Mystic can be a noble one. However, Mystics become mar-
tyrs when the symbolic ritual sacrifice made to the gods
becomes distorted and twisted into the sacrificial self-abuse of
their own denial.

Another shadow expression of the Mystic is found in the
addictive personality who seeks spiritual ecstasy by getting
high on such things as drugs or alcohol. Rather than obtaining
mystical union through personal growth and spiritual development, this individual seeks an altered state of consciousness
through artificial means. How fitting that the word spirit,
which describes our divine vital essence, is also defined as "a
strong alcoholic liquor." When people restore the spiritual
dimension to their lives, and replace the "spirit" of liquor with
the "spirit" of their divine nature, it can have the effect of
diminishing the overpowering hold that their addictions seem
to have on them. This may account for much of the success of
Alcoholics Anonymous, which uses a spiritual Higher Power in
its recovery process.

I've also seen people have strong mystical experiences that
had a similar healing effect with regard to addictions. My client
Jenny was plagued with alcohol and cigarette addictions while
consistently sacrificing her own needs in order to take care of
other people. Jenny had the planet Neptune, which is associated with the Mystic archetype, near the Ascendant at the time
of her birth. Neptune was the Roman god of the sea and his
watery home is symbolic of the transcendent ocean of energy to
which the Mystic is attuned. One Christmas eve, while dealing
with a particularly frustrating situation, Jenny went outside to
smoke a cigarette. While looking with awe at the starry night
sky, she was infused with a sense of love and peace beyond anything she had ever known before. In this expansive state, she
realized that she no longer needed to fill herself up with
unhealthy substances to feel good. She also saw clearly that she

could love others and help others without feeling enmeshed in their problems. Jenny put the cigarette down and hasn't felt the desire to smoke since then. Sustained by this feeling of love and serenity, her alcoholic depression lifted because she no longer experienced the need to hide and deny her problems with drink. Jenny was also able to maintain good personal boundaries by saying no to people's demands when she needed to. This is a dramatic example of the powerful role that Spirit and the Mystic archetype can play in the healing of one's addictions.

When the Mystic is expressed in an unbalanced way, it can also lead to asceticism or religious fanaticism. The subpersonalities that can emerge with the Mystic archetype are the Victim/Martyr; Monk or Nun; Rescuer; Caretaker; the Addict, an addictive or obsessive aspect of the personality; and the Dreamer/Space Cadet, who is ungrounded or in a fantasy world.

### Ruler (King/Queen) Archetype

The King, Queen, or Ruler archetype is the essential wise leader who makes life decisions or laws based on ideals that serve the greater good of the whole. The Ruler is empowered, confident, and has a sense of knowing she deserves the best. She is able to have clarity of purpose, to see the goals that need to be accomplished, and take the organized steps that are necessary to obtain those ends. There is a sense of justice and equality in this process and a capacity to adhere to a high standard. This archetypal influence can help you manifest your true power and authority, and enables individuals to be great leaders, business directors, and statespersons.

The Ruler has the ability to balance and weigh the different elements of a situation and decide what truly will allow the whole to benefit and grow stronger. Many fine leaders have started out with this dream only to be disenchanted or seduced by a corrupt political system that greedily caters to only one interest group. The Ruler has the responsibility to use his power wisely and justly, rather than for personal gain or for the betterment of the privileged few.

In addition to external leadership, the symbolic Sun King represents the Self, the ruling consciousness which directs the whole psyche. It signifies power and mastery over your world and the ability to be an instrument through which a higher spiritual power can manifest. In our inner world, this aspect can help us make decisions that benefit our whole being, rather than letting one aspect of the personality dominate.

Shadow expressions of the Ruler include the individual who, like a dictator, acts as a dominating, pompous authority, greedy for his own power. This is the tyrant, driven by his own ambition, who gains control by keeping others subservient to him. The Ruler can also be aloof, detached, and out of touch with those she serves, like the fairy-tale Wicked Queen who is cruel and lacks compassion. When the Ruler energy is repressed, individuals may deny their own authority or be passive people pleasers who are easily influenced by others and unable to make decisions. A person expressing the Ruler archetype can also be a rigid traditionalist, interested in keeping the "status quo," and resisting or limiting change that could be beneficial.

The immature King/Queen expression can result in the person who is a spoiled little Prince or Princess, accustomed to royal treatment. This individual is often shallow, weak, conforming, and wants everything to be easy. Such a person may act like a spoiled Brat at times, insisting that the world revolve around them. Other subpersonalities that can emerge with the Ruler archetype are the Judge, Protector/Controller, Pusher/Perfectionist, Critic, and People Pleaser.

If the King or Queen rules with wisdom, then he or she becomes a Wise Elder. The Elder is an older authority and presence who embodies the wisdom of experience as well as the deep spiritual understanding accompanying it. The Wise Elder can be found in various forms, including the Wise Crone and the Grandfather or Grandmother figure of Native American traditions. Along with the insights that age can bring, the qualities of the Wise Elder include discernment, self-discipline, and a mature sense of responsibility. The Elder is patiently willing to share the knowledge that she has gained in order to help others, and to give back some of what life has given her.

In our American culture the wisdom of our elders is often lost in a society focused on youthful appearance. Families are often separated by distance with children and grandchildren denied an elder's knowledge and perspective. The elderly are many times exiled to nursing homes rather than being encouraged to continue a useful and fulfilling life. I can't help but wonder if such things as Alzheimer's disease, which involves increasing loss of functioning, is not a reflection of our loss of the elderly being able to function in their rightful role in our society.

When the Elder archetype is distorted or unbalanced it can be negatively expressed as cynicism, rigidity, and criticalness. It can result in the critical nag or the advice giver who attempts to control how others do things, rather than empowering them on their own life path. Another shadow expression is found in the person who is burdened by responsibilities or has become hardened by the years and no longer feels a sense of joy or excitement for life. When the Wise Elder energy is repressed, an individual may be disconnected from his own inner wisdom, remain immature and selfishly self-centered, or be uncomfortable with advancing age. Subpersonalities that can emerge with this archetypal energy are the Protector/Controller; Critic; Know It All; Pusher/Perfectionist; Cynic/Skeptic; the Pessimist; and the Old Fogy, a rigid, sometimes stoic, and extremely conservative aspect that has lost a sense of the joy and spontaneity in life.

The planet associated with the Ruler and Wise Elder archetypes is Saturn. As stated previously, Saturn represents a traditional elder power and authority and is named for the powerful god of Roman myth, also known as Father Time. This seems appropriate since, in third-dimensional space, time seems to "rule" the structure of our lives. Like the Ruler archetype, time can be used in a way that provides helpful organization, or be distorted into a framework that limits and restricts us. As mentioned earlier, the wisdom of the Crone is symbolized by the Moon, particularly in its waning phase, and the Sun King is, of course, associated with the Sun.

## Teacher Archetype

The Teacher is the philosopher who seeks knowledge of the essential truths of life while sharing what has been learned and experienced with others. The Teacher has a broad perspective of life that unites various philosophies into the universal truths of creation. Integrity and truth itself are very important to those carrying the Teacher archetype. Acting as a guide or mentor in a process of self-discovery, the Teacher helps individuals to learn, grow, have faith, and believe in themselves, while inspiring them to find spiritual meaning or a personal philosophy for their lives. The Teacher experiences everything in life as an opportunity to learn and grow. Thus, this archetype can use travel, education, or anything that provides a new perspective in order to bring about its expansion.

On an internal level, we all have an Inner Teacher, the Higher Self, through which we receive guidance and wisdom. Although we may find outer teachers useful in our process of personal growth, it is the voice of this Inner Teacher that is our ultimate navigator and guiding force. The best kind of teacher is one with integrity, patience, and compassion who demonstrates through his own actions what he is striving to teach others. There is nothing more confusing or disheartening than the hypocrite who doesn't practice what he preaches. When the Teacher energy is distorted, it can become self-righteous or judgmental and result in the know-it-all who is constantly giving advice by telling others what to do and the one and only "right" way to do it. Another shadow expression is the individual who is constantly up on her soapbox philosophizing, or much like a debating champion, always mentally fencing and arguing a point.

Many spiritual teachers express the archetypal Teacher energy. When it is negatively expressed, it can result in a manipulative guru type who needs followers he can control and tell how to live their lives. This person will use the undying devotion of his followers to empower himself, rather than leading them to their own inner truth. Another shadow expression of the Teacher is found in the attached devotee who has no sense of self and needs to be constantly filled up by her master's presence. This type of individual can also operate as a spiritual groupie, rather than doing the work of true self-development. There are also teachers who maintain control by withholding information and only letting people know half-truths or distortions.

The subpersonalities that can emerge with the Teacher archetype are the Know It All; Judge; Rambler; Pusher/Perfectionist; Protector/Controller; Critic; and Nun, Monk, or Guru.

The planet associated with this archetypal soul energy is Jupiter. Jupiter was the Roman name for the Greek god, Zeus, who kept order in the cosmos through upholding the highest truth, justice, and virtue. As the most massive planet in our solar system, Jupiter provides a physical representation of the expansion and growth that we gain through the learning processes of archetypal Teacher.

With the planet Jupiter ascending on the horizon at the time of my birth, the essence of the Teacher is a very important one for me. This is true not only in my role as a teacher to others, but also in the life lessons that I have had to learn through my role as a student in relationship with other spiritual teachers, educators, and mentors. I have learned as much about being a teacher through my negative experiences as I have through my positive ones, sometimes even more. With Chiron near the Midheaven and Venus also close to Jupiter at the Ascendant, my healing work provides an important avenue for bringing love through in my teaching.

# DISCOVERING YOUR ARCHETYPAL SOUL PATTERNS

The following process will assist you in identifying one or more of the archetypal soul energies operating in your life.

1.  What is the thing that you dream of doing? What is your passion or talent (painting, travel, the performing arts, community leadership, teaching, writing)? What were the aspirations you may have had as a child or what things did you enjoy doing or playing (magician, nurse, astronaut, ballerina, cowboy hero, Indian warrior)? These dreams, passions, and childhood aspirations often represent an archetypal presence seeking expression through you.

    Examples: "People say I'm a good listener and that they feel better just talking to me, that I understand." Archetype: Healer.

    "As a child, I always liked reading about the lives of the saints." Archetype: Mystic.

2.  What is your shadow, the thing about yourself that you fear expressing or feel negative about? What would it look and feel like if this was transformed?

    Examples: "I'm shy. I would be a confident and effective speaker." Archetype: Communicator.

    "I'm afraid of being in a position of authority, even though I feel like I'm a good organizer. I would feel empowered to pursue leadership roles." Archetype: Ruler.

3. Is there an adversary in your life, a repeating pattern you constantly have to deal with, perhaps a repeating pattern in your relationships? Any primary figure that frequently appears in your dreams or daytime fantasy?

   Examples: "My current boss is always after me to be more assertive in my sales approach. My wife gets upset when I don't aggressively go after what I want. They both make me so angry." Archetype: Warrior.

   "I keep dreaming about babies, that I'm responsible for helping an infant who is sick or malnourished in some way." Archetype: Child.

4. After using the previous questions to discover some possible archetypes operating in your life, choose one and write a description of what this essential archetypal soul energy would look like if it was embodied in a form. If it was a person, for example, what would he or she look like or how would he or she appear to you? (Other forms may also present themselves such as animals or mythical beings.) If you prefer, draw a picture of how you imagine the archetypal energy to be embodied or find a piece of artwork or a picture that represents it for you.

5. What limiting myths, concepts, or feelings do you have with regard to giving expression to the essential soul qualities that this archetypal energy represents?

   Examples: "I'm not smart enough to be a Teacher."

   "I'm afraid that if I express this Warrior energy, people will go away and I'll end up alone."

   Now imagine what it would be like to express these essential qualities successfully and experience positive results in your life. As you do this, notice how you feel in your body, what your emotional experience is, and what you think

and feel about your life as a result of successfully expressing this energy. Affirm your intention for giving expression to this essential soul quality and for transforming
those things within you that will enable this to happen.

6.  Take a few relaxing breaths, close your eyes, and imagine
    that you are going on a journey to meet with the essential
    archetypal soul energy that you have chosen. Hold an
    intention that everything you experience will be for your
    highest good. Now, imagine that you are walking along a
    path in nature. You feel very grounded and centered in
    your own being, here, as you feel the earth beneath your
    feet while walking on this path. You're able to fully and
    completely be here with nothing else to do. The warmth
    of the sun feels good on your skin and you can just relax
    and let go into the beautiful stillness of this place.

    As you continue along this path, it leads you to a cave. As
    you stand before the cave opening, ask the archetypal
    presence to come forth from this cave to meet with you.
    Notice what you experience. Be aware of how it feels
    emotionally and physically to be with this archetypal
    energy. What message—through words, feelings, or
    actions—does the archetypal presence have for you at this
    time? If you feel comfortable with this archetypal pres-
    ence, ask if he, she, or it would be willing to assist you in
    giving expression to the essential quality it represents. As
    the process seems complete, begin to come back to exter-
    nal awareness, and when you are ready, open your eyes.

7.  You may now find it useful to record your experience and
    write about your feelings. What have you discovered
    about yourself and the purpose of this archetypal energy
    in your life? Are you aware of any subpersonalities oper-
    ating in your life that in some way relate to the expres-
    sion of this energy? Name one thing that you could do

for yourself or change in your life this week that would help you more fully give expression to this archetypal soul energy. For example, you could give expression to the Healer in you by finally signing up for that herbology class that you've been interested in or by doing healing things for yourself such as getting a massage. You might help the artist in you come forth by purchasing some watercolors and art paper. The Warrior's energy could be expressed by having the courage to assert yourself in telling one person what you believe or feel you need. In addition, be alert to any synchronistic experiences that may occur relating to this or any other archetypal soul energy.

As you proceed through the rest of *The Energy Body Connection*, remain mindful of these archetypal patterns that you have now discovered and the positive soul qualities that you are seeking to embody. In this way, you will continue to deepen with these energies through the other processes presented in the book. In Part III of this book, you will discover how to clear any subpersonality dynamics or other contamination that may be blocking your true soul expression. In Part IV, you will have an opportunity to further integrate these soul qualities as you embody more of your own spirit essence.

---

## Notes

1. Alexander Lowen, *Bioenergetics* (New York: Penguin Books, 1975). Ron Kurtz, *Body-Centered Psychotherapy: The Hakomi Method* (Mendocino, CA: LifeRhythm, 1990). Barbara Brennan, *Light Emerging* (New York: Bantam Books, 1993).

2. Edward C. Whitmont, *Psyche and Substance: Essays on Homeopathy in Light of Jungian Psychology* (Berkeley, CA: North Atlantic Books, 1980), pp. 73–74.

3. Carl G. Jung, *Memories, Dreams, Reflections* (New York: Random House, 1961).

4. Hal Stone and Sidra Winkelman, *Embracing Ourselves: The Voice Dialogue Manual* (Novato, CA: Nataraj Publishing, 1993).

5. George Vithoulkas, *The Science of Homeopathy* (New York: Grove/Atlantic, 1980).

6. Ibid.

7. David E. Larson, M.D., *Mayo Clinic Family Health Book* (New York: William Morrow Co., 1990), p. 694.

8. Percy Seymour, *The Scientific Basis of Astrology: Tuning to the Music of the Planets* (New York: St. Martin's Press, 1992), p. 225–226.

9. Some scientists may argue that the gravitational effect of the attending doctor on the baby is greater than, for example, that of the distant planet Pluto. However, this scientific argument is repudiated by Ronald Laurence Byrnes, who explains that gravitational influence must not be measured solely by simple force or attraction. Escape distance and gravitational field potential, the energy required to move an object beyond the grip of a planet's gravitational influence, must also be considered. When the formula for gravitational field potential, $[-Gm/r]$, is used, it is found that the distant planet Pluto does indeed have a stronger gravitational field potential than the baby's doctor. See Ronald Laurence Byrnes, "The Physical Basis of Astrology: The Influence of Gravitational Field Potential." *The Mountain Astrologer*, April/May, 1994.

10. Michel Gauquelin, *Neo-Astrology: A Copernican Revolution* (London: Arkana, 1991).

11. In addition, there are imprints from the mother's consciousness and physical state of being. Arthur Janov, *Imprints: The Lifelong Effects of the Birth Experience* (New York: Coward-McCann, Inc., 1983).

12. Barbara Brennan, *Hands of Light.* (New York: Bantam Books, 1988).

13. Astrological charts can be obtained through Llewellyn Personal Services, P.O. Box 64383-K926, St. Paul, MN 55164-0383. See also, Steven Forrest, *The Inner Sky: The Dynamic New Astrology for Everyone* (Rpt.) (San Diego, CA: ACS Publications, 1989); and William W. Hewitt, *Astrology For Beginners: An Easy Guide to Understanding and Interpreting Your Chart* (St. Paul, MN: Llewellyn, 1997).

14. John Bradshaw, *Homecoming: Reclaiming and Championing Your Inner Child* (New York: Bantam Books, 1990).

# PART II

# THE MIND

# 3

# THE TOOLS OF
# CONSCIOUSNESS

*Manifesting Your Intentions*

**WHAT IF EVERY TIME YOU THOUGHT** or said something, it instantly manifested right before your eyes? At first, this might sound like a wonderful thing. You could manifest a million dollars instantly and never have to worry about money again. However, what about the unhappy thoughts and worrying that you do? What would it be like if these things manifested instantly, too?

The fact is, your thoughts and words actually do create an effect. On some level and in some way, they are constantly manifesting certain results. Remember, the energy that everything is composed of is intelligent and responsive. Although you may not see the results of your thinking manifest physically, your thoughts and verbal intentions are like radio signals sent out into the universal matrix of energy all around you.

Much like clay is formed into various shapes, this alive, conscious, and creative energy substance is molded by your thoughts and intentions. Thus, you continue to shape your experience and reality through your thought processes.

How might your thoughts manifest in ways that you don't immediately recognize? Our bodies are a great storehouse of much of our thinking and of our conscious and unconscious beliefs. The cells of our body are like sponges soaking up the thoughts and experiences of our day. The worries and negative thoughts about ourselves are taken in just like the food we eat. If this is the only type of nourishment we offer our bodies, it will eventually lead to disease or an unhealthy state. I'm reminded of an Oscar Wilde story, *The Picture of Dorian Gray*, which I saw as a movie. The central character in this drama is a young handsome man who had a large self-portrait of himself painted. As he continued to become more self-centered, dishonest, and manipulative, changes began to take place in the painting, until finally it became a picture of an ugly, vile, and decrepit person. The painting acted as a mirror, reflecting the effect this man's negative consciousness was having on his life. This is a case where fiction isn't that far from the actual reality of things. It certainly represents the effects that negative thinking can have on the body. On the other hand, if such thinking influences one's experience, then it is also true that healing imagery can be consciously used to affect positive changes in your life and physical form.

The universal matrix of energy binds all of us in an interconnected network of consciousness. As we think, our thoughts also go out and affect one another along this network. So, even though a thought doesn't apparently manifest in your life, it does affect the collective mind and planet on which we all live. These thoughts can then affect others or return to you from the mass mind consciousness to be recycled once again as your own thoughts. This obviously creates a vicious unconscious cycle.

Our thought processes thus act like magnets, creating self-fulfilling prophesies of experience. If an individual thinks that his efforts are never appreciated or recognized, then most likely, he will experience life situations that prove this belief to him over and over. He may choose a mate who doesn't appreciate him or be unable to recognize it when his partner actually does acknowledge his efforts, because it is filtered through the lens of his negative thought pattern. In a situation like this, it is important to examine how such beliefs originated, and heal the core experiences from which they formed.

However, what we actually have available to us here is a tremendously powerful tool. Imagine the things that could be accomplished by humanity if we collectively focused our consciousness on creating harmony and peace on the planet. Many individuals have already realized this potential and have begun to meet in large and small groups with this intention in mind. By understanding how to use this powerful tool of consciousness, you can begin to create the kind of life that you would like to have. We are co-creators. This means that we can work together with the creative power in the universe to manifest our own creations. We use the power of our words, which are made of the substance of our consciousness or knowing, to do this. Any thought, intention, or internal prayer will be amplified and empowered by consciously verbalizing it as the spoken word.

If you find yourself having a negative thought, you can uncreate it and replace it with a positive image, thought, or intention of what you do want to create. If you have a fearful thought, for example, about being involved in a car accident, you can negate it by imagining the thought dissolved in a brilliant flash of light. Then, replace it with an image of what you do want to manifest. In this case, you might want to envision yourself driving safely with no problems and affirm, "It is my intention to be safe and protected in all that I do this day." This doesn't mean that you can arrogantly ignore the physical realm.

If you need your car brakes fixed or have worn-out tires, take care of it.

This type of clearing process can also be done at night by reviewing the experiences of your day and using light and affirmations to transmute any disturbing thoughts or actions that may have occurred. Begin by writing down any unresolved feelings regarding the events of your day. Lovingly accept your feelings and ask Spirit that the experiences involved be transformed. Record anything about the situations that you would now do differently, or simply recreate them in a new way internally through visualization. Next, imagine a ball of white light, like a sun, moving slowly through your whole energy field and body from your head down through your feet, clearing the difficult experiences and/or negative thoughts from your consciousness. Then, see this orb of light shoot up into the sky and drift farther and farther away until it becomes very small in the distance and simply disappears. When this is complete, affirm any new patterns that you now want to establish for yourself.

## AFFIRMATIONS

Affirmations are a method of putting forth an intention of what you would like to create in your life. They are wonderful to use when strengthening a new pattern that you are establishing in your process of personal growth. It is important to deeply, completely, and clearly focus the power of your consciousness on your intention. This sends a very clear message to the creative force so that your true desires can be manifested, rather than giving form to negative thought patterns. It is, therefore, helpful to take time to quiet yourself and still the mind first, bringing your consciousness deeply inside, to the core and center of who you are.

A good affirmation is directly personal, positive, and is stated in the present tense with feeling, knowing, and acceptance.

Directly personal means that it is stated in a way that is directly related to you. For example, instead of saying, "May world peace be manifested on Earth," say, "I give thanks that peace is now manifesting directly in my life and in the world." Even if it is a general and nonspecific affirmation, it will be helpful to personalize it by using "I." Nonspecific affirmations are great when you don't know what to ask for, or aren't sure what the best results might be in a particular situation. Affirmations such as, "I give thanks that Spirit is now bringing forth perfect results in this situation in a way that is for the highest good of all involved," or "I accept that divine order is now being restored in this situation," can be used in such cases. Sometimes I make an affirmation asking for a specific thing and then add, "or anything more wonderful the universe has in mind for me that I haven't even imagined yet!"

The positive aspect of an affirmation is important. You want to make sure that you are affirming what you do want to manifest and not verbalizing what you don't. So, instead of saying, "I accept that I won't go broke," affirm, "I give thanks that financial abundance is now effortlessly manifesting in my life." This emphasizes the positive dynamics that you want to experience. Stating things in present tense language keeps you present and connected with the affirmation in an immediate way, and states it as something that is happening in the here and now, not in some future or unreal time. Avoid using phrases such as "going to" or "trying." For example, the statement, "I accept that I am going to try and be more loving," doesn't have much power behind it. This is because it is not about something that is actually happening in the present. Notice the difference when it is stated as, "I give thanks that each day I am experiencing more love in my life, and expressing that love to others."

Feelings are what connect us to the knowing and consciousness of our core. For this reason, it is important to give this feeling quality to your affirmation. This means that you really feel

✱ use affirmations
according to what
is defined —
think
say
feel
create
demonstrate

it, accept it, and know it to be true. I have heard individuals stating affirmations with absolutely no affect, as if they were reciting math multiplication tables. This will not be as effective because there is a lack of conscious feeling and connection to both your own Higher Self and what you are asking for. I have found that speaking forth the words of your affirmation from the solar plexus, the center of emotional power and will, helps to connect you with your feeling self. Visualizing yourself experiencing the new pattern that you're affirming will also assist you in connecting with your feelings, and accepting that your prayer is answered and already manifesting in your life. I have worked with people who say an affirmation or put forth an intention and then continue to negate it through constant doubt and worry. This will cause confusion about whether you really want to manifest the affirmation or the doubt-filled thought.

Doubt and worry are often reflections of the subconscious dynamics that exist regarding the issues related to your affirmation. Emotional healing concerning such issues may sometimes be necessary in order for the fullness of your affirmation to manifest. This is similar to opening the curtains in a dusty, darkened room and letting the sunlight in. You can then see the dirt that was not noticeable when the room was dark. In much the same way, when you create an affirmation or prayer, it shines a light on anything that has prevented you from manifesting that intention in your life, illuminating the dust of your distorted core beliefs and emotional patterns. These dynamics emerge to be transformed and released, so that your intention can be fulfilled. For this reason, it is important to use affirmations in conjunction with some type of emotional clearing process. Otherwise, you may be trying to impose a new pattern on the subconscious mind without addressing the feelings that reside there; for example, in the form of childhood pain.

Something else that will help you with the acceptance of your intention is including a sense of gratitude and thanks in your affirmation. This implies that it is already done and also elicits a sense of love and humility, which creates a receptive state or condition within you.

When doubts, worry, or fears surface for you with regard to your affirmation:

1. Write down the affirmation as well as your doubting reaction on a piece of paper. Record any feelings that you have relating to this doubt you are experiencing.

2. Continue to explore your response. Is the reaction or doubt a familiar message? Who or what does it remind you of? When was the first time you remember having this particular feeling or belief, and what was your experience at that time? This will help you look at the subconscious patterns that you have regarding these issues.

3. Put forth an intention or prayer that Spirit assist you in the deep healing of your mind and heart to bring you into alignment with your affirmation. As part of this process, a subpersonality dialogue regarding a negative internalized message may help you to clear things emotionally so that you can be confident about your affirmation. (See chapters 5 and 6 for information regarding the use of the Embodiment Dialogue process.)

## *Making an Affirmation*

The following steps will assist you in making any affirmation, intention, or prayer a powerful statement that will manifest in your life.

1. Find a relaxed, comfortable position, centering yourself inside by taking a few full breaths into your abdomen.

2. Reach forth to your highest sense of spiritual consciousness and love. Make conscious contact with the Creative

Source as your know it and go into your own heart and being, your highest sense of Self within.

3. State your intention and put forth the pattern that you want to create by speaking the words of your affirmation from your solar plexus with power and feeling. Say it mentally and verbally, with authority and knowing. Feel it in your body as you say it.

4. Accept that your affirmation is manifesting. Feel yourself receiving it and visualize what it's like to have it so. See, sense, or imagine what it will be like to experience the affirmation manifesting in your life.

5. Give thanks to the Creative Source, if this was not already a part of your affirming statement or prayer.

6. Let go. Assume that your prayer is answered. You can relax and know that it is being accomplished, just as you do when you order a catalogue item by phone or mail, and simply assume that it will arrive without having to worry about it every minute.

## Examples of Affirmations

In addition to the personally designed affirmations that you create, here are some others which you may find useful:

1. I am a divine being and there is a divine plan of love for me.

2. I give thanks that each day I am experiencing greater love and compassion in my life.

3. It is my intention to accelerate my personal growth and spiritual development, and I give thanks that each day I am opening up to experience more of Spirit's presence in my life.

4. I can trust the divine guidance from my Higher Self and the wisdom of my own instincts.

5. I give thanks that each day I am experiencing and emanating greater health, joy, and vitality in my life.

6. I give thanks that financial abundance is now effortlessly manifesting in my life.

7. It is my intention to experience love, joy, peace, and safety in all that I do this day.

8. I ask for the deep healing of my mind and heart with regard to this issue, and I accept that Spirit is now bringing me all the assistance that I need to resolve and clear it.

9. I give thanks that Spirit is now bringing forth perfect results in this situation in a way that is for the highest good of all involved.

## RESOURCES *draw on an archetype to...*

You can also use your conscious mind to assist your process of personal growth by becoming aware of your internal and external resources. Resources are things, activities, or inner qualities that act as a support and instill a sense of comfort, well-being, and wholeness. When you are feeling upset or disconnected from your own essential being, resources can provide a feeling of inner integrity and strength. Affirmations and prayer, for instance, are powerful spiritual resources that you can use at such times. You accessed yet another resource in the last chapter when you connected with the positive qualities of your archetypal soul essence. These inner qualities can now be drawn upon whenever you need them. For example, one client, who is a school teacher and very good with children, was able to draw upon this Teacher aspect in herself when dealing with the difficult childlike characteristics within her own personality. Another man let the Artist in him bring greater creativity to his mundane job.

Resources can be especially helpful when difficult feelings arise or when you are going through a period of stress, depression, or anxiety. They act as an anchor, returning you home to the more centered, strong, or expansive feelings that are available within you. Difficult memories and feelings from past events can be resolved in this way because new resources are present that were not available at the time the original painful situation occurred. For example, the experience, skills, and wisdom we have gained as adults can now be used to assist the more vulnerable part of us inside to deal with certain fears which are based on wounding childhood events. Resources can thus empower us by providing the tools we need to deal with the inner and external challenges of life. In addition to internal resources, we also have external resources available to us such as support groups, inspirational books, or uplifting activities such as physical exercise.

Working consciously with internal and external resources can greatly benefit individuals who don't know how to nurture themselves. Many people from abusive families lack the ability to take care of themselves in this way. Such individuals may have no sense of what comforts or relaxes them, or even what makes them feel happy. For some, these things have simply not been a part of their experience. If you are one of these individuals, it will be especially important for you to become conscious of your personal internal and external resources. Here are some things that will help you in this process.

### External Resources

To increase awareness of your external resources, make a list of five things that make you feel comforted, relaxed, or a little bit better in some way. It may be helpful to spend a few quiet moments centered inside yourself, and from this place, remember a time when you felt very nurtured, fulfilled, content, or peaceful. Notice what you were doing at the time you felt this way. What activities or things help you feel this way spiritually, mentally, emotionally, and physically? (This may also include expansive inner sensations and feelings that you can resource. See page 116 for Internal Resources.) When you are feeling lonely, sad, or anxious, you can look at this list and remember to do those things which comfort, nourish, and relax you.

As an example, here are some things that individuals have listed as possible external resources.

- Write about your feelings or write a letter to God, expressing how you feel.

- Make a cup of hot tea and sip it while sitting in the sunshine, snuggled in a cozy blanket.

- Do some outdoor activity or physical exercise you enjoy (swim, bike, a walk in the park).

- Talk to a loving friend.

- Get a massage or rub your own feet.

- Spend time with your favorite dog, cat, or other pet.

- Soak in a warm bubble bath. (Candlelight is a great addition to this.)

- Go to a place in nature (a meadow, park, forest, or lake).

- Dance to rock music or African rhythms; do yoga or other stretching to music you enjoy.

- Go to a playground, zoo, or do something you loved to do as a child.

- Work in the garden or repot some house plants.

- Read an uplifting book or a heart-warming story.

## Internal Resources

In addition to accessing the positive inner qualities of your archetypal soul essence, another internal resource can be experienced through the reverie of recalling a time when you felt peaceful, relaxed in some way, or felt an expansive feeling in your body. Using creative imagery to simply imagine yourself in some type of pleasant experience—perhaps walking in the forest, sitting in a warm mountain meadow, or enjoying a day at the ocean—can accomplish the same thing. I often have clients internally visualize and feel themselves in a place such as this, one that they've actually been to or one which they creatively imagine, in order to access feelings of comfort, relaxation, and safety. They can then go to this "safe place" internally whenever they feel overwhelmed or need to reconnect with a sense of peace and their own internal center. Several of the meditations in the next chapter can also be used for this purpose.

When you have an uplifting experience of a spiritual nature, feel a sense of peace, joy, unconditional love, or simply feel good about yourself, you can notice all the bodily sensations connected with this experience. This will help your body hold the memory of this expansive experience and you will more readily be able to access these good feelings once again by returning to the memory of the experience.

Our bodily sensations and feelings are actually one of the most powerful internal resources we have. Connecting with expansive somatic feelings, for example, can help us relax, while it is often our gut-level body sensations that help us to determine when a situation is uncomfortable or potentially dangerous.

The ability to feel these things somatically is thus an internal support that we can call upon to help us through various life experiences. I discovered a whole new level of somatic support for myself when I started receiving bodywork. One particular experience I had, after a Rolfing session on my upper body, provides an excellent example of this. Instead of my old pattern of collapsing emotionally and also physically through the chest area when confronted with difficult experiences, I was able to actually feel my chest muscles supporting me and holding me up as I moved through various challenging situations. Feeling the physical sensations of muscular support in my body enhanced my new sense of emotional strength and self-confidence. Bodywork such as this can be an excellent way to consciously access and work with this type of internal support. The somatic awareness processes contained in chapter 5 will also enable you to experience this type of internal resource that the body provides.

Keep your list of external and internal resources readily available and, as you continue with the processes in this book, remember to use your affirmations and resources to support your journey of personal growth and healing.

Meditate and think of a question that you need your Higher Self to support you on . . . go to the massage therapy session; go to that level and let ~~whatever is spoken~~ the Higher Self reveal it self.

unconscious

# 4

# AWARENESS
# AND MEDITATION

*Quieting the Thinking Mind*

THE MIND IS INDEED A POWERFUL TOOL. However, this power must be harnessed and disciplined if we are to unlock its full potential. Our conscious thinking mind actually represents only a limited part of the creative intelligence that is available to us from other parts of our psyche. Awareness and meditation are two processes that can assist us in accessing this fertile resource within us.

Awareness means being totally present and fully conscious of what you're experiencing in each moment, perceiving how you feel mentally, emotionally, physically, and energetically. It involves a conscious feeling, sensing, and seeing, rather than a mental focusing. However, disciplining, focusing, and quieting the thinking mind will allow you to center into this state of consciousness more readily. Awareness is an important aspect of personal growth and spiritual development because all of us have, at many points in our lives, removed our conscious awareness from our experience, our feelings, our bodies, and our environment. We originally distanced ourselves in this way during wounding situations in order to avoid the pain that we were experiencing at the time. The process of healing and growth involves reclaiming these areas of our lives (body, feelings, etc.) through returning our conscious awareness to them once again.

How do we accomplish this? First, by showing up in our lives and paying attention! This requires having consciousness in the here and now present, rather than dwelling in the past or worrying about the future. This type of mindfulness and being in the present moment is a foundational part of Buddhist philosophy and meditation practice.

One of the most powerful consciousness-raising exercises I know of involves going through your day while keeping your mind attentive to what you are doing while you are doing it. For example, when sitting down to a meal, your consciousness is fully present with the experience of eating, thinking of nothing else as you enjoy the visual appearance of the meal's presentation as well as the sensations of all the individual textures and flavors of the food. While you're driving your car to work, your mind is focused totally on the process of driving. When washing the dishes, you are fully aware of everything involved in that act, such as feeling the warmth of the sudsy water and the movement of your hands over the dish or pan. This is easy to say, but not so easy to do. This exercise will, however, immediately demonstrate the amount of time that you spend in the whirlwind grip of the thinking mind, rather than in a present-centered state of awareness.

# KEEPING A JOURNAL

One of the most effective means for healing, growth, and the development of conscious awareness is the practice of journal writing. Keeping a personal journal—a written account of your thoughts, feelings, and experiences—provides a structure for consciously connecting with your inner self. It allows you to access the intuitive guidance from deep within your own being and creates a sacred space for your innermost feelings and perceptions. I'm constantly amazed at how much can be revealed in the process of sitting down to write with pen and paper in hand, even when I think I have nothing to say! In the process of writing, in simply being willing to begin, a doorway opens that allows wisdom, insight, and creativity to be stimulated. Since you will be using a journal as you proceed through the various processes in this book, here is some general information on keeping a journal that you may find useful.

A journal can be used in many ways to assist you in your process of personal growth and spiritual unfoldment. Many times, journal writing can bring clarity and resolution to situations that seem to dominate your consciousness. Perhaps you find yourself thinking about an issue over and over in your mind. Journal writing can provide not only a channel to express your true feelings, but can also help you connect with the underlying issues involved and help you discover new choices and directions.

You will obtain the greatest benefits in this endeavor by connecting with the feelings you have rather than just relating external events. As you do this, you will begin to more fully understand the patterns in such events and the meaning they may have in your life. For example, rather than just intellectually describing the argument that you had with your friend and what was said or done, it would be useful to explore the emotions it evoked and write down the feelings of anger, sadness, shock, et cetera. Through doing this, you might realize a repeating pattern in relationships of not having your feelings heard, and relate it to anxieties from your past about not being accepted. Not only might the argument with your friend then have less emotional charge, but you could also make more conscious choices regarding expressing your needs and feelings in relationships.

A journal can be a place to record the profound realizations and peak experiences of your life as well as the things you might judge as trivial or mundane. All of these things are important and can lead you to a deeper connection with your own being. Your journal can be a loving and nonjudgmental companion that is always there to listen. It can also provide a safe place to release and clear feelings when you need to, rather than inappropriately venting those feelings on others. I often have clients journal feelings in the form of a letter to individuals with whom they have unresolved issues. This journal letter can be written uncensored and without concern for saying everything in a grammatically perfect fashion because it is written solely for the person writing it and is not actually meant to be sent. This process empowers people, helps them clarify their true feelings, and enables them to transform the situation involved, so that they can let go of it.

Your journal can also be a place to describe, record, and explore your dreams, visions, and meditation experiences. Dream symbols often unfold their meaning over a period of time as the conscious mind more fully realizes different levels of the wisdom they contain. For this reason, it can be very helpful to have a written record of your dreams in your journal, so that you can refer back to them later. Dreams are most easily remembered immediately upon waking, so this is a good time to write them down. You will often find that if there are pieces of the dream you can't recall, the missing parts will emerge in your consciousness later in the day. You don't have to write down all your dreams by any means, but you will find it beneficial to at least record the ones that seem significant, impactful, or emotionally charged for you.

It is also helpful to record any synchronistic events that emerge for you in your process of personal growth. One time, after a session with my therapist that involved my relationship with my father, I experienced a very confirming synchronistic event. This particular session focused on taking my power back from my father. I was now no longer a passive child who had to endure his alcoholism, but an empowered adult woman. The day after the session, my father called and left a message on my telephone answering machine. He related that there was an ice storm back East where he lived and at that moment all the electric power was off in his house. His exact words were, "I have no power!" For a long time, whenever I was feeling down or having doubts about myself, I would go back to read this experience in my journal to reconnect with the empowerment of that session. Keeping a journal can give you this kind of perspective and help you to see the overall pattern of what is taking place in your process.

Your journal can also be used in an autobiographical way to "tell your story," and reflect on your process of personal growth and spiritual development up to this point. One man used his journal to write the story of his life. He included his childhood experience and how, through therapy, he was able to heal the rigid emotional legacy inherited from his father, as well as what he now understood about life as a result. He planned to give it to his children in order to share with them what he had learned.

For those with a history of physical, emotional, or sexual abuse, telling the story of what happened to them is a very important part of their healing process. Often, children who are sexually abused are threatened with harm if they tell anyone about the abuse. Being able to tell this dark secret is a very empowering step in recovery. A journal provides a private and confidential place where the truth can finally be told and feelings can safely be expressed.

Journal writing also allows you to bring forth new information from your meditations, enabling you to more fully understand these experiences. In contemplative states, in the reverie of nature, and at other times as well, you can receive guidance through words, images, feelings, or sensations. Writing the process down helps bring the meditation experience more fully into your consciousness and assists you in integrating its elements into your daily life. Also, different pieces of information relating to a common theme will often emerge throughout your various meditations. Having the information written down and dated helps you to keep track of these connected elements and the unfolding process that is taking place.

The writing process can also be the meditation itself. Quiet yourself for a few moments, ask Spirit a question, and start writing the answer. I have a friend who calls this "a letter from God," and it can be a very powerful and insightful process.

Journal expression includes more than words, and many times when I receive images in my dreams or meditations I will draw them in my journal. This type of creative expression can be fun and provide further insights. Your journal is also a great place to write down your goals, visions, and intentions for your future. What is your true heart's desire for yourself? What would your ideal life be like and what would it include? How would you like to see yourself in the next three months, six months, year, or more? Imagine it, feel it, and then write it down and make it real! You can then create and record in your journal specific affirmations that will assist you in manifesting these life goals.

These are only some of the examples of how a journal can be used. Your journal is a reflection of your own uniqueness, so be creative. The most important thing is to be honest, no matter how nasty sounding and not "nice" that may be at times. Let your journal be at least one place where you can just be you without all the "shoulds" and "should nots."

## *Journal Exercise*

The following journal writing exercise will not only help you get started in your journal, but will also create a greater conscious awareness regarding your process of spiritual awakening.

Take some time to write and reflect on your process of personal growth and spiritual development up to this point.

- How has your life path led you to the point where you are right now?

- What are the realizations that led you to major life enhancements or shifts?

- Have you had any experiences that felt uplifting, expansive, or transformative in some way either spiritually, mentally, emotionally, physically, or energetically? (This could be an ecstatic moment—perhaps the birth of a child, or a life-altering experience such as a healing process.)

- What was the spiritual belief of your upbringing (or lack of it), and how did this affect you?

- What other spiritual paths, philosophies, or personal growth processes have you explored and what did you gain? What worked for you and what didn't?

- What is your current relationship with Spirit or the Creative Force as you understand it and what are you seeking to gain at this time from further growth and spiritual development?

# MEDITATION

Many times, when I ask people if they meditate, I hear a series of moans or statements such as: "Oh, I tried that once and I couldn't do it. It doesn't work for me." The individuals who I find are disappointed or frustrated with meditation fall into three primary categories.

1. They have preconceived ideas, expectations, or misunderstandings about it.

2. They are using a technique that doesn't work for them.

3. As part of their meditation practice, they are trying to conform to a particular lifestyle, spiritual belief, or philosophical system that they're uncomfortable with.

First let me clear up any misunderstandings about what meditation actually is and how it works. Meditation is a tool for quieting yourself so that you can gain clarity and awareness by becoming more receptive to information from deeper states of consciousness. It is a time of stillness when you can be inspired, receive guidance from Spirit, and feel nourished by the love of creation. Through meditation, you can have a deeper realization of your own being and come to know yourself more fully. You can also connect with a creative power source that can assist you in your own growth and help you manifest the desired changes in your life.

Meditation is not dependent on any one particular form or technique, religious or spiritual belief, or philosophical system. In fact, meditation can simply be relaxing and observing what you are internally aware of in the present moment. That's all the technique that is required. You can probably even recall a time when you did this, perhaps relaxing after an exercise session, listening to meditative music, or while enjoying a peaceful nature setting. This type of meditation can be done anywhere and at any time. Gradually, by consistently taking time to quiet the thinking mind and direct your consciousness inward in this way, you can learn to strengthen your concentration and gain a greater sense of peace and self-awareness.

There are actually many different types of meditation available. You may feel drawn to one particular form or try several of them to see which best fits your particular needs. One type of meditation technique helps people strengthen their concentration by having them focus their consciousness on a meaningful or inspirational object. This could involve meditating on a beautiful flower, a candle, a crystal, or a spiritually uplifting picture or mandala. I meditated on an orange for years and was amazed at the realizations that constantly emerged for me. For example, the separated individual sections of the orange, held within the unified circular shape of the outer skin, signified all the different aspects of my being integrated into one whole Self. It also represented how all people are individuals, yet, are also united as part of a much greater whole. I was also fascinated by the amazing life force potential of each tiny seed holding the creative pattern of an entire orange tree within it, just as each of us holds the essential seed of spirit within us. It's possible to be so absorbed in this type of practice, that everything else around you fades away as you become one with the object you're concentrating on. However, it is also very effective and relaxing to simply gaze at the object while keeping your consciousness focused on it with an alert receptivity.

Other forms of meditation practice have individuals focus on a particular word or phrase, which is sometimes repeated. As you focus on the specific word or phrase, it becomes imprinted on your consciousness and the energy or quality of it begins to unfold so that you have a greater realization of its meaning within your own being. I find that people are often naturally drawn to a particular inspirational quote, a phrase from a book, an affirmation, or prayer which is meaningful to them. In some cases, a specific word or sound "mantra" is given by a teacher with the intention of bringing about a particular experience for the one reciting it. Each of the various mantras in Hindu tradition, for instance, is used for a specific purpose such as strengthening a spiritual quality, uniting with the energy of a particular deity, awakening a chakra center, or providing spiritual protection.[1]

By meditating on the predetermined mantra, one can attune to its particular energy or the state of consciousness associated with it. This is possible because each word, whether spoken or not, is composed of certain sounds and, like all sound waves, carries a certain vibrational frequency. Through repeating the sound or word of the mantra, you can bring your consciousness into resonance with its particular vibratory rate, much like the sound emitted by one tuning fork can cause another one to vibrate with a similar tone.

Chanting sounds such as the "OM," can have this effect. In Hindu philosophy, the OM is considered the primordial vibration from which all creation originated. It is believed that all matter and energy in the universe is composed of the smaller frequency waves that came rippling forth from this original vibrational sound emerging from the stillness of the void.[2] The OM is often chanted repeatedly in order to connect with this consciousness of the One, the totality of All That Is.

In addition to sounding the OM in this way, you can also use it as a centering exercise in preparation for other meditation. To do this, break the OM sound down into the three syllables— Ah-O-MMM—and extend each part for as long as you comfortably can while sustaining a single breath. Open your mouth wide for the Ah part, round your mouth for the O sound, and then close your mouth for the MMM. As you begin, inhale through your nose and take a full breath into your abdomen. As you exhale with the Ah sound, let it come up from your belly and resonate in your heart area. Then form the O sound and let it resonate in the clavicle/throat area. As you sound the MMM, let it vibrate on the roof of your mouth and resonate in your crown chakra. Repeat this twice, reciting the OM a total of three times, and then sit in the stillness and feel the energy flow through your whole body.

Certain other meditation techniques involve concentrating on the breath or using specific breath exercises. For the most beneficial effects, such meditative breathing is best done through the nose. One such breathing meditation involves maintaining awareness of each inhalation and exhalation while sitting quietly. This can include awareness of the whole breathing process—for example, the expansion and contraction of the lungs and the rising and falling of the ribcage with each breath. It helps to breathe more slowly and rhythmically as you count out each breath cycle up to ten and then repeat it. This can be done by counting one on the inhalation, two on the exhalation, three on the next inhalation, and so on, up to ten. However, most people prefer to inhale one slow breath while counting to five and then exhaling on six through ten. If you become distracted or your mind wanders, gently bring your conscious awareness back to your breathing and start counting from one again. If you are a more kinesthetic person, focusing on the physical breath in this way may be easier for you. Likewise, if you need to connect more fully with the life force of your physical body, this type of breath meditation can be helpful.

The stillness of meditation can also involve contemplative movement practices. If you find it hard or uncomfortable to sit still, this type of meditation might initially be easier for you. Walking meditation, for example, can be done anywhere but is most effective in a quiet nature setting. While walking, keep your consciousness focused fully on the process of walking; for instance, the way you place your foot on the ground, the smell of the air, or the flower that you stop to touch. You can also combine walking meditation with other techniques such as breath or mantra meditation. Other methods that can be used for movement meditation are Sufi dancing, which involves a rhythmic whirling motion; certain types of meditative yoga; and T'ai Chi, an ancient Chinese practice consisting of continuous postures executed through a relaxed, flowing movement and slow, deep breathing.

Another type of meditation involves focusing on the chakra energy centers or imagining yourself immersed in a particular color. If you did the chakra meditation at the end of the first chapter, then you've already had one experience of this type of meditation.

It is also a very comforting meditation experience to simply sit within the silence of your own being and call forth the loving presence of the Divine. Open to receive this unconditionally loving energy of the universe while giving thanks, just soaking in the love as you gently breathe it into your heart. I recommend this process especially at those times when other meditation practices may seem too difficult.

## Avoiding the Meditation Pitfalls

The biggest mistake I see people make with regard to any type of meditation is thinking that they must be doing something wrong if their mind is full of thoughts or if they start experiencing annoying feelings and bodily sensations. When you begin to still the thinking mind or attempt to focus it after a lifetime of the mind having total control, the first thing you become aware of is how uncontrollable your mind seems to be. Suddenly, a parade of noisy mental chatter fills your head.

Quieting the mind or having a peaceful mind doesn't necessarily mean that your consciousness is empty of any thoughts, feelings, images, or sensations. In fact, when these things emerge, they can be significant information for you. Learn to just observe the flowing river of feelings, sensations, and thoughts without judgment. This type of unattached reference point is often referred to as the witness state or the objective observer aspect that can simply experience what is, without mental or emotional reaction and interference.

Trying to fight the thinking mind is very much like flailing your arms around at a swarm of angry hornets. What you resist, persists even more strongly. When you find your mind getting distracted, rather than getting into a big internal battle of judgment and self-recrimination, simply bring your consciousness back to the present and continue observing. Each time you gently bring your wandering mind back to a present-centered state of awareness, it strengthens your ability to focus your consciousness. So, no matter how many times you initially have to do this in a meditation session, the process is always working for you, regardless of what your thinking mind tries to tell you.

In addition, although meditation eventually results in a calming revitalization, a sense of anxiety or discomfort can sometimes emerge when all the outer activity stops and one's inner feelings can finally be heard. Once again, as one's illuminating consciousness is directed within, subconscious forces may be brought to light and be seen and felt for the first time. Initially, this may not seem very relaxing. However, you will be receiving important information that will allow you to heal the source of the uncomfortable feelings. It is helpful to simply recognize and acknowledge feelings when they do emerge for you. Avoid denying or resisting your experience or judging your feelings and sensations as good or bad. Acknowledging your true feelings is the first step in beginning to understand them. At the same time, remember that your emotions or sensations are only a part of who you are in your totality. Simply observe these things without attachment and think of your conscious awareness as sunlight that is coming into your inner room, allowing you to see what is there and more fully know yourself.

The first rule of meditation is that there are no rules. In other words, don't make this another perfectionistic performance issue or an excuse to beat yourself up over some rigid concept. Try to balance commonsense discipline with a sense that meditation is a joyful time for you to shut out the noise of the world and go within. Think of meditation as your time to just relax, receive, and soak in the nourishing energy from the universe.

Since everyone is a unique individual, each person's needs may vary in regard to the self-discipline needed for meditation. If you tend to be compulsive, perfectionistic, or rigid, remember to be gentle with yourself. It may be important for you to be flexible and have a day off. Sometimes I suggest that people meditate for six days of the week and have one day when they aren't required to do anything. Eventually, you will appreciate the benefits of meditation so much that you won't want to be without it. However, if it becomes forced drudgery, you are probably trying too hard. Conversely, if you are a person who lacks structure, and you tend to procrastinate or be lethargic, then part of your process may involve working more consciously with developing self-discipline in your meditation practice. This is especially important when your initial enthusiasm begins to wane and things seem stagnant or boring. There can be periods when it may appear as if nothing is happening for some time, and then suddenly, you may notice that you are feeling less burdened and stressed, or that you seem to feel really good more frequently. You may also find that you want to go inside in meditation for the answers to your life questions, rather than being dependent on external sources and validation from others.

## Getting Started

Begin by making space for meditation in your life. I mean this quite literally. Create an actual space in your home as your meditation sanctuary. This could be some place away from the distracting activity of things such as a corner of the bedroom or just an assigned area where you can spend some quiet time. Make this place special to you by placing some meaningful or uplifting things there such as an inspirational picture or book, a candle, sacred objects, flowers, healing stones, or sea shells. You will also want to include a chair or cushion to sit on in your meditation space. The meditation place that you create in this way is symbolic of the sacred inner space of the divine Self and the conscious connection that you are now making with this part of yourself.

When choosing a time to meditate, consider your schedule and energy patterns so that you structure things in a practical way and can therefore be successful. Also consider the significance of sunrise and sunset. These are powerful times for meditation because they are nature's transition periods between the world of day (consciousness) and night (subconscious). Meditating in the morning can set a peaceful and positive tone for your entire day. However, if you have trouble unwinding after your workday, you might find it useful to meditate before bedtime. I have found that early morning or evening periods work best for people. It is easier to still your own thinking mind at times when the world isn't so active with everyone's busy mind in high gear, mucking up the mass mind airways. Meditating at about the same time every day in the same place is also helpful because it establishes a specific pattern that becomes easy to follow each day.

It is important to sit in a position where your back is straight, so that the energy can flow properly along the spine. It is not necessary to sit in a lotus posture with legs crossed and folded underneath you, no matter how many Eastern gurus or Zen masters you have seen depicted in this way. It is just as effective and conducive to the energy flow to sit in a chair with feet flat on the ground. Having your feet on the ground can also strengthen your connection with the Earth by making you more consciously aware of the life force energies moving into your body through your feet. Laying down to meditate is not recommended because it is too easy to fall asleep. You've been laying down to fall asleep all your life and it has created a very strongly established pattern that is difficult to resist.

In the beginning, start out with a meditation time of only three to five minutes a day. I've known many people who thought they had to meditate for an hour each day to be doing it correctly. People such as this struggle with such a lengthy time, then become discouraged and give up meditation practice all together. It is better to start out slow and then build your time gradually as you become more accustomed to meditation. For example, meditate for five minutes for two weeks, then ten minutes for the next two weeks, and then fifteen minutes for the month after that. Increase your time to twenty minutes a day when you feel you are ready. It is initially more effective to consistently meditate for shorter periods of time, at about the same time and place each day, than it is to meditate sporadically for longer periods of time.

As you begin your meditation session, get comfortable and take a few slow, cleansing breaths deeply into the bottom of your belly. If you are comfortable with it, it is better to breathe in and out through your nose or to at least inhale through your nostrils and exhale through your mouth. However, if your nose is stuffed or you don't feel relaxed breathing this way, it is better to breathe through your mouth. As much as possible, let the breath expand fully into not just your diaphragm, but also into your abdomen and pelvis. Breathing into your abdomen in this way, unlike upper respiratory breathing, will help you enter a body-centered state of relaxation. Then just breathe naturally, letting your breath be soft and easy.

Next, intend, feel, or imagine yourself surrounded in light. Some people find it easier to do this if they visualize a circular or egg-shaped bubble around them and then see it filled with bright light. This acts as a protection for you and also enhances your meditation experience. You may also want to state a particular intention for your meditation work. For example, your intention for your session might be to discipline the thinking mind and focus your consciousness, to learn to relax, to obtain personal clarity and guidance, or to have a deeper realization of Self.

# WEEKLY MEDITATION PROCESS

To help you get started, I've included a series of weekly meditation processes that will assist you in gradually developing your own meditation practice. This will also give you a chance to experience several different types of meditation techniques. These processes, developed and adapted over the years from my work with various teachers and organizations, have been used successfully by many individuals.

## *Week One*

Find an object that is spiritually meaningful to you or evokes a sense of beauty, reverence, joy, or wonder. A candle, picture, flower, or other gift of nature works well. Spend three minutes each day meditating on the object. Have a sense of allowing your consciousness to gently rest upon the object and enfold it. As you do this, let your consciousness stay totally concentrated on the object. If your mind drifts to thoughts of other things, then gently bring your consciousness back to enfold the object once again. Use the same object for the entire week.

At the end of week one, record your experience in your journal. What have you become aware of this week? Remember, don't be discouraged if it has felt like your mind is out of control. You are beginning to discipline the thinking mind and that is a step in the right direction. Soon, your ability to do this will be strengthened.

## Week Two

Imagine a place that you would like to go to, perhaps a place that you know of or one you would enjoy visiting. For five minutes each day, go there in your consciousness. Think of your consciousness as a magic carpet that can take you anywhere you want to go. Then, focus on the specific place you have chosen. Immerse yourself in the experience—see the colors that are there, hear the sounds of the place, and even smell the fragrances in the air. Once again, if your mind wanders to other subjects, gently bring your consciousness back to your chosen place.

One by-product of this meditation is a growing awareness of the fact that what you experience is often a result of where you put your consciousness. You are, in fact, always involved in this process, usually in an unconscious way, through what you place your consciousness on. During this week, be mindful of what type of experiences you create as you direct your consciousness in this way.

At the end of week two, record your experience with the meditation. Did you enjoy going to your place in consciousness this week? To what degree were you able to experience yourself actually being in that particular place? During the week, did you have any realizations regarding the connection between what you were experiencing and what your consciousness was focused on at the time?

## Week Three

This week you are going to meditate for five to ten minutes each day on one quality that you would like to embody, such as peace, love, joy, abundance, wisdom, beauty, grace, truth, or freedom. Before beginning, take a few slow and relaxing breaths into the bottom of your belly and let yourself drop into a place deep inside you. As much as possible, allow yourself to feel in your body the quality that you choose. For instance, feel yourself enfolded by the quality of love. Have a sense of breathing this loving substance in and feel it circulate through your whole body. Feel it absorbed into each cell as it permeates every part of your being. Feeling the quality kinesthetically in this way will help you to experience it more fully.

You can also imagine what it would be like to emanate and manifest this quality. For example, envision yourself as very peaceful and serene. Imagine what your life would be like if you emanated this feeling of peace, how you would act, and what it would feel like in your body. If your mind strays from the quality that you are meditating on, gently bring your consciousness back to focus on it again. Throughout the week, remind yourself of your quality at different points during the day, and notice if it helps you to resonate with that particular feeling.

## Week Four

This week you will be doing a color meditation. Every day of the week you will be meditating on a different color for eight to ten minutes each day. The colors you will be using are those associated with the chakras and you will be meditating on them in that order. So, day one will be red, day two will be orange, day three will be yellow and continuing on through the week with green, blue, indigo violet, and white.

As you begin, take a few full breaths to center yourself. As you exhale, let the thoughts and tensions just drain right out of your body as you sink deeper inside. Then imagine yourself surrounded with the colored light for that specific day of meditation. The colors should be vibrant and clear, like a red marble or a yellow lollipop. It may help you to find such objects as this in order to have a clear sense of the colors you will be working with. I have found it helpful to use samples of colored glass, which can be obtained at any stained glass supply store. Recalling the effect that these colors have on you emotionally when you see them or wear them may also enable you to experience the colors more fully.

In the meditation, feel the color enfold you, breathe it in and feel the colored light absorbed into your whole body. Experiencing the color in this way will help you to feel it and sense it so that you're not trying to "think" the color into existence. Remember, you will only be doing one color each day and will be using a different color each day of the week.

Notice what your experience is and how you respond to each color. Are there any colors that are harder to visualize or stay focused on? Did the various colors have different qualities or have different effects on your experience? For future reference, note the colors that seem to be especially effective and nurturing for you. You may want to bring these colors into your life in other ways—perhaps in your environment or in the clothes that you wear—in order to take advantage of their benefits.

## Week Five

On the first day of week five, you are going to create an inner spiritual workplace and healing space for yourself. Then, for the remaining days of the week, you will be going to that place within to contact your Higher Self for guidance. On day one, do the following guided meditation.

Take a few cleansing breaths, letting yourself sink a little deeper inside and then just allow your breath to become soft and easy. Allow any distracting thoughts or tensions to gently fade away with each exhalation.

Now see, sense, or imagine yourself surrounded in an orb or sphere of soft healing light. Put forth an intention that you be guided by your Higher Self to a place of healing and spiritual growth. Now, imagine yourself walking along a pathway in a very serene natural setting. You have nothing else to do right now and can just relax here, fully letting go into the beauty and peacefulness of nature all around you.

Feel the warmth of the Sun on your skin. Savor the rich fragrance of the earth. Enjoy the rippling grass dancing in the wind.

After a time, you notice that the path you are on leads to a spiritual workplace, a sacred healing space that you can use to heal, receive guidance, and grow spiritually. This place is designed perfectly for you and can be anything that you want it to be, for example, a healing temple or house. It may even be unlike anything that you have ever experienced before, such as a structure composed of crystals.

Because this spiritual workplace is filled with tiny particles of light, its form may also appear somewhat ethereal. However, it should feel comfortable, loving, and expansive.

As you enter, take time to explore your spiritual workplace. Set it up just the way you want it to be. You can have all the colors that you love and just the right kind of comfortable furniture. As you look around here, you notice colors that feel healing and uplifting, and objects that are sacred to you or have meaning in some way. Everything in this environment is totally soothing, comforting, and nourishing to your entire being. Take a few moments, then, to feel yourself sitting in your spiritual workplace enfolded by a presence of unconditional love.

Before beginning your meditation on days two through seven, choose a specific issue or concern you would like to receive guidance on, or perhaps just pick something that you would like more information about such as your process of spiritual growth. You can also simply put forth an intention to enter into the stillness within you to experience more of your higher wisdom and the presence of the Divine. When you are ready, surround yourself with light and ask that everything you receive be for your highest good. Feel, sense, or imagine yourself walking along the pathway to your inner spiritual workplace. Take a few moments to really visualize and feel yourself in your healing space. If there is anything that you want to change about the environment, feel free to do so.

Call on the presence of Spirit and your Higher Self to assist you and ask for guidance regarding your question. Then just let your mind become neutral and receptive, like a still pool of water. Simply observe your experience without judgment and remain open to receive wisdom in whatever form it may come. This is nothing that you have to work at or try to do. Remain passive, yet alert, and allow impressions to present themselves. You may have insights, hear words (either your own unspoken words or another voice unlike your own), see images, have feelings emerge, or have a strong sense of something being true. These things may seem subtle at first or vague. However, just allow yourself to receive the impressions without trying to cognitively understand them all at once. More may be revealed to you at a later time. Meditate in this state of receptivity for ten minutes each day.

Record the information that you receive in your journal. How did you experience guidance coming to you? Have you ever received insights or had intuitive feelings in this way before? It is important to acknowledge this type of guidance whenever or wherever it comes to you. (I very often receive guidance and insights in the tub or shower!)

The more you recognize and respond to this type of inner guidance, the stronger and more frequent it will become. Continue to use your inner spiritual workplace whenever you would like.

## *Week Six*

As you still your mind and drop into your center, imagine that you are sitting in a vibrant ray of sunshine. Feel the sunlight pour into and around your whole body. As the golden sunlight from above comes streaming in along your spine, see, sense, or imagine it forming a ball of light at your solar plexus. Take a moment to feel the warmth and energy of this radiant orb. Now, allow this ball of light to expand, so it becomes brighter and more charged with energy, until it encircles your whole body. As you sit in the vibrant warmth and radiance of this orb of light, let yourself soak in its nourishing energy and be revitalized. Do this meditation for ten minutes each day and throughout your day, visualize and feel this vibrant golden energy surrounding you in order to consciously connect with this vitality and light. Record your meditation experiences in your journal.

This meditation can be very beneficial at times when you need to strengthen your energetic boundaries or when you feel particularly susceptible to other people's energy emanations for some reason. Did you notice any changes in your energy level, emotions, or mental outlook as a result of this week's meditation?

## *Week Seven*

For this week's meditation, you are going to feel yourself enfolded in what I call the womb of the Great Mother. This womb is a totally safe, nourishing, healing, and compassionately loving environment which the Mother of all creation provides for you. All you have to do is rest in this energy and allow yourself to receive. People report that this meditation produces a very healing experience for them. It can be used at times when you want to create a sense of safety and love for yourself.

Begin by centering and feeling yourself surrounded by an unconditionally loving presence. If you have difficulty connecting with the love, it may help you to remember a time when you felt love for someone or something, or when you felt that love for you from another. While doing this, some people like to imagine themselves totally enfolded by a soft pink cloud. Others experience a type of gossamer healing cocoon of sparkling light and love all around them. The important thing is to connect with a feeling of unconditional love and healing that is totally supporting and nourishing to your being. Breathe this loving and nurturing substance into every bone, muscle, organ, and system of your body, especially your heart. Feel it absorbed into every cell as soothing waves of comforting love infuse your whole being. From this place, feel and receive the affirmation, "The universe is a safe, warm, loving place for me and I can rest in that love."

Do this meditation for ten to fifteen minutes each day and record your experiences in your journal.

### Week Eight

For week eight, you are going to do a breath meditation while focusing on the spiritual nourishment of the breathing process. Do this breathing meditation for ten to fifteen minutes each day.

Sit comfortably, relax, and while breathing through your nose, begin to follow the movement of your breath in and out of your body. As you inhale, feel the breath move in through your nostrils and up into the top of your head, and then allow your breath to continue down your spine and expand out through your whole body.

While breathing, welcome Spirit, in the form of breath, wholeheartedly into your entire being as you would a beloved partner. Have a sense that Spirit intimately knows you and lovingly nourishes you. To assist with this, repeat the words, "I am here and I love you, know that I care," as you breathe fully and receive in this statement as Spirit's words to you.

## Meditation Process Review

How has your meditation experience progressed over the last eight weeks? Have you noticed any changes in your ability to concentrate and still your thinking mind? If you feel that you need to strengthen your concentration, you can repeat the meditation for week one for approximately ten minutes each day. One option is to visualize the object this time with your eyes closed, rather than looking at it in front of you. As you hold this inner image in your consciousness, notice all of the qualities and characteristics of the object such as the color, and texture. See and feel it with your inner eyes and senses. You can also alternate between visualizing the object in this way with your eyes closed, and looking at the object before you while resting your consciousness on it.

Continue to use these meditations or explore any of the previously mentioned techniques that interest you. When you feel ready, gradually increase your meditation period to at least twenty minutes. As your ability to concentrate improves, you will be more comfortable with meditating for longer periods and will be able to simply sit in the stillness of your own being to receive. Whatever type of meditation you use, allow yourself to receive of the spiritual nourishment and wisdom that is available through this practice.

Now that you have some experience with quieting your thinking mind through this chapter, you will be able to use this new level of awareness in your process of going deeper inside into the body and emotions in Part III.

------------

## Notes

1. Jonathan Goldman, *Healing Sounds: The Power of Harmonics*, 2nd ed., Rev. (Rockport, MA: Element Books, Ltd., 1996).

2. Deepak Chopra, M.D., *Quantum Healing: Exploring the Frontiers of Mind / Body Medicine*. (New York: Bantam Books, 1989).

# PART III

# THE BODY AND EMOTIONS

# 5

# SOMATIC AWARENESS

*Listening to Your Body Self*

**YOUR BODY IS AN EXQUISITE JEWEL** crafted by your soul to facilitate your presence here on Earth in third-dimensional time and space. Despite any perceived body concepts or actual physical limitations due to injury, surgery, or disabilities, your body is perfect in the eyes of your soul. Every cell in your physical body carries the imprint of your true soul purpose here in its genetic coding, and that information can be unlocked through listening to the messages that your body is constantly transmitting. This chapter will increase your awareness of your physical body and help you translate its messages, thus opening a transformative doorway to your true spirit nature.

It may surprise you that body awareness is something that you have to learn about since you have, after all, been walking around in your body all your life. The fact is, however, that besides rigorous attempts to change our physical forms through diet, exercise, and trips to the beauty salon or plastic surgeon, many people do not know or communicate with their body self. It is usually not until some physical symptom or disease develops that we begin to pay attention to this very important part of us. At such a time, most people get impatient and angry that their busy schedules are disrupted by this bodily annoyance. In this mechanized, computerized culture, it is very easy to ignore the physical body that we take for granted, expecting it to function continually.

Another reaction to illness is often fear and a sense of helplessness when individuals feel they can no longer control what is happening to their bodies and to their lives. Yet, there are things that we can do to help restore balance to the body-mind system. In fact, it can be a very rewarding experience to consciously utilize the sensations, symptoms, and messages of the body through a communication with your own body-mind. By participating with your body self in this way, you can experience greater health, vitality, and a sense of emotional well-being. However, this type of communication does require a shift out of the hurried, mentally dominated consciousness that is so familiar to us in this culture. In order to experience body-centered processing, one must be still and listen—to "be" instead of "do." For hard-driving and impatient Type-A personalities this may be a challenge.[1] If you are used to relying on your analytical processes, consciously participating with your body may at first seem like a slow process. However, it is worth the initial effort.

Your body has been patiently and eagerly waiting to aid you in your process of healing and growth. It has a story to tell. That story may contain some pain because the body tends to hold physically what you don't deal with emotionally. If there isn't resolution, completion, or a clearing on the emotional level, disease and other physiological symptoms can occur. There is, however, a loving and healing intent to these messages of the body. Your aches, pains, illness, and other body symptoms serve you in a valuable way. These phenomena point the way to greater health, emotional well-being, and spiritual transformation. Communicating with your body can provide the answers you need to obtain all these things in your life. You will also find that as you heal and remove the blocks to expressing your true self in this way, your consciousness will naturally expand to include an experience of your spiritual being.

I also feel that the body awareness skills presented here are particularly important in a culture where we are primarily taught to think with our analytical minds and not intuit with our instinctual perception. At this time, reclaiming this instinctual wisdom is an important part of our individual and collective healing process. As we learn to respect and listen to our own body consciousness, we will become more attuned to our planetary body, Mother Earth. We have kept our physical bodies estranged from our spiritual self for too long, and our relationship with the planet reflects this. If you currently have physical concerns, such as an illness or a chronic condition, this section will provide you with information that will help you to be more consciously aware of your bodily experience, enabling you to participate more fully in your own process of healing. Since the body can be used to access limiting core patterns held in the subconscious mind, these techniques can also provide an abundance of material that can greatly facilitate anyone's process of personal growth.

The following processes will assist you in obtaining full presence in the moment and will give you a chance to practice the conscious feeling, sensing, and seeing that true awareness requires. You will also be learning ways to amplify the body sensations that you are working with and methods of communicating with your body in order to deepen and connect with the feelings involved. This will assist you in clearing emotional blocks from your body and subconscious mind, and will help you release any energy that your body has been holding concerning such issues. You will then be able to integrate positive new patterns based on your true soul essence.

The processes in this chapter can all be done on your own. However, you may want to have a partner present to assist you and give you support. Sometimes, it can be comforting just to talk to someone who has felt similar feelings or dealt with the same kinds of issues as you have. For this reason, and because body-centered processes can access powerful feelings, you may even benefit from the assistance of a support group or therapist while doing this work. This is especially true if you have feeling states that seem overwhelming or if you have a history of physical, emotional, or sexual trauma.

For those with a history of trauma, anxiety can sometimes arise if the process of reconnecting with painful bodily-held feelings is going too fast. It is important to work with such situations in a way that allows for slow progressive integration of the experience to avoid retraumatization. If states of panic, dissociation, or emotional overwhelm occur for you when doing any of the processes in this chapter, return to your resources from chapter 3 and obtain the assistance of a professional experienced in working with trauma and abuse.

While doing this work, it will also be helpful to record your experiences in your journal, so you can have a written account of your process. You will gain new insights in this way, receive further validation for your experiences, and be able to refer back to them later.

# THE BODY SYMBOL

The body actually provides us with many types of symbolic information. The most obvious, of course, are disease and illness. The type of illness and body area it affects, is a significant reflection of what the body-mind is trying to communicate. For instance, as I mentioned in chapter 1, individuals sometimes have strange heart palpitations, bringing their attention to childhood heartaches that need to be addressed. As these individuals are able to heal these emotionally painful events, the strange heart symptoms cease. Many body-mind books and metaphysical texts have lists of specific physical symptoms along with their correlating mental/emotional "cause." Although this information can be useful, the particular meaning of your illness may be different than those indicated. For this reason, direct communication with your own body will be extremely beneficial in this process of self-discovery.

A second type of body information is somatic character armoring. As mentioned earlier, myofascial structures respond to emotional and physical stimulus, which results in the formation of a fixed muscle tension or armor. In this way, the body reflects physical, emotional, and mental habit patterns and styles of behavior. It is the visible physiological response to dynamics present in other dimensions of the body-mind system.

Contracted musculature in the body may contain the response to self-limiting thought processes, repressed emotions, unfulfilled spiritual needs, as well as physical trauma. The habits and patterns that the body reflects, are learned from culture, society, and our own family systems. These things may restrict our instinctual functioning and be in opposition to the archetypal soul expression that is moving from our core. Thus, we embody the reflection of parents, society, and others rather than our own essential selves. By looking at how we are somatically organized, we can learn many things about ourselves and how we block the movement of life from within us. This chapter will enable you to observe and process these body patterns in order to discover the message they contain.

A third type of somatic information comes from mannerisms and body language. Fritz Perls, the founder of Gestalt therapy, stated the importance of body language in this way:

> But consider for a moment this fact: everything the patient does, obvious or concealed, is an expression of the self. His leaning forward and pushing back, his abortive kicks, his fidgets, his subtleties of enunciation, his split-second hesitations between words, his handwriting, his use of metaphor and language . . . all are on the surface, all are obvious, and all are meaningful.[2]

It's still amazing to me how much information and healing can emerge from one tapping index finger!

The body also provides us with information through the five senses of feeling, seeing, hearing, tasting, and smelling. This includes not only what we sense externally, but also what we perceive internally. For example, outwardly you may feel a prickling sensation on the surface of your skin, while a feeling of frustration is present inwardly. Outwardly, you might smell a strong cologne, while inwardly remembering the smell of alcohol on your parent's breath. Outwardly you might hear the wind blowing in the trees while inwardly hearing an intuitive voice speaking to you. A relaxed, present-centered state of awareness allows such feelings to emerge and creates more receptivity to inner images and sensations.

Somatic experience in all its forms—disease, armoring patterns, mannerisms, and sensations from the five senses—provide a focus for communicating not only with the body but also with archetypal energies. Through listening to the body's messages, the purpose and meaning of an archetypal presence can be realized. As part of this healing process, it may be found that body symptoms represent unresolved situations from birth, childhood, and even past lives. By clearing the body and the subconscious mind of these places of blocked energy, physical health can be restored, and the way is made clear for a fuller realization of your true self. Becoming familiar with the developmental stages of childhood and the psychosomic effects of the birth process, as well as past life dynamics, can be useful in this regard.[3]

The experience of biological birth may be especially significant because it operates as a bridge between the persona consciousness, along with the experiences of this life which have formed it, and the pure spiritual essence which we are before entering into physical form. Processing of in-utero and birth experience can thus act as a doorway leading into a greater consciousness of your true spiritual essence. The birth process is, by its very nature, a life and death experience that is potentially hazardous and often traumatic. The imprinting of in-utero sensations and the pain of birth into the infant's developing nervous system can shape both physiology and personality.[4]

Additionally, the physical as well as the emotional state of the mother can affect the developing fetus. The mother's feelings of stress, depression, pain, and anxiety can thus be transmitted to the fetus. The child then comes into the world having acquired such feelings as rejection, fear, and worthlessness with no apparent cause.[5]

The overall internalized message of a positive birth experience can be that life sometimes involves struggle and with effort you can succeed. However, this scenario is often not the case with many birth experiences. Thus, emerging body-mind phenomena can relate to different aspects of biological birth that need to be addressed in order for healing and spiritual awakening to occur. It can be helpful and often quite illuminating in this regard to get as many details as possible about the events surrounding your birth from your mother or other relatives.

Beyond the doorway of physical birth into this life, lies past-life experience. As individuals become increasingly sensitive to archetypal energies in the process of embodying more of their own soul essence, they may have past-life memories. These experiences may come as vague impressions of living in a different time or can involve intense and overwhelming feelings, sensations, and images that are relived in a very real way. Such experiences can bring to light various spiritual, mental, emotional, and physical issues that are part of an individual's present life. The emerging archetypal theme of these experiences often represents a soul gift that can be reclaimed after the past-life experience is healed and the soul lesson is learned. As the past-life session with Joan (presented in chapter 2) shows, body phenomena are often the first sign of these emerging patterns. If past-life and/or birth issues surface for you while working with the body, you may find it useful to explore different methods of birth and past-life regression, such as hypnotherapy or breathwork, to assist you further.

## GETTING TO KNOW YOUR BODY

The following awareness processes have a twofold purpose. First of all, they can help you become more consciously aware of the physical dimension of your being and thus assist you in being more present and grounded in your body. Secondly, they are steps that can progress into a dialogue process and facilitate the expression of emotions which are a necessary part of your growth and healing. These awareness processes may be used alone for the purpose of increased somatic awareness, or the body information that emerges from them can be amplified to help you more fully connect with bodily-held feelings. You may be more drawn to some of these methods than others or find that certain ones work better for you. Try them all or just do the ones that feel right for you. For the purposes of this chapter, I have divided somatic awareness, amplifying methods, and dialogue into separate parts. However in actuality, they often blend together and your process will sometimes move back and forth between them.

Somatic awareness involves being consciously present with bodily sensations and feelings. It can be as simple as noticing a place in your body that is drawing your attention—perhaps a place that is tense, heavy, or where the movement of breath and energy seems blocked or congested in some way. However, some people, especially those with abusive family backgrounds, don't have a strong feeling sense in their bodies. In this type of family, there may not have been much healthy, safe touching or physical contact. Such individuals may have learned to dissociate or cut themselves off from their body and feelings as a means of survival.

If you feel that you are one of these people, you may not be immediately aware of bodily sensations. You may have to resensitize yourself and relearn the language of bodily feelings, sensations, and images. Getting to know what the body looks like; where soft tissue, bones, and organs are located internally can help. I often have people refer to anatomy and physiology books so that they can get familiar with the physical body in this way. *The Anatomy Coloring Book* is fun and easy and *The Human Body In Health And Disease* is also a good reference.[6] I then have individuals touch or massage their own body to help them associate the visual image that they know with what they feel. If you feel disconnected from your body or have noticed that when doing the relaxation processes in previous chapters that your awareness of physical feelings and sensations is weak, the following exercise can help you become more sensitive to your body experience.

## Exercise: Somatic Awareness

Put your hands on your lower rib cage, feeling externally the rising and falling of your rib cage with your breathing. Feel the expansion and contraction of your rib cage and diaphragm as the lungs fill with air. It may help you to think of it as an accordion, bellows, or balloon blowing up. Then, put your hand on your abdomen and feel it moving up and down as you breathe into this area. As you do this, sense the internal organs in your abdomen (the stomach, intestines, etc.), moving as you breathe. Next, put your hand on your chest and feel the beating of your heart. As you feel the beating, allow yourself to imagine the blood being pumped by the heart and circulating throughout your whole body. Can you feel the blood moving through the vessels in certain parts of your body such as your neck? To help with this, touch the carotid artery of your neck with your fingers and feel the pulse at your wrist.

Touch or massage the muscles of your feet, legs, arms, and face. Feel the muscle tissue and bone structure. Notice how the sensation of touch feels on your muscles and bones. Then, get a visual sense of what you are feeling with your hands. You may want to use a picture of the muscle and skeletal systems from an anatomy or physiology book to assist you with this. After looking at such pictures of the bones, muscles, and organ systems, close your eyes and visualize the muscles and bones you are feeling as you touch them.

It may be helpful to go through this exercise before doing some of the processes in this chapter. However, as you do the other processes, you will also find that it strengthens your connection to your bodily senses and feelings. I also recommend that, throughout the day, you check in periodically to notice how you're feeling in your body. If you're talking to someone, engaged in a particular activity, or experiencing a specific situation, notice how the energy feels and how you feel in your body as you're doing it. What bodily feelings, sensations, or responses are you aware of? Don't judge or try to analyze what you're receiving, just allow yourself to experience it. If you become aware of a physical sensation sometime during the day—such as a headache, nausea, or other pain—notice what was happening and what you were feeling or thinking right before it occurred. Is there a relationship between what happened and the physical sensation? Record in your journal the insights that you gain about your body and your self from these experiences.

### Exercise: Body Drawing

Body drawing is another method that can help you get more familiar with your body self.

Get a large sheet of paper and draw your basic body form on it. If you are working with a partner, it can be fun to do this in full life-size by having the person draw an outline around your body while you lie on one or more sheets of butcher's wrap or other type of paper that comes in large rolls. If you are working alone, draw your body to any scale that you are comfortable with. Don't worry, this drawing of the contour of your body doesn't have to be precision correct or an artistic masterpiece for this exercise. However, even this basic drawing process can be affected by your self-perceptions and can bring forth issues concerning your self-identity and body image that provide information about certain somatically held feelings. For example, there may be certain areas of your body that you have uncomfortable feelings about drawing. If this is too charged an issue for you, start with a generalized body form that you trace from a magazine or from an anatomy or physiology book.

Once you have a body outline, use a yellow colored marker, pencil, or crayon to shade the areas on the body outline where you feel alive or present in your body and where the energy feels full. You may notice these areas as more relaxed, pleasurable, warmer; perhaps they are places where you enjoy being touched.

Next, with the color blue, shade in areas that are uncomfortable or are places you retreat from. These areas may be places of tension, pain, stress, chronic illness, or where there is a lack of circulation.

This body drawing process will help you to be more consciously aware of places of blocked energy in your body or areas where there are possibly somaticized emotional issues. It can also be used as a helpful exercise for those with a history of abuse, particularly sexual abuse, in order for such individuals to indicate where they do and don't like to be touched. This helps such individuals realize that they have a right to control their own bodies and assists them in establishing a sense of physical boundaries.

## Exercise: Body Scanning

Body scanning is a method of moving your consciousness through your body in a relaxed, inwardly focused state to experience what you are aware of in your body at the present time.

It can tune you in to your physiological and emotional state of being. Things that can be ignored in an everyday busy state of consciousness can come more fully to your attention. In the same way that you might observe yourself externally in a mirror head to toe, you use your inward eyes and senses to internally observe what you're aware of throughout your whole body. If you are visually oriented, you may see internal images. If you are more of a feeling person, you may be aware of certain sensations you feel in your body. Sometimes these sensations may occur as very tangible physical sensations such as an area of tension or pain. At other times, the sensations or images may seem vague at first and you may wonder if you're making it up. Whatever the basis of the phenomenon is, it came from within you and can be invaluable information in your body awareness process.

It is important not to judge or try to analyze your experience at this point. So for now, don't worry about whether the experience is real or imagined. As you continue with this type of awareness process, the feelings, sensations, or images that you receive will become clearer and stronger, and you will more readily be able to validate them.

Here is a good general outline for scanning, however you may come up with a system that works better for you. Feel free to experiment and be creative. Body scanning can be done in a sitting position, laying down, or even standing up—although laying down is probably the most relaxing position for the body. Whatever your body position, make yourself as comfortable as possible. Closing your eyes will also enable you to focus inward.

Before beginning, take a few full breaths. Let your breath expand fully through your rib cage, abdomen, and pelvis as you consciously breathe into the bottom of your belly. After taking a few cleansing breaths this way, begin to breathe naturally, allowing your breath to be soft and easy as you continue to be aware of the movement of breath in and out of your body. Let yourself be supported by the surface beneath you, allowing each exhale to let you sink a little deeper into your cushion or chair, a little deeper into your body. This is nothing that you have to work at or try to do, just allow a letting go.

Take a moment to feel what it's like being in your body right now. With your inner eyes and consciousness have a sense of scanning through your whole body. As you do this, notice if any part of your body seems to need your attention in some way or if there is any feeling, discomfort, or other sensation that seems to emerge. Observe any places of tension, stress, or chronic sensations that bother you. Also be aware of any areas of your body that feel vague and disconnected from the rest of you, or where breath and energy is constricted, stagnated, or lacking. In addition, notice the places in your body that feel alive and full of energy right now.

It may be helpful for you to have a sense of being in a stream of liquid light. As the stream of light flows over the different parts of your body from the head, notice how those areas feel. Are they soft, relaxed, tense, or tight?

Allow yourself to become aware of the external shell, the outer layer of your body, and notice what you feel on that level. Be conscious of the muscles of the scalp, face, jaw, throat, and the long muscles of the neck, shoulders, and arms. Are these muscles able to softly respond to the rhythm of the flowing liquid light? Be aware of how freely the whole body—head, neck, chest, abdomen, and pelvis—are moving in response to your breathing. Feel the light fluid flow down and move into the lower half of your body. While doing this, be aware of any areas where the flow is constricted.

As you continue to scan through your body, allow yourself to move inward and experience your core, a deeper more internal place of being. It may be useful to visualize or imagine yourself as very tiny and walking through a door in the outer shell of your body, down a stairway of steps into your core. Be aware of what you feel here, at your core, in the area of your internal organs and the deep muscles near the spinal vertebrae. Notice any sensations, feelings, or images connected with these areas.

Allow yourself as much time as you need to do this. A quick scan can take only a minute or so, but it is a process that usually takes between three and five minutes. When you are ready, open your eyes and take time to get reoriented to your external surroundings. Write down in your journal what your experience was and what body information was brought to your conscious awareness. If you prefer, draw a picture of your experience and how the body process felt or looked.

Another method of body scanning is used in conjunction with your current issues. In this body scan, take a particular issue or feeling that you're experiencing right now or a predominant feeling that you've been having (anger, sadness, joy, fear), and notice where you feel this emotion in your body, as well as how you experience it somatically. For example, you may tighten your abdomen when you feel pressured, clench your jaw in anger, or raise your shoulders when anxious.

You can also use a particular dream image or disturbing issue that you've been dealing with and notice where you experience this in your body. For example, the issue of having to talk with your child's teacher again may be felt in your body as a knot in your stomach, a constriction in your chest, or a headache. A lion dream figure may be felt in your throat as a need to roar.

The information you received in the body scan can now be explored further through methods of amplifying the somatic experience and by using the Embodiment Dialogue process. However, after finding a place in your body that needs your attention in some way, you can also breathe energy and light into the area for several minutes, filling it with gentle, loving kindness. This, in itself, will often provide a shift and alleviate or lessen any physical discomfort.

### Exercise: Body Reading

Body reading is a way of experiencing what is happening in the muscular-skeletal system by observing how energy is contained, constricted, or expressed through the body. It can give you a better understanding of your somatic patterns and how your mental-emotional experience is expressed physically. Traditionally, body reading has been used by bodyworkers including massage therapists, Rolfers, and Bioenergetic therapists to determine what kind of work is needed for the client.

I highly recommend any of the many types of bodywork available as beneficial additions to your program of personal growth and spiritual development. Systems of deep connective tissue manipulation such as Rolfing are particularly helpful because they reorganize fascial layers, freeing the energy bound up in old armoring patterns. This not only makes more energy available to you on all levels, but also allows you a more conscious experience of your body. I find that clients involved in this type of bodywork generally experience a much more efficient and accelerated process of healing and growth.

Often, body reading is used in conjunction with a particular system of somatic character typology.[7] These systems of body interpretation can provide useful information leading to a deeply felt realization about one's self. However, avoid latching on to such interpretations in merely a cognitive way. Such intellectual "answers" may tend to block the emergence of further important material from the body and subconscious mind. To increase your understanding, I have provided some basic information here regarding certain general emotional and energetic tendencies associated with various somatic patterns. However, when actually doing a body reading, it may be more beneficial for you to free yourself of all preconceived ideas and simply observe. You can then gain further insights for yourself by amplifying the somatic patterns or through a direct communication with your body.

In order to observe your natural patterns, body reading is best done for you by another person. However, if this isn't possible, you can do it for yourself by looking in a full-length mirror. Dance studio mirrors are great for this because you can watch your body as you move across the floor. If you don't have a partner to assist you, your backside can be more easily observed by using two facing mirrors such as are often found in department store dressing rooms.

Another drawback with doing a body reading yourself is that it is often hard for people to be objective about their own bodies. This is especially true of individuals who have been abused, have issues about food, have an obsessively negative view of their bodies, or have feelings of shame connected with their bodies. I have worked with individuals for whom the very thought of looking at themselves in a mirror was anxiety producing. If you have any of these issues, you may be more comfortable starting with one of the other exercises such as body scanning, or working with a supportive friend or therapist rather than attempting this alone. When choosing someone to assist you in this process, pick someone objective, loving, and nonjudgmental.

Avoid looking at your body in terms of good or bad. Self-criticism can get in the way of discovering what is really there. Also, the critical judgment of the mind shuts down the somatic feeling senses that you are seeking to engage. I sometimes have people actually talk to their critical voice inside, often an internalized critical parent, before beginning a body reading. By telling this Critic subpersonality to take a temporary "time out," these negative messages can be suspended so that a more compassionate aspect can be present.

In doing a body reading, you may see or experience things that your body has been holding. Remember, however, that no matter what you see, your body has served you well throughout your whole lifetime and is deserving of your love and appreciation. Approach your body patterns as doorways to information. As you observe, listen to these postural messages of the body with compassion as you would listen to the story of a hurt child who you were helping to feel better. If you have negative feelings about a particular part of your body, such as "my hips are too fat" or "my feet are ugly," use this information to help focus your consciousness within.

For example, if you're unhappy about your hips, take a moment to focus your attention inside to the hip area. What are you aware of or what do you sense from this internal body place? If, for instance, it is your feet you are uncomfortable with, take a moment to shift your consciousness to a place deep inside your feet. What do you sense, see, or feel from here?

This will shift your attention from what you mentally think about your body to what you actually feel from your body within. If you are having a body reading done by someone else, it will also help you to do an internal body scan during the reading. This will lessen any self-consciousness you have about being looked at and you will access your own internal information as well.

Body reading is most easily done while nude. If you feel uncomfortable with this, wear your underwear, a bathing suit, or spandex leotard. The more of the actual body surface you can see, the better. However, clothing can provide useful information. Notice how the clothes hang on your body and you will see a lot about the body underneath. Places of body tension and energy blocks are often reflected by how the clothing material lays on the body.

Body reading should be done in a nonjudgmental, relaxed way with a soft gaze rather than an intense stare. Stand back from the mirror a bit in order to do this. As you look externally at what you see, you can also stop periodically to feel what you experience internally. If you are reading someone else's body, allow yourself to receive the impressions from the person's body by positioning yourself at a comfortable distance from the individual so that this is possible.

Some things to be aware of while observing your body are alignment, proportions, overall vitality, skin color and tone, movement of breath, and areas of muscular-skeletal tension. Tension areas may appear contracted, tight, or hard. Skin color and tone can tell you a lot, also. Tension areas may appear mottled or darker in color with a tint of yellow, green, or purple. Weak areas may lack tone, be smaller, and have similar coloration.

Begin your body reading by walking around the room. Notice what you are aware of in the way that you move and carry yourself through space. Perhaps there is a sensation or imbalance that draws your attention. Your movement may be strained or graceful, or there may be a sense that you glide, stomp, or lumber along.

After observing your movement while walking, get an overall impression of your relationship to your body. Do you look comfortable or at home in your body? Do you feel present in your body? Notice if there is an overall appearance of aliveness and strength, or if the body seems weak or contracted in some way. If a certain body area looks tight and held, then the feelings connected with that area may be blocked from awareness.

Observe in what areas of the body the breath is moving freely and in what areas the flow of breath is restricted or blocked. Where there is breath, there is energy. So, there will be more feeling and aliveness in areas that are moving in response to your breath.

After the initial impression, begin to look more specifically at alignment. Be aware of your sense of balance and basis for support. Notice if if some body areas lead while others follow, whether some body areas are higher or lower than others, a shoulder or hip for instance, or if there is any torquing or twisting of the body.

When you observe proportions, be aware of left/right, top/bottom, and front/back splits, as well as other large segmented displacements seen between the head/body and torso/limbs. For example, the top of the body may be large and muscular while the bottom is thin and weak, the front may be open and relaxed while the back is tense and contracted, or the torso might be strong and average in size while the arms seem weak or smaller. Sometimes, the left and right sides of the body will look like they belong to two different people because of one side being higher, more constricted, or projected forward. The left side of the body, relating to the right brain, is associated with our intuition, holistic perception, creativity, feelings, and receptivity. The right side of the body, which relates to the left side of the brain, is associated with the rational mind, logical thinking, and an assertive quality. Differences in the right and left sides of the body often involve conflicts between these two aspects of our personality.

The front of the body represents our persona, the part of us that we let people see. The backside relates to what is hidden or not seen. Tensions in the back can relate to stored feelings that we don't want to deal with or have others see. These emotions, often the nonsocially acceptable ones of anger and fear, then get "backed up" along the spine. When painful things happen in life, we are often told, "put it behind you." No wonder so many people have back problems! If you see a front/back split it may indicate a conflict between how you want to appear (front) and what your real, yet possibly denied, feelings are (back).

The bottom half of the body relates to support, our grounded connection with the Earth, and a more introspective or private aspect of ourselves. The top half of the body, on the other hand, relates to self-expression and social contact via communication and touch.

Similarly, the torso represents our central core, the more vulnerable areas of the body that we protect or retreat into. The limbs are how we reach or step out to interact with the world, perform functions, and get our needs met. I've found that disproportionate top/bottom or torso/limb segments often relate to the "being" and "doing" parts of our nature in some way. Frequently, disproportionate head/body splits relate to conflicts existing between the thinking mind (head) and gut-level feelings (body). Because body splits are often indicative of two different aspects of our being in this way, they can provide excellent material for a dialogue process.

For example, in observing Sally's somatic organization patterns in a body reading, I saw a noticeable left/right split with the left side appearing more tense and contracted than the right. Sally reported having several injuries and accidents to her left side. I touched her feet to sense the energy flow in her body and noticed that the left side felt shut down and had a weak flow of energy.

I developed this ability to sense the body's energy by doing energy healing and bodywork. You can sense it for yourself by rubbing your hands together briskly for about twenty seconds and then holding them several inches apart. You will probably feel some type of sensation inside your hands such as an emanation of heat, a vibration, tingling, or a sense of attraction or resistance. Then have a partner rub his hands together and place your palms directly over and one inch above his palms. Notice what you experience now. The body awareness skills in this book will also make you more attuned to this energy in yourself and in others.[8]

I had Sally focus inside to bring her awareness to the left and right sides of her body. She had vulnerable feelings associated with her left side. The right side produced a feeling of competence and seemed analytical. Synchronistically, Sally reported that a few days previous to this session, she had been to a psychic artist who saw two distinct and separate aspects present in her aura. Sally also experienced some tension in her left buttock and I wondered if there might be a connection between this place and the split. I gently applied some pressure to her left buttock with my hand to amplify the holding pattern of the muscles. As I did this, Sally spontaneously started crying. She realized that her left side was like the hurt, scared Child inside of her. Sally had connected with this more vulnerable part of her and felt the love which that part of her had to express. By listening to this Child within, she learned that this feeling aspect of her being needed more time and attention. In this way, she was able to bring balance between the competent/analytical and vulnerable/feeling aspects within her.

After looking at your general alignment and proportions, bring your attention to specific areas of your body. As you continue through the body, keep in mind the chakra centers and the specific body areas associated with each one. Look at the legs and feet. Notice how you are positioned to receive support from the earth, and what you feel about your contact with the ground and reality. Is there a sense of being planted firmly on the ground, being solidly present here on Earth, or is there a sense of holding on desperately with arches high and toes dug in?

The feet may also be pointed inward, outward, or perhaps go off in different directions. This can represent inwardly directed, outgoing, or conflicted energy. Observe the knee joints and whether they seem flexible—able to support, yet bend and yield. The knees, like all joints, are intersections of energy connecting two different parts of the body. Joint areas can thus indicate how gracefully you deal with change, transitions, and with different aspects of yourself.

In observing the torso, notice the position of the pelvis and whether it is tilted forward or backward. (Observing from a side view will help you see this.) Most people have some misalignment of the pelvic area, a reflection, no doubt, of the distorted sexual messages that most of us have been raised with. In addition, the pelvis provides a foundational support with other parts of the body building upon it, therefore emotional support issues can be embodied here. Also, regardless of what you see in the fashion model magazines, there is nothing wrong with a soft, round belly. This usually indicates a soft, warm, sensual quality. However, there will sometimes be lines of tension or discoloration around the abdominal/solar plexus area, often accompanied by the type of shallow breathing that blocks the expression of feelings. Because the solar plexus is also the connecting place between the heart and sexual organs, if heartfelt feelings are cut off from one's instinctual emotions or sexual energy, it can result in such tension in this area.

As you bring your awareness more specifically to the top half of your body, notice the chest and back area. The chest, area of the heart, is often protected through various body postures including rounded shoulders, an overexpanded upper body, or a collapsed chest that appears as if there is a weight on it that needs to be unburdened. My client Peter, with Venus close to the Ascendant at birth, provides an example of this second dynamic. His body structure shows an inflated chest, which presents a powerful image designed to protect his sensitive heart feelings and artistic nature. As a young man, he had abandoned artistic pursuits because it hadn't seemed like a practical way to provide for a family. He put this part of him aside while further armoring his upper body through a regular workout regimen. This somatic pattern was accompanied by a protective mechanism of control and a quickness to anger. With Mars near the Nadir point, he often expressed his Warrior energy in this distorted way by unconsciously acting out his anger. The expanded chest, control issues, and powerful emotional outbursts of anger were all part of a pretense of strength, an unconscious protection meant to keep him from more sensitive feelings that he perceived as weak and painful. This particular psychological strategy is often associated with this type of body pattern.

As mentioned earlier, the back can also tell quite a bit about what is hidden or backed up in a person's life. The back may sometimes appear tense or contracted in areas, especially on either side of the spine. Also, observe the shoulders. Are they broad, narrow, retracted, raised up, weighted down by unseen burdens, or protective of the heart and chest? The arms and hands may seem weaker in appearance, unable to reach out and receive, or they can seem like overdeveloped vehicles of acting and doing.

The cervical segment of the neck and throat acts as a bridge, a mediator between heart and head, between feelings and thoughts. What do you feel in this area and observe about your neck, head and face. For example, the neck may seem shortened and held in turtle style, as if retreating into the torso, or it may seem to tilt the head forward, "head first into the world." The jaw is another major area where tension is stored. Underneath this tension is often withheld feelings of sadness, anger, or an urge to scream. Many times a clenched jaw is indicative of the amount of emotional control necessary to hold back or swallow these feelings. (To relax your jaw, it is often helpful to consciously rest your tongue on the floor of your mouth or to slightly curl the tip of your tongue toward the back of it. This will automatically drop the jaw.) A strongly set jaw can also reflect one's sense of will and self-determination.

After looking at specific body segments, determine whether any of the things that you observed or felt relate to one another. Perhaps you observed both a concave chest and weak arms that relate to a sense of overall neediness that you feel. You may also see somatic patterns that relate to energetic patterns that you first got a sense of when doing the chakra meditation in chapter 1. For example, the sense of alienation and ungroundedness that you felt as a root chakra imbalance may now be experienced through the physical expression of underdeveloped legs and high arches.

Before completing this process, connect with the areas of strength, vitality, and aliveness in your body. Then, close to the mirror, look into your eyes and into the soul of who you really are and send loving acceptance to your body and all the parts of yourself. Breathe this love in and really feel yourself wholeheartedly receive it with a sense of gratitude for your body self.

Record in your journal the things that you observed and any insights that you gained from doing the body reading. This process has probably brought your awareness to a great deal of symbolic body information. Any of this body information can now be further explored and amplified to discover the essential message that these somatic patterns hold for your process of healing and growth.

## AMPLIFYING SOMATIC EXPERIENCE

Sometimes, just by using the awareness techniques already mentioned, you will experience a deepening that will produce an immediate connection to a particular issue and the feelings involved with it. In other cases, your experience of the body phenomenon may still be vague, and amplifying it will be beneficial. Amplification, also known as magnification, is a Gestalt method used in therapy experiments to exaggerate a particular experience so that the issues and feelings relating to it can be explored.[9] It allows the energy connected with a body dynamic to be concentrated and magnified so that the experience is fuller and more concrete. For example, in the session with Sally (page 167), I used touch to increase the sensation so that she could have a more vivid experience of it. This led to emotional release and a connection with her Child subpersonality. However, touch is just one way to amplify body phenomena. The following material illustrates some other methods for doing this and will also give you a clear understanding of how these techniques can assist you in gathering more information about your body experience. Any of these amplifying methods can then be used as part of the guided Embodiment Exercise found later in the chapter.

Exploring bodily sensations by amplifying them is primarily a somatic-feeling process of gathering information rather than a cognitive one. This means that things are known or experienced through the body, feelings, and senses. In whatever way you amplify your experience, it is important to notice how it feels in your body. Be aware of the feelings that you have when doing it and what it brings forth for you. Avoid intellectual analyzing. Instead of trying to figure it out, let the feelings, sensations, and images emerge from your body and subconscious mind.

You may, quite naturally, want to ask yourself, "Why is this body phenomenon happening?" However, asking why you are having a particular body experience deals with causes and tends to engage the cognitive functions. "Why" questions are, therefore, not as useful as "what" and "how" questions dealing with process that tend to bring you into an internal state of awareness. For example, "what" are the characteristics of your physical complaint and "how" does it feel mentally, emotionally, and physically? Also, if you are assisting others in this work, use present-tense language, which brings people into the "here and now" and more deeply into their body. For instance, say, "What are you noticing, now, in this place, here, in your shoulder?"

When amplifying body experience, allow yourself to enter a relaxed and inwardly focused state. You may already be in this place through the awareness process leading up to this point. If not, just take a few moments to close your eyes and take a few full breaths into your abdomen. Begin to follow the movement of breath in and out of your body. Have a sense that each exhalation allows you to clear the thoughts from your mind as you sink a little deeper into your body and into a deeper, more relaxed place inside you. Once again, breathing into your abdomen in this way will produce a body-centered state of relaxation that will help you connect with your senses and feelings. The amplifying process will then be more effective from this internal state of awareness. Also, as you are using the amplifying process, go slowly and take time for the information to emerge from the subconscious mind, rather than trying to interpret or find meaning in what you are experiencing too quickly.

You may want to have a partner with you to help you feel safe and assist you if you get stuck. If you are assisting someone, avoid analyzing the person's process or interpreting it for them. Simply help the person to stay aware of what is happening by feeding back to them what they say and perhaps writing it down for them.

## Amplifying through Breath

Breath is an important aspect of amplifying somatic experience because it can bring energy into areas where energy and consciousness have been lacking, thus acting upon the psychosomic patterns of muscle tension and holding that reside there. As mentioned earlier, these somatic armoring patterns contain the contents of our mental and emotional experience. When breath is brought into the body and the energy increases in these areas, the feelings and issues residing there are brought to consciousness. Most people do not breathe fully; full conscious breathing can actually be felt throughout the whole body. When armoring patterns are released, the muscles of the head, neck, shoulders, chest, diaphragm, abdomen, and pelvis can be felt moving as part of the breathing process.

Because breathing is both a spontaneous and a consciously controlled process, it acts as an interface between the central and autonomic nervous systems, between the conscious and subconscious mind. This makes it a powerful vehicle for consciously accessing elements from deeper subconscious levels.

Breath can be used in a exaggerated way to amplify body dynamics. For example, if there is a tense or constricted area of the body where breath is perhaps shallow, a full deep breath can be brought into that place allowing the area to expand with your breath. Putting a hand on the area first and having a sense of letting your breath come up and push against the pressure of your hand can help. Repeat this several times while noting what you experience or what feelings it brings forth for you. Using your breath in this way can not only help you deepen into your body, but by bringing in energy, it helps establish a conscious connection to your experience. You may even find that you have a spontaneous expression of emotions as tension patterns are released from your body through this type of amplified breathing.[10]

I used this method with Peter (page 169), to help him explore the dynamics behind his overexpanded chest. While standing, I had him take several large breaths into his upper chest, blowing it up to magnify the sensations of his armoring pattern. Upon doing this, he immediately spread his feet apart, taking a broader base of support. Peter then began to slightly move his weight back and forth from foot to foot, like a tennis player awaiting a serve, ready to dart in the necessary direction at any moment. He definitely looked mobilized for action as I asked him to tell me what he experienced through the amplifying process. Peter said that he felt a tension throughout his body and that the amplifying process made him very self-conscious and anxious. There were feelings surfacing that he couldn't control and that made him anxious. He realized that the amplified breath had magnified an anxiousness and pain that he often felt inside of him. In the past, he had tried to cover up these feelings and run away from them. Now, he was ready to confront them.

The armored tension in Peter's chest area was bracing him against the pain. With the energy focused in his upper body and drawn up out of the solar plexus and second chakra, it left him with a lot of jammed-up life force energy in the first chakra. He was cut off from the emotional nourishment of the second chakra as well as a balanced expression of instinctual feelings and emotions through the solar plexus. Peter would deny his real feelings, which blocked true emotional intimacy with others, and then would eventually explode in spurts of reactive anger. The Lover (Venus) and Warrior (Mars) were always in conflict within him, with his Protector/Controller subpersonality making sure that he never got too close to the painful feelings inside. Through our work together, Peter was able to safely reconnect with his true feelings and emotions. By resolving the pain of the past and allowing more of his softer, artistic side to be expressed, both emotionally and through his creative art, Peter was able to eventually let down the protective guard to his heart. In this way, he was able to express the love and creativity that Venus represents while also having the heroic Warrior's ability to act upon his true feelings with impeccability and balance.

## *Amplifying with Qualities and Characteristics*

Another very effective method of amplifying body information involves getting a sense of the qualities and characteristics of the physical sensation or issue. This can bring out aspects of your experience that were not known before. For example, Sarah mentioned that in a recent bodywork session with her Rolfer, she had felt vague sensations in her pelvic area. Although she very much wanted the work to continue in that area, she felt mildly protective of it. Something seemed to be keeping this part of her from fully participating with the rest of her body. Through our work together, she wanted to explore these feelings further.

I had Sarah bring her awareness into her pelvic area in order to connect with the feelings and sensations that she experienced there. I then asked her to notice the qualities and characteristics of the body experience, any shape, texture, or color that seemed to emerge for her. She described a nebulous blackness that was vaguely round, but with no firm edges or boundaries. I continued by having Sarah breathe into the pelvic area and deepen with any feelings or other sensations this nebulous blackness brought forth, any feelings that were connected with it in any way. She said it felt like a tension that didn't want to let go. In having her explore what would happen if it did let go, she reported that, "It would have no force in place, no control." However, at the same time, Sarah felt like she no longer needed this tension, which was linked with an old way of being in control. This vague tension was no longer serving her and, after asking her, I found out that there was no inner part of her resisting its release or that still needed it in any way. It seemed like an empty shell.

As a result of Sarah's previous therapy, her need for such inner controls had been eliminated. (If this had not been the case, there might have been some subpersonality negotiation or emotional clearing to do before a shift could take place.) However, even though this emotional healing had taken place, a deeper level of muscular holding in the dense physical body remained. And so, this accompanying energetic shell still existed. The Rolfing session assisted the physical body in aligning with the new intention of relaxation and openness in the pelvis, and now the old energetic pattern could be released, as well.

I had Sarah notice what she experienced when she brought light into the nebulous energy in her pelvis. She said she now saw only a sparkling brightness, a jewel with a fountain of energy and light above it. I then asked her how the jewel felt to her, what the qualities of it were. She reported that she felt flow, love, and joy. I then had Sarah enjoy these pleasurable sensations, allowing the feelings of love and joy to flow through her whole body, letting it settle into every part of her, so that she could deepen with the expansion that this new energy brought. The qualities and characteristics of pleasant sensations can also be fully experienced in this way in order to help you expand with enjoyable feelings through your body.

The following questions will assist you in using this method to amplify your body experience. Remember to go slowly and take time for information to emerge while exploring these qualities and characteristics from a place of relaxed internal awareness. Rather than thinking about an answer, notice what you sense and feel from inside and allow your body and subconscious mind to reveal their wisdom from this place of being.

1.  What is the quality of the sensation you're experiencing? For example, it may be sharp, dull, burning, poking, stabbing, throbbing, tingling, cramped, knotted, edgy, churning, focused, or radiating.

2.  What are any other characteristics of the pain, sensation, or experience? Does it have a shape, texture, or color? For instance, it may be hot, cold, large, small, thick, flat, long, round, square, rough, smooth, hollow, dense, stringy, lumpy, sticky, bright, dark, red, black, green, or gray. Perhaps the body sensation or symptom even has a sound associated with it. For example, it may have a thumping beat, a high-pitched tone, electrical static, a scream, wail, crash, drone, or hum.

3.  If your body experience had a form, what would it look like? Such things as a knotted rope, deep pit, box, wall, or flying bird may emerge. Notice what feelings this image or any of the other characteristics listed bring forth in you. Take time to connect as deeply as possible with these feelings as you bring your consciousness to your experience. Notice if any of these sensations, sounds, feelings, or images are familiar in any way or if they remind you of a particular issue, pattern, or person in your life.

If you tend to be visually oriented, you may more readily access a form or image. If you are a kinesthetic type, it may be easier for you to connect with a physical sensation such as a stabbing pain. People who are more auditory in nature will most likely hear sounds or words. If you tend to be a feeling type, emotions may present themselves more easily. Although you may be more predominantly oriented to one of these aspects, they all represent possible pathways of information that you can access as part of your process. Be open to any or all of them.

## Amplifying Somatic Patterns

Somatic armoring and specific tension patterns can also be amplified through exaggeration. For example, rounded shoulders can be exaggerated by letting the chest contract more and more as the shoulders round in. A barrel chest could be inflated, raised, and puffed up even more by pushing the shoulders back. Misaligned hips could be amplified by lifting the raised hip even more. This technique can also be used with mannerisms and other body experiences. Let's say you connect with a feeling of inadequacy, and as you experience this in your body, you drop your head. To amplify this, you would drop your head down further and further until, perhaps, you were in a ball. This contracted ball position will most likely have more impact than the slightly dropped head.

While amplifying the posture, notice what's happening inside of you, what it feels like. Does it remind you of anything? You might notice that you've felt like this before. For example, the contracted ball posture might feel compressed or compacted. It might remind you of how constricted you feel at work and how angry you are at your boss for making derogatory remarks. Amplifying the body posture would enable you to get in touch with the anger that you were feeling toward your boss for making the derogatory remarks that resulted in your feelings of inadequacy. You could then appropriately give expression to these feelings through a journal dialogue or through other methods of emotional clearing. (See the information on emotional clearing later in this chapter.)

A client I'll call Bill gives an excellent example of this type of amplifying process. As he was talking about his relationship with his wife, I noticed that something happened to his breathing. It sounded like he was trying to catch his breath. When I brought this to his attention, he wasn't aware of what he was doing. He did relate, however, that starting around the age of four, he had bad allergies with respiratory problems and had trouble breathing. At that time, his breathing was very shallow and he couldn't breathe through his nose at all. As a result, he had very little energy. He even had his tonsils and adenoids surgically removed, but it hadn't alleviated his symptoms. To this day, he sometimes still had trouble with his sinuses, which affected his breathing.

As he was talking about this childhood illness, his shoulders began to sag with his body stooped forward. I had Bill focus inside and notice what this body posture felt like to him. He said that this is what his posture was like when he was a child because he couldn't breathe very well and he was always tired. I had Bill exaggerate this somatic pattern by collapsing his upper body even further and telling me what he experienced. Bill related that it brought up feelings of worthlessness, of being defeated and disappointed. He said that this is how he felt when his wife nagged him and he felt the same way when his father lectured him when he was a child. Instead of understanding his breathing difficulties, his father would yell at Bill to stand up straight, threatening to get a body brace for him to wear if he didn't.

Amplifying this body posture helped Bill connect with the underlying feelings that were affecting his relationship with his wife and creating his breathing difficulties. He was then able to resolve these feelings relating to this experience of his father and his childhood illness.

## *Amplifying through Movement and Artistic Expression*

Movement and artistic expression are two other methods that you can use to amplify your somatic experience. Let your body move in the way it wants to or in a way that would feel good. Do the arms want to reach out? Does your hand want to make a fist? Would the legs like to kick or get up and dance? Do the hands want to cover or protect another part of your body such as your stomach, heart, or face? When amplifying this way, it can help to repeat the action or movement and, as you move, notice what you are aware of and how it feels in your body. What feelings, images, or beliefs emerge for you. Do these things seem familiar in any way?

Dancing and movement can be a very empowering process. I once had a client with back problems get up and respond to her body ache through movement. As this evolved, she began doing an African-type dance. Through the dance, she was able to connect with her feminine instinctual nature, feeling the power and support it gave her. At the end of her dance, she stood up erect and aligned in her body, walking upright in a way that she had never known before.

With this amplifying process, you may sometimes need to go very slowly, making small slow-motion movements, as you move consciously with awareness. A movement session I did working alone illustrates this process. At a time when I was working a lot, without much recreation time, I began to feel a lack of joy and aliveness in my life. When noticing where I felt this in my body, it seemed centered in my hips and pelvis. While bringing my consciousness fully to this place, I focused on any movement I could bring to this area that might assist a sense of joy, playfulness, and expansion. Spontaneously, I began to make small movements, slightly rotating the pelvis forward and then backward. This led to increasingly larger movements that eventually involved the legs and upper body. Soon, I was responding to a rhythmic wave moving through my whole body. Immediately, I felt a surge of quickening energy flow up all along my spine from the root chakra to the crown, accompanied by feelings of ecstasy and self-love. These feelings and sensations lasted for several minutes and the expansion that they brought lasted for days. Through this movement process, I had connected with the creative force and the essence of all love, bringing joy back into my body and into my life.

Art is also a wonderful method of amplifying body conditions. Draw or color a picture of your body sensation, symptom, or experience. There may be unconscious material relating to the body that can be made conscious in this way through certain symbolic elements that reveal themselves in the artwork. For example, if you drew a picture of an ocean scene with a rock, the ocean may represent certain flowing or more malleable elements of your personality, and the rock more solid or rigid elements. This can be particularly useful for people who are artistic or visually oriented. They may have a greater realization of the body phenomenon through being able to see it in this way. Experiment with any artistic medium that you're drawn to.

One woman, Jane, used this method at home when she was up very late at night with stomach problems. She felt bloated. To amplify the sensation, she decided to draw a picture of how she felt. The picture she drew looked like a young child had drawn it—it was of a female figure with a weeping heart and a large round circle for the lower part of the torso. There was a dot in the middle of this round part, with frantic circles around it and lines shooting out in all directions. There was an arrow pointed toward this area with the words, "This is where everything is stuck."

Jane asked about the stomach problem in a journal dialogue. She gave the figure in the drawing a voice, and received an answer to her question: "It's bursting because you are trying to stuff everything in to get enough of what I need to survive." Jane often found that she ate compulsively, especially when she was tired or stressed. Now this voice was telling her that she was eating out of another need, emotional survival. It was just this type of eating that had created the bloated stomach. Jane realized that she was trying to fill an empty hole inside of her with food.

Sometimes working with one amplifying process will lead to using a different one, as my session with Barbara illustrates. Barbara is a sixty-year-old woman who had separated from her husband after forty years of marriage. Her body appears dense, compact, and somewhat rigid. Her back, along the vertebrae, looks braced and held in. I had Barbara focus inside and notice how she was feeling in her body. She said she was aware of feeling braced and held back. I had her continue by breathing fully into her back area, feeling it expand and open with her breath. I asked her what she was aware of as she did this. She said that she had a painful sensation running down her right arm. I then asked what type of movement her arm might like to make in response to the sensation. Barbara said it wanted to strike out, and that she sometimes felt angry but held it back. This had been a reoccurring issue for her lately with regard to her relatives and other people who expected explanations and perfect answers about her separation. They were not supportive of her decision and she wanted to be left alone. I encouraged her to let her arm strike out to express the frustration that she was feeling. Barbara then saw an internal image of a man standing up on a hill overlooking the sea. She said she felt like she was waiting for her "ship to come in." However, she now knew that she would have to look within, instead of outside to her husband or relatives, for support.

The braced body pattern was symbolic of Barbara's lack of external support and her need to develop a positive inner support for herself. This was being somatically expressed through the tension along the vertebrae of her back, which provide skeletal support for her body. The man who appeared in Barbara's inner vision turned out to be an inner guide for her. Barbara was breaking a lifetime pattern that began even before her marriage, during her childhood with a stoic father. The archetypal masculine guide came to help her on this journey of self-discovery. It came to help her develop a positive male aspect that could give structure to her life in a way that was supportive and not rigid.

Interestingly, even though this woman was not familiar with tarot symbology, the vision that she related describes the three of wands card of the tarot. This card relates to being able to envision new possibilities through getting some distance on a situation and gaining a new perspective. It signifies the development of strength and will, yet often requires focusing inward while one waits for things to unfold outwardly. It can involve the test of time and distance in a relationship. This seems to describe Barbara's situation of getting some emotional distance from her family in order to develop a connection with the strength of her own inner masculine. Through working with this aspect of herself, she would then have the ability to creatively bring the things she envisioned into reality.

## EMBODIMENT DIALOGUE

After becoming aware of a somatic experience and getting a fuller sense of it through the amplifying process, you can progress into a dialogue. Dialogue is a method of consciously inviting elements of the psyche to speak. It is a central part of Gestalt therapy and is also used in Voice Dialogue and the Jungian process of active imagination.[11] The dialogue process can be used with body symptoms, dream symbols, archetypal energies, subpersonalities, and also to communicate in an internal way with people you have unresolved issues with. In the guided meditation at the end of chapter 2, you actually had a short dialogue with your archetypal soul essence when you asked if it had any guidance for you. In this way, the archetypal energy was given a voice to deliver its message to you.

In a dialogue with your body, you find out what it is trying to communicate to you by simply asking your body's symptom, sensation, or experience what its purpose, meaning, or message is for you. For example, if your body had a voice or expressed itself in words rather than sensations and illness, what would it say? Your headache could be letting you know you're angry about something. A back pain may be saying you need support and to stop trying to do things all by yourself. A cold may be telling you to slow down and take a rest.

I once developed a cervical lump. I was very concerned about it and knew it could be serious. When I saw my regular physician, he referred me to a surgeon. In dialoguing with the lump, I was told that I was pushing myself too hard. I needed to celebrate, have more joy in my life, and take a vacation. Within twenty-four hours, I had my vacation ticket in hand to let my body know that I was taking what it said seriously. By the time I got to the surgeon at the end of the week, the lump had almost totally disappeared. Within another few days it was gone. This shows it's definitely worthwhile to talk to your body and listen to what it's telling you.

Not all dialogue with your body will have such miraculous results, nor should you look for instant cures. However, if you do have physical difficulties, this type of communication will help you stay connected with your body's needs in order to have a more empowered role in your own healthcare. For instance, in addition to help with the emotional components of your physical illness, you might receive information on a healing modality that would benefit you; about certain foods, vitamins, or minerals that your body needs; or the timing for scheduling a medical procedure.

Dialogue is like a type of roleplay where you shift your consciousness over to speak as the body or another character, yet still keep a part of your awareness present in the background as an objective observer or witness to the process. By becoming your backache, for example, and letting it speak through you, you can discover its meaning. Maintain a state of contemplative receptivity as you do the dialogue and let your imagination flow with the process. Because dialogue is more effective if done in a relaxed meditative state, it is helpful before beginning to center yourself by taking a few relaxing breaths so that you can quiet the thinking mind and enter a state of internal awareness. With the thinking mind stilled, the intelligent forces of the subconscious mind and the creative imagination can flow as you remain actively receptive.

It is important to let the dialogue experience develop in this creative state without judgment, analysis, or mentally controlling what happens. Using the somatic awareness and amplifying processes preceding a dialogue will assist you in centering into your body and feelings and help you avoid mental analyzing. Instead, your dialogue process can flow in a nonjudgmental way.

If you do this type of dialogue without first doing an internal awareness or amplifying process, be sure to take a few moments to relax and center inside. Spend some time in meditation or do some relaxed breathing. As you breathe, have a sense that each exhalation allows you to sink a little deeper into a more relaxed place inside you. Begin the dialogue from this place of internal awareness.

When using the dialogue process in working independently with your body, record both parts of the communication in your journal as you go along. Write down your feelings, comments, and questions as you say them, then shift your consciousness over to speak as the body symptom or somatic experience and record the responses that you receive. This helps you stay focused and able to keep track of things as they're happening internally and gives you a recorded account of your process.

After becoming familiar with this type of dialogue, some individuals are more comfortable allowing the process to unfold internally, without the interruption of writing the conversation down, preferring to record what happened in their journals when the dialogue is finished. This takes a more disciplined, focused awareness and an ability to clearly separate different intrapsychic elements. When you feel confident with the dialogue process, you can experiment with this method. The Embodiment Exercise at the end of this chapter will also assist you in doing this type of dialogue in the form of a guided internal process.

It is important that you are willing to listen to the information that you receive in a dialogue. My cervical lump is a good example of this. Often, if you have ignored your body or repressed a certain symptom for a long time, your body self may not want to talk at first. In such a case, you may want to express feelings such as, "I know that I haven't paid attention to you in the past. However, I want to listen to what you have to say now." Answers can come in the form of images, feelings, or other body sensations—not just in words. It is important to participate with these feelings and images as they emerge. Find out what the body symptom is, how it feels, and what its purpose is for you. Ask what it is trying to say or what it needs or wants of you and find out what you want to know. Respond to the information that you receive by saying how you feel, as well as what your needs are with regard to what is being said.

The following work with Chris illustrates how the process of amplifying sensations can help you connect with feelings that naturally progress into a dialogue. Chris came into a group session feeling agitated and anxious. She had been having panic attacks throughout the day. Several weeks earlier, she had filed for divorce from her abusive husband, Chet. Chris reported that she'd had her ups and downs, but nothing that would explain the extent of this anxiety. She worked in the field of traditional medicine and was very skeptical about this type of body-centered process. She didn't even think she could relax enough to settle into her body to do it. I had her take a few slow, deep breaths to help her relax, and then continued.

| | |
|---|---|
| Pam: | Chris, just close your eyes and take a moment to notice how you experience this agitation and panic in your body. |
| Chris: | My heart is beating really fast and I feel very tense. There is a tightness in my chest. |
| Pam: | Bring your breath into your chest area and notice what the character of that tightness is, if it has any particular form or shape to it. |
| Chris: | It feels like a rubber band tightened around my heart. I have a headache too, like a pre-migraine. |
| Pam: | Describe what type of sensation this head pain is. |
| Chris: | It feels like all these gears, cogs, and wheels tightening. It keeps getting turned tighter and tighter. I felt like that today. I couldn't even settle down enough to think. It's like I'm so overwhelmed, I can't put words or language to the feelings. It's just a mess and I can't sort it out. |
| Pam: | Just notice, now, if there is a connection between the tightening in your head and the rubber band tightened around your heart. |
| Chris: | Yes *(starts to cry)*. I married Chet because I loved him. I still love him. I saw all his faults before we were |

married. I was scared and unsure about it, and had all sorts of problems like colitis and fatigue. I couldn't sleep, either. But I married him because I believed in love and marriage. Now I'm afraid of making a mistake again. That's what the anxiety is about. I'm afraid I might be making a terrible mistake.

Pam:      Like the one you made before you decided to marry him in spite of your doubts and bodily response.

Chris:    Yes. Is it okay to divorce him if I still feel this love for him? Is it okay to end the marriage?

Pam:      Perhaps your body and heart have a message for you in this regard.

Chris:    *(Relating the message from her heart and body.)* I love him, but he's abused and hurt me. I need to let go of this marriage. I didn't listen to myself and what my instincts were telling me the last time. It's okay to leave this marriage. I can still have love in my life. It's okay to believe in that. I don't have to give that up.

After receiving this message from her heart, the tightness in Chris' chest was gone. The terrible, anxious feeling stopped and she felt calm and relaxed. Chris continued to feel confident in her decision to terminate the marriage. She was amazed and elated that her symptoms had been relieved through this process.

Chris was able to accomplish three important things as a result of this work. First, she was able to resolve the inner conflict between her heart and head, and confirm that ending the marriage was the right path for her. Second, she was able to clear the feelings around her disappointing experience with love and the original decision to marry. The body-mind was assisting her in working through this dilemma again to bring resolution. It is quite possible that if this kind of work had been done originally, she would have chosen not to marry this man. Finally, she established a new pattern of listening to her core bodily instincts and feelings, as well as the intuition and guidance from her heart. Much of the body dialogue you do will give you information and provide resolution, as in Chris' case. Other times, it will provide you with pieces of information that will need continued work.

To illustrate how Embodiment Dialogue can be used when working alone with your own body issues, here is a dialogue that I did during a menstrual period when I was experiencing some especially painful cramping. These days of the month are an excellent time for women to do internal work of this nature; there is a natural movement inward to the feminine instincts that provides a fertile ground for connecting with the body, intuition, and the subconscious mind.

I started by centering, relaxing, and bringing my conscious awareness into my uterus. As I breathed into this area, I soon had a memory come up of when my daughter was born two months prematurely. After giving birth, the placenta didn't release and it had to be scraped from the walls of my uterus. It took a very long time and the frustrated doctor was being rough with me and it hurt. I decided to dialogue with the uterine area and placenta to find out more.

Pam:     It was so painful, what was wrong? Why wouldn't you *(placenta)* come out?

Placenta:     I have to stay here. I have a job to do. I provide protection and nourishment for this child. It's not time yet. I didn't want her to leave yet. *(I had a spontaneous release of emotions here and started to cry. It was a sobbing that came from a place deep within me. It felt like my body self was mourning.)* I didn't want her to be born yet, but I had to respond to her spirit and there was so much then that was not yet healed. *(This was referring to the unhealed issues of my own childhood.)*

Pam:    Yes, I wanted a normal birth too. I thank you for being a good protection for my baby and I understand that her spirit wanted this experience for some reason. You had to respond to her spirit and my unhealed will and emotions. This experience was to help me heal my issues too. I love you, body. *(I then sensed that this situation was still unresolved. I was not hearing words but feeling impressions from my body and psyche. I then knew that I was experiencing the painful cramping because I was still psychically stuck, trying to release the placenta. I wanted to complete this for myself and knew that I needed my body's help.)* . . . I'm wondering if there is another way now for you, body, to release the energy of this afterbirth, now that my baby has been safely born and your job has been completed?

Body:    Yes, tell the doctor to stop scraping. *(I then had an image of myself talking to the doctor.)*

Pam:    *(to doctor)* Stop being so rough. Don't you realize what I've been through? I've been here over twenty-four hours. My baby has been born two months early and I don't know if she'll even survive and all you want to do is get this over with. I need you to be gentle and I don't want any Valium because I want to go up to see my baby in intensive care after we're through. You stand there and watch. If you talk to the body and work with it, it will respond. And that's what I'm going to do.

I then called on the presence of my archetypal Healer guide, Minoa, and put my hands over my abdomen. As I affirmed my intention to heal this issue, I felt a very gentle comforting feeling in my uterus and saw an image of shimmering light surrounding the placenta and uterine wall.

Then, in my mind's eye, I saw the remaining afterbirth separate from the uterine wall and release from my body. I had a sense of being able to be with my baby daughter immediately afterward, which I had not been able to do in the original situation. I visualized myself with her in the way that I wanted it to be. I felt guided by my body and Higher Self during this whole process. The experience enabled me to resolve and complete this old situation and to release the energy my body was holding as a result of it. The following day, as tissue came out of my vagina, I felt a real confirmation of the work I had done the previous day. My body had finally released the old placenta energy and accompanying feelings. As a result of this work, the painful cramping I was experiencing with my periods subsided, and then ceased.

This dialogue is a good example of how communicating with the body can shift to a dialogue with an external character—in this case, the doctor. It was important for me to express the anger that I was feeling toward this insensitive doctor who was hurting me. These dialogue experiences are a gentle balance between responding to the subconscious elements of the psyche and creating what feels right to you. This is your internal world, and there are things you can do here for your own healing in order to resolve issues from the past. Other aspects of the personal subconscious, such as Mom and Dad, will often show up and have to be dealt with. I feel it is better to resolve these things in your internal world than to act them out in the external world. This type of internal work makes it less likely that unconscious acting out will occur. For example, my relationship with doctors greatly improved after this process.

When working alone, feelings involving an external person, such as my doctor, can be expressed by writing them down in a journal communication to the individual involved. This can also include a dialogue process in which you listen to the other person and give them a voice in the conversation by imagining or intuitively sensing what they would say. In my case, by listening to what the doctor had to say, I may have even gotten a sense of regret or an apology on his part. This can often facilitate completion and letting go of the past. It is okay if this is something you don't want to do or feel incapable of doing. This can be a difficult process when it involves separating very charged emotional feelings.

When working independently, there are also times when actually shifting your consciousness over to speak as another person in a dialogue might be inappropriate, for example, with an individual who has been violent or abusive in some way. In such a case, you will want to have help from a caring therapist who can facilitate the work for you and help you feel safe and supported. If you are working with body elements independently and start feeling scared or dissociated, you may have tapped into some very charged issues. Pay attention to these feelings. They are telling you to get assistance in order to make it safe for yourself before going further.

In this dialogue with my body, I was dealing with archetypal Mother. Until this session, I had been feeling guilty that I wasn't a good mother because I didn't carry my child to full term. This dialogue gave me a new understanding in which guilt and blame had no part. The placenta's holding on was actually an aspect of motherhood, the instincts of my body still trying to protect my child. I felt a gentle mothering presence that enfolded me as I saw the light fill my uterus.

You can consciously invoke this type of archetypal energy and call upon it when needed. If you need a soothing healing energy, visualize and somatically feel a Healer with you. I did this when I called on Minoa. A Warrior can bring protection and safety and a wise Ruler can help decide the consequences for wrongdoers. A Mother's presence can provide comfort and nurturing. Allow yourself, in this creative way, to use visualization in the dialogue process.

As this session shows, often sensitive issues and vulnerable feelings emerge in this work. For this reason, it is important to have a safe place where you can feel free to express what you need to for your own healing without interruptions. Turn the phone off and put a "Do Not Disturb" sign on the door if you need to in order to create this sacred space. Something else that helps create a feeling of safety is to sense or visualize a soft healing light around you before beginning. Call on the presence of your Higher Self and ask to be guided in a way that is for your highest good. This prepares the subconscious mind for the work and also provides protection and guidance through your process.

## THE EMOTIONAL BODY AND DEEP CLEARING

Emotional expression often happens spontaneously when we go deeply into our body and feelings, connecting with the issues that reside there. Other times, expressing emotions can be difficult because we receive so many messages against it from our society or from overly restrictive caretakers. For this reason, you may feel a little shy or embarrassed about it at first. Because we have been taught that showing anger is not "nice," that we must be "good" or "polite," the vulnerable part of you that may have internalized such messages may need to hear that it's okay to cry or feel angry at times. These are human emotions and it's a natural part of being human to feel them and express them. By denying them, you cut yourself off from a whole part of your being, your feeling self. Holding back these feelings, this life energy, can be exhausting—it takes a great deal of energy to keep this powerful force from moving forth. I do not mean that you should vent emotion irresponsibly without awareness. Rageaholics do this quite regularly to no avail. Rather, true healing and transformation come from connecting deeply with your feelings in a consciously aware way. This allows for a deep healing process in which emotionally held energy can be released and cleared from the body and the subconscious mind.

Sometimes, while doing a dialogue, you may get a sense that you are having feelings that you can't connect with in a full body-felt way. When this occurs, stop and notice if there is a place in your body where you experience the energy of this issue, event, or the person/figure with whom you're dialoguing. Is there a place where this issue seems to reside physically within you, or a specific area of your body that participates with it in some way? Notice what you are aware of from this place in your body and what sensations or feelings emerge from here.

There may also be times when you experience a numbness or confusing fog and think that you don't know what you're feeling. When this happens, sit down and get quiet. Breathe fully into your belly for a minute or so and have a sense of dropping down into your body and what you're experiencing, even if you don't have a name for it yet. It may help you to have a visual image of dropping down below the fog. After breathing and sinking into your body in this way, you will most likely be able to identify a feeling such as sadness, anger, fear, or excitement. It's okay if you don't know why. Psychology has put a lot of emphasis on analyzing things to find out the "whys." However, sometimes feelings will come up with no immediate connection to the content of what they're about. Often, it is only by allowing feelings to move and have expression that greater understanding can come. Some therapists also make the mistake of overemphasizing emotional release, making it the end goal of therapy. A deep connection to feelings doesn't always involve a giant catharsis. Sometimes, a much subtler, yet equally powerful shift can take place in the shedding of one tear.

You may naturally experience emotional release during a dialogue or while amplifying your somatic process. When emotional energy comes forth, you may begin to cry or feel so angry you could scream. At this point, allow yourself to be with these feelings and cry, scream into a pillow, or let your body respond with movement in some way. This release can in itself provide a shift and clear emotionally held content from the body. Other times, especially with very charged issues, you will need assistance from a therapist or trained facilitator whom you trust. This will create safety and allow you to go deeper into the feelings so that important issues aren't neglected. Safety is an important part of deep emotional clearing. Individuals from abusive homes may have been punished for expressing their feelings and violence often resulted from showing any kind of disagreement or anger. Even in more emotionally healthy families, expressing anger was often considered bad behavior. A safe, trusting environment is essential for one to feel comfortable with emotional expression. Support groups are wonderful for this.

Having a physically safe environment is also important. Give your body enough space to move around during emotional processing. You may find that you want to kick your legs, swing your arms, or take on different body positions. It's also okay if you don't. Be sure there isn't anything hard, sharp, or breakable near your body when you're doing this. It may also be useful to make a list ahead of time of things that you can do to safely and appropriately release emotions when you're feeling upset. Writing about the feelings in your journal is often helpful. You may also want to have big pillows that you can hit or scream into. If you have been a reserved person for a good part of your life, the sound of your own voice screaming can be a shock. For this reason, you may prefer screaming into a pillow so that the sounds are muffled. You can also use a towel by biting down on it while making sounds. Other ways to safely release emotion including slapping a towel against a bed, stomping around on soft ground, or kicking your feet against pillows on a bed.

It may also be helpful to be aware if there is a movement or sound that your body would like to make to help clear emotional energy from your body. Sound is a way to move energy as it creates a type of bridge or channel through which the energy can move. It may help you to remember this image when you are using sound for this purpose. Breath is also an important part of this sound process. Through breathing, you receive the life energy of oxygen into your body. Remember that breath can bring energy into areas that are constricted or energetically stagnated, thus releasing the pattern held there. Breathing into an area of the body where a particular feeling resides will help you form a sound in order to clear these somaticized emotional patterns.

To use sound to move emotional energy, bring your breath into the area. Have a sense of allowing the breath to push the held energy out by making a sound. You may not know the type of sound that you will make until it comes out, and the sound may come with words. Let yourself give in to the sound as much as possible without restricting it or holding back. If this is difficult, you can creatively use archetypal energies in the process of emotional clearing. Imagining a Warrior or Powerful Goddess with you and feeling the energy of such a presence may assist you in releasing anger.

In the process of emotional clearing, certain bodily sensations may be experienced as shifts take place in your system. There may be twitching, shaking, or spasms as the body releases held energy. You may also experience heat, cold, tingling, or the vibrating sensations of energy streaming through your body. Radiating sensations may be felt emanating from specific chakra locations such as the heart or solar plexus area. Breathing patterns can also become unusual. It is important to remain aware of your breath, continuing to breathe fully. Avoid holding your breath or breathing shallowly as release continues to help facilitate the process of full emotional clearing through the body.

When held energy of this nature is released from your body, you can ask Spirit to transmute it, visualize it dissolved in light or consumed by fire, or simply ask that it be returned to its right place. Any heavy or negative-feeling discharged energy can be cleared from your room by opening the windows and burning incense.

Sometimes after deep emotional release, taking a sea salt and baking soda bath can be useful to assist in the process of clearing the released energy out of your auric field. In her book, *Light Emerging*, Barbara Brennan gives a good recipe for this type of bath; she suggests dissolving two cups of sea salt and the same amount of baking soda in a bath of medium hot water, then soaking your body for twenty minutes. After the bath, rinse with fresh water and rest.

Because of its detoxifying effects, this bath may initially drain your energy and can even make you feel light-headed. For this reason, be careful that you don't make the water too hot, especially if you have blood pressure problems. Until you get used to its effects, you can also shorten the amount of time that you spend in the bath, particularly if you feel weak, or reduce the amount of sea salt and baking soda to as little as one cup each if the larger amount seems too strong.

This bath is also an excellent remedy if you accumulate any negative-feeling energy in your auric field. As a substitute for the sea salt, or by itself, epsom salts can be used if that's all you have available. The flower essence crab apple may also be added to the water for its cleansing and purifying effects.[12]

Moderate sunlight can also be used to revitalize your energy system after emotional clearing. This process can be assisted by consciously breathing the light and warmth of the Sun into your energy field, chakras, and body with the intention of absorbing its healing vitality.

# REORGANIZATION

It is important after emotional release and deep clearing to fill your whole body with gentle, loving kindness by breathing light and love into every part of your being. This healing process provides comfort, realigns your energy system, and assists your physical body in reorganizing with the new pattern being created.

Dialogue and emotional clearing help move emotional blocks out of your body and resolve issues from the past. Optimally, through these processes, a shift will have taken place in which an old pattern has been transformed. Reorganization is the process of bringing in a positive new energy to replace the old pattern. In a relaxed, inwardly centered state of awareness you can feel the new mental, emotional, and/or physical experience sinking into the tissues and the very cells of your body. This may involve deepening with a quality such as self-empowerment, enjoying a new sense of relaxation in the body, or savoring an expansive feeling state.

Visualizing light and feeling light and love as part of this process allows your physical body and auric field to be charged with energy. The subconscious mind and the very cells of your physical body are then infused with this matrix of light, seeded with the pattern of the new conscious intention. This is a profound transformation that deepens the shift in consciousness into the body-mind in a very powerful way. Be sure to take time for this process at the end of your work and allow light and love to flow into every part of you.

After this type of healing reorganization, you may feel your muscular-skeletal system changing and relaxing. Body areas may feel bigger, lighter, or more spacious. You may notice an actual change in your appearance, such as brighter, clearer eyes or a softer, more relaxed look to your body. Such reorganization work can sometimes take you into very deeply relaxed states or a type of light trance. Be gentle with yourself afterward and be sure to give yourself time to come back to external awareness.

## INTEGRATING MIND AND BODY

To further assist the reorganization that is taking place in the body-mind system, it is important to create a bridge of understanding between the conscious mind and the subconscious dynamics of your process. This helps the conscious mind get "up to speed," so to speak, with the new imprint that is being created. It is accomplished through journal writing, affirmations, and other methods of integration. Through this process of integration, the transformation that has taken place in your body and subconscious mind can be brought into the actual experience of your daily life, helping you to consciously establish new patterns.

Journal writing is an important part of this type of integration. Writing down the things that have happened, putting it in black and white before you, helps make it more concrete and real. You may have already discovered that this practice assists you in bringing internally processed dynamics more consciously into your external experience. After recording the feelings and insights that you have had as a result of your experience with your body-mind processing, note what changes this will make in your life. It may be useful to explore the following questions.

1. What are the old patterns, behaviors, and belief systems that are changing?

2. What are the new patterns that you are establishing and how do you want things to be in your life, now, as a result? It may be helpful for you to identify one specific thing that you can do to help yourself establish this new pattern in your life and directly apply any new understandings that you have gained. For example, one woman had an old pattern of feeling thwarted and victimized by life. In a session that she had with me, she was able to connect with a new, assertive way of being that allowed her to go after what she wanted. After doing some goal setting, this woman decided that she wanted to go back to school. She then applied for and received a grant for financing. By setting her goals and applying for the financial aid, she took practical steps to change her old behaviors and integrate this new assertive pattern in her life.

3. If you've obtained information in your process that needs further work, have a sense of how it would look and feel if the situation were resolved. What might need to happen for this to be accomplished? Envision yourself six months to a year into the future, seeing the body symptom or other issue healed. Notice the characteristics of this transformed state. How would you feel and move in your body? What would others observe about you? As you imagine this and experience these new feelings and sensations within you, allow yourself to look back from this future place and see what specific steps you took to accomplish these things in your life.

Something else I have found useful in the integration process is the symbolic reminder. Find something that is symbolic or represents the transformation that has just taken place within you. It may be a picture, a gemstone, or something from nature. Carry it with you and hold it occasionally, or put it in a place where you will see it and be reminded of the new pattern or attribute that you are integrating. On walks and hikes, I often find little gifts from nature that are symbolic of my experience in some way. Once, during a period of deep healing, I found a walking stick while on a hike. Later, during a meditation, I found that it was symbolic of my own healing, and that it was meant to be a staff of power. As my healing process continued, I carved and sanded the stick, decorating it with feathers, shells, fur, and other meaningful objects. Just as the stick was transformed into a rod of power, so did I heal and transform, taking on my true power of Self. I experienced a noticeable shift in regards to this, just as my staff was completed.

Drawing a picture of your experiences can also help you integrate aspects of your process. The picture can then be put somewhere you will see it and continue to be reminded of the essence of your work. Remember, also, to be aware of dreams and other synchronistic events that relate to your experience and your process of transformation.

Affirmations are also very useful in the integration process, helping you to seed positive new patterns into the subconscious mind so that they can manifest externally. They can be used to replace negative internalized messages with loving, supportive ones. For example, an excellent affirmation for the woman mentioned above might be, "I give thanks that each day, I am experiencing greater confidence, courage, and direction in my life."

## EMBODIMENT EXERCISE

The Embodiment Exercise is a guided process for your body awareness work, including amplifying methods and dialogue. Read through the exercise fully before beginning to become familiar with it. You can also record it on audio tape or have a partner assist you by reading it to you as you proceed.

## *A Guided Meditation: Embodiment Exercise*

Sit comfortably in a big chair or lay down on a cushion or mat. Allow at least thirty minutes for the entire exercise, process times may vary and you will want to take as much time as you need to complete each part. Through this exploration, you may connect with feelings, have insights without any further communication, or have a dialogue without emotional expression. Your experience may vary each time that you do it. This exercise is meant to be a guide. Follow your own process and be flexible with it.

Begin by stating your intention for your process. Your intention may involve a specific issue or be general in nature, such as an intention to listen to your body and heal. You can then call on Spirit or ask for the presence of your own Higher Self. Visualize yourself surrounded in a soft healing light and ask that this experience be for your highest good and healing.

Close your eyes and breathe fully into the bottom of your belly. Follow the movement of your breath in and out of your body for a moment, letting each exhalation take you deeper into your body. Allow yourself to relax and settle into your body as you feel the rising and falling of your abdomen with your breath. Any thoughts or cares from your day can just drift out of your mind with each exhalation as you drop more deeply into your body self.

Imagine that, just like a tree, you are sending roots down deep into the ground. Visualize or sense these energetic roots extending down from your feet (if you are sitting), or a root extending down from your coccyx, like a tail (if you are lying down). As you sense these roots going deeper into the earth, allow yourself to sink even more deeply into your own body.

When you're ready, scan through your body and notice any area that seems to draw your attention, perhaps a place in your body that feels tense and constricted or where breath and energy aren't moving as freely as possible. If you are working with a particular issue or feeling, notice where in your body you experience this feeling, what part of your body participates with it, or where the energy of the issue seems to reside physically. Bring your consciousness to rest here, fully focusing your awareness on this place in your body.

Take several full amplified breaths into this area of your body. *(You can also experiment with amplifying the experience by massaging the area or by exaggerating a somatic pattern.)* Notice what you feel and experience as you do this. Simply be mindfully receptive and allow any sensations, images, or feelings to present themselves. Focus on the quality of the sensations.

This body experience may have a color, shape, temperature, or texture. If it had a form, what would it look like? Notice how you feel in your body and what emotional feelings are evoked as these things emerge. Perhaps it is a familiar feeling in some way or reminds you of something.

You may find that today your body has a message for you regarding the purpose of this body experience, something it needs you to know. Let any form that may have previously emerged have a voice. If, rather than expressing itself through sensation and pain, this body experience could speak, what would it tell you? You may have something to reply, a response or question. As you communicate with your body, notice what feelings this experience brings forth in you. Are these familiar feelings or do they remind you of some other life issue?

As you give full expression to the feelings that emerge, it will help you to release any blocked emotional energy that has been held in your body. Have a sense that this energy can drain out of your body, down into the earth through the roots you visualized earlier. There may also be a sound or movement that you or your body would like to make in response to these feelings. If so, let yourself express the sound and let your body move in any way that would feel good. Use pillows or anything else that you need to assist you or support your body.

When this feels complete, visualize, sense, or feel a soft radiance, a healing, loving light, enfold you and fill your whole body. Perhaps it has a color. Allow your body, your whole being, to absorb this loving light and drink it in. Take some time to just immerse yourself in it. Breathe in the love and let it fill every structure, organ, and tissue of your body, particularly the specific areas of your body that you have been working with. Feel every cell bathed, soothed, and nourished with this healing light as it flows into every part of you. Allow yourself to expand into the new energy and life patterns emerging for you. Savor these new feelings, sensations, or qualities as they deepen within you, breathing them right into your very cells.

Notice, then, how the nature of the energy in your body may have changed. You may experience the particular area of your body that you were initially drawn to as a little softer, lighter, or more open now.

After completing this exploration, allow yourself time to return to external awareness as you would after a meditation. Be gentle with yourself. Write your experience in your journal and record what you have learned from your body. How does this experience relate to other events and issues in your life? What new patterns would you like to bring into your life as a result? Compose two affirmations that would assist you in applying the insights that you have gained through this process and write them in your journal. Declare your affirmations throughout the day for the next week, using the guidelines in chapter 3.

---

## Notes

1. Kenneth R. Pelletier, *Mind As Healer, Mind As Slayer: A Holistic Approach to Preventing Stress Disorders* (New York: Dell Publishing Co., 1977).

2. Fritz Perls, M.D., Ph.D., *The Gestalt Approach and Eye Witness to Therapy* (Palo Alto, CA: Science and Behavior Books, Inc., 1973), p. 75.

3. For the developmental stages of childhood, see John Bradshaw, *Homecoming: Reclaiming and Championing Your Inner Child* (New York: Bantam Books, 1990); and Jack Rosenberg, Marjorie Rand, and Diane Asay, *Body, Self, and Soul: Sustaining Integration.* (Atlanta, GA: Humanics, Ltd., 1985). For birth dynamics, see Arthur Janov, *Imprints: The Lifelong Effects of the Birth Experience* (New York: Coward-McCann, Inc., 1983); and Stanislav Grof, M.D., *The Adventure of Self-Discovery: Dimensions of Consciousness and New Perspectives in Psychotherapy and Inner Exploration* (Albany, NY: State University of New York Press, 1988). For past-life experiences, see Roger J. Woolger, *Other Lives, Other Selves: A Jungian Psychotherapist Discovers Past Lives* (New York: Bantam Books, 1988).

4. After only a few weeks in the womb, the fetus can neurologically react to and store the input of sensations. Yet, at the time of birth, the higher brain functions are not developed. This means that the fetus can feel pain but can't cognitively process and integrate it. Pain-killing endomorphines also repress the conscious memory of the trauma. However, knowledge of the pain is still stored in the memory of the subconscious mind and in the cellular memory of the body through the autonomic nervous system. Arthur Janov, *Imprints: The Lifelong Effects of the Birth Experience* (New York: Coward-McCann, Inc., 1983).

5. Every emotion contains a physical component through the chemical substances produced in the brain, nerve endings, and at other body sites, in addition to the hormones released by the endocrine glands. When these substances cross the placenta into the fetus' bloodstream and developing nervous system, the child receives the physical manifestation of the mother's subjective feelings. Arthur Janov, *Imprints: The Lifelong Effects of the Birth Experience* (New York: Coward-McCann, Inc., 1983).

6. Wynn Kapit and Lawrence M. Elson, *The Anatomy Coloring Book* 2nd ed., Rev. (New York: Harper Collins Publishers, Inc., 1993). Gary A. Thibodeau, Ph.D. and Kevin T. Patton Ph.D., *The Human Body in Health and Disease*, 2nd ed. (St. Louis: Mosby-Year Book, Inc., 1997).

7. Alexander Lowen, *Bioenergetics* (New York: Penguin Books, 1975). Ron Kurtz, *Body-Centered Psychotherapy: The Hakomi Method* (Mendocino, CA: LifeRhythm, 1990). Barbara Brennan, *Hands of Light* (New York: Bantam Books, 1988). Barbara Brennan, *Light Emerging* (New York: Bantam Books, 1993).

8. For more specific information on sensing the body's energy field in this way, see Barbara Brennan, *Hands of Light* (New York: Bantam Books, 1988).

9. Erving and Miriam Polster, *Gestalt Therapy Integrated: Contours of Theory and Practice* (New York: Random House Inc., 1982); Gay Hendricks, Ph.D. and Kathlyn Hendricks, Ph.D., *At the Speed of Life: A New Approach to Personal Change Through Body-Centered Therapy* (New York: Bantam Books, Inc., 1994); Arnold Mindell, *Dreambody: The Body's Role in Revealing the Self* (Portland, OR: Lao Tse Press, 1997).

10. Cyclic amplified breathing methods such as Holotropic Breathwork and Rebirthing also exist. See Stanislav Grof, M.D., *The Adventure of Self-Discovery: Dimensions of Consciousness and New Perspectives in Psychotherapy and Inner Exploration* (Albany, NY: State University of New York Press, 1988); and also Leonard Orr and Sondra Ray, *Rebirthing in the New Age* (Berkeley, CA: Celestial Arts, 1983); and Leonard Orr, *The Healing Power of Birth and Rebirth* (Stanton, CA: Inspiration University, 1994).

Through this type of sustained amplified breathing, one can experience sequences of biological birth and childhood events, past-life patterns, and transpersonal phenomena, along with accompanying archetypal images. However, discernment must be used since the psyche contains powerful forces that one can open up to through this type of breathwork, which is continued for extended periods. Deep psychological material is often accessed and follow-up work is usually necessary to help with processing and integrating the experience. Ideally, breathwork of this type should be done in conjunction with counseling or psychotherapy. If you are considering this type of sustained amplified breathwork, make sure that the practitioner you choose has a firm grounding in psychospiritual process, as well as proper training and certification.

11. Erving and Miriam Polster, *Gestalt Therapy Integrated: Contours of Theory and Practice* (New York: Random House, 1982). Hal Stone and Sidra Winkelman, *Embracing Ourselves: The Voice Dialogue Manual* (Novato, CA: Nataraj Publishing, 1993). Robert A. Johnson, *Inner Work: Using Dreams and Active Imagination For Personal Growth* (San Francisco: Harper San Francisco, 1986).

12. Mechthild Scheffer, *Bach Flower Therapy in Theory and Practice* (Rochester, VT: Healing Arts Press, 1988).

# 6

# Healing Fragmentation

*Creating Wholeness*

**If you are working with body** issues involving a somaticized complex, you may find that some form of subpersonality or archetypal energy emerges in the process. Often, they stand as guardians at the gate of your healing and transformation. The Embodiment Dialogue process from chapter 5 can also be used to communicate with these subpersonalities and archetypal energies.

## WORKING WITH SUBPERSONALITIES

You may experience subpersonalities through certain feelings, hear statements associated with them when working with the body, or internally visualize them embodied in a form. Dialoguing with these inner personalities is often a process of creative bargaining or "horse trading" as Robert Johnson calls it.[1] This type of interior negotiation resolves conflicts and brings cooperative agreement so that all the parts of yourself can work together as one whole self. Through a dialogue process of this type, you can reclaim disowned or lost parts of yourself and transform shadow material.

In the book *Embracing Ourselves*, Hal Stone and Sidra Winkleman discuss their Voice Dialogue process. This is an excellent guidebook for working with subpersonalities and I highly recommend it. They illustrate that, through dialogue, you can become conscious of your subpersonalities and give them appropriate expression under the guidance of an aware ego. I have found that this type of dialogue is very effective when combined with the internally focused body-centered processes presented here. Such a relaxed, meditatively receptive state will be helpful in allowing you to access the creative, feeling elements of the subconscious mind.

Imagine how you would feel if you were locked up and hidden away for a long time? After being repressed and denied, shadow aspects and subpersonalities are often in an unpleasant state. However, even though subpersonalities may initially appear nasty or opinionated, there is usually a positive intent behind their behavior. There is often a trauma or an emotionally painful experience that has created the shadow behavior. Very often the negative attitude of a subpersonality is a patterned defensive response operating as a protective mechanism,  preventing further pain. The key is to find the positive intent of the subpersonality and heal the issue involved. Thus, by loving these parts of yourself and seeking to truly understand them, healing and integration can occur. The true archetypal essence can then emerge. This type of dialogue will not only help you resolve conflicts within your personality, but can also enable you to heal past emotional issues, and allow you to give expression to an essential aspect of your own soul.

To better understand a subpersonality, it will help you to explore what the function, protective mechanism, or positive intention of it is. Does it help you or serve you in any way? How long has this subpersonality dynamic been operating in your life? Is there a way its negative qualities could be more positively expressed or used in a more balanced way? For instance, your Perfectionist subpersonality may be protecting you from making a mistake because at sometime in your life you were very hurt and embarrassed, or even punished, for making a mistake. Now that you are no longer in that situation, your Perfectionist may be better able to assist you by helping you to focus on a task that needs your conscious attention or by lovingly encouraging you to achieve practical goals in your life.

To determine the positive expression of your subpersonality, it will be helpful for you to go back to chapter 2 and look at the essential qualities of the archetype with which it is associated. Start by looking at archetypal Masculine, Feminine, and Child and then go on to others that might apply. For example, the Critic, Judge, or Skeptic subpersonalities can help you with their discriminating ability to evaluate things—a positive quality of the Masculine archetype. They can, for instance, help you to determine if the new car you are thinking of buying has all the features you desire at a fair price, or whether the offer the telemarketing salesman is making to you is as good as it sounds. The Caretaker's strength as a Feminine nurturer for others can instead be used to find activities that are self-nourishing and nurturing to your soul. Your Seducer/Seductress can align with the Lover's ability to find pleasure in a variety of activities, helping you to express your sensuality by savoring the fragrances of nature or through the appreciation of artistic beauty.

I find that, when working alone, individuals can do well in communicating with their subpersonalities if they write down both parts of the dialogue in their journal as they proceed. In fact, these inner personalities often reveal themselves during a dialogue of this type with the body. Some people even find it helpful to sit in two different chairs as they dialogue with the subpersonality, to help them separate the two distinct aspects of their personality. However, there are times when it will be difficult for people to separate these internal elements of the psyche, and the assistance of a facilitator will be needed for the dialogue process. If you feel stuck in some way during a dialogue or find that you are having trouble distinguishing who is who, please seek the help of a therapist or other partner that you trust.

When you dialogue with a subpersonality, be aware of its qualities and characteristics and what your response is, especially on a sensate-feeling level, to the dynamics involved. Like any conversation, there can be questions, concerns, suggestions, and disagreements within the dialogue. When you shift your consciousness over to speak as the subpersonality, you will also gain information from noticing how you experience it in your body. If you have any doubts about what you are hearing in a dialogue, get a sense of how what is being said feels to you. When you take it in, does it resonate in some way, ring true with a kind of, "Ah, yes," or do you feel a knot in your stomach or other negative sensation? These responses are your way of knowing whether the information being communicated feels true and right for you, or at least a way to determine what feelings need to be addressed before that truth is revealed.

It is important to stay connected with your feelings in this way because, on the surface, things can often be deceiving. An ugly or nasty sounding inner figure may be a wounded part of you that needs to be heard. On the other hand, a sweet angelic character may have misleading information based on beliefs that are no longer useful. Use discernment and pay attention to your authentic feelings. When feelings come up for you, see if you can get a sense of what they relate to. Bring the feelings that you are having into the dialogue, and express any concerns or needs you may have in the situation so that resolution and healing can take place. Conflicts that emerge in the dialogue can usually be resolved through interaction of the different points of view.

It's also important that the more vulnerable parts of you, such as the Child within, feel safe and protected when working with stronger and more dominating inner aspects such as the Critic or Protector/Controller. In such a case, you can create a feeling of safety through creative visualization. For example, if you feel overwhelmed during a dialogue with an intense sub-personality, you can imagine yourself in an impenetrable bubble or other protection. You can also imagine that the character you are dialoguing with is very small and you are very big, or call forth the presence of an archetypal ally to aid you.

When doing somatic processing, you can consciously call on the symbolic presence of a particular body phenomenon and invoke these subpersonalities or archetypal energies for a dialogue by asking to talk to the one influencing, or in charge of, your ailment or sensation. It may be helpful to imagine what your body experience would be like if it was embodied as a person or other figure and notice what it would look like and say.

The following dialogue I did with a client, Jackie, illustrates how this can work. During a session when Jackie was talking about her anger toward her sister, she started having a bad headache. I had her close her eyes, center into her body, and bring her awareness into her head area.

Pam:    Jackie, I'd like you to just breathe into that area of your head and tell me what kind of pain it is, what the quality of it is.

Jackie:    The pain is at the base of the skull, at the side of the occiput.

Pam:    I wonder if you have a sense of what it looks like, how it appears to you?

| | |
|---|---|
| Jackie: | It looks like a round ball at the occiput, like a big boulder blocking a hole there. |
| Pam: | I'd like you to call on the presence of the one who is in charge of this boulder and head pain and just notice, now, if you sense anyone here associated with the boulder or your headache in any way. |
| Jackie: | Yes, there is a troll or kind of gnome-like person. |
| Pam: | Yes, what is this gnome/troll's job? |
| Jackie: | He says, "I'm holding in the rage." |
| Pam: | I wonder if the gnome will tell you why it is important to do this? |
| Jackie: | I had a memory of a time when I got real angry at my sister and pushed her through a glass door. |
| Pam: | Jackie, I'd like you to have a sense of shifting your consciousness over to the gnome, to talk as the gnome . . . *(And then to the gnome)* Sounds like you're protecting her, gnome. |
| Gnome: | Yes. I don't want her to get hurt. |
| Pam: | You're protecting her from getting hurt or hurting anyone else. |
| Gnome: | Yes. |
| Pam: | Well, it seems like she is hurting now. Her head hurts a lot. |
| Gnome: | Hmmm. |
| Pam: | I'm wondering, gnome, if you would be willing to keep her from hurting now? I'm wondering if you would allow her to express some of her anger now if you could be in charge of making sure it was done in safe, appropriate ways that didn't hurt Jackie or anyone else? |

Gnome:    Yes, I'll do that.

Jackie:    The gnome is moving the boulder. I can see some black stuff streaming out. It's going to my sister. There is not as much pressure built up behind the boulder now.

As the session continued, it shifted to a dialogue between Jackie and her sister. She was able to express to her sister the anger that she felt over her betrayal. After the session, the head pain was gone. Dialogues such as this can remove the emotional charge relating to a situation and resolve it internally so that emotional conflicts aren't acted out externally on another person. It can then allow any external communication to be clearer or eliminate the need for it altogether. A few days later, in fact, Jackie was able to have a very successful external communication with her sister concerning these issues from the past.

The gnome was initially perceived by Jackie as ugly and troll-like. It then became more elf- or fairy-like in her inner vision as the session continued and its positive healing intent became known. The gnome represented an unconscious defense mechanism that originally provided protection but was now obstructing Jackie's healing. It operated as a Protector/Controller sub-personality preventing Jackie from expressing the assertive aspect of her Warrior essence. With the Sun and Mars together (conjunct) on the Midheaven at birth, it was important for Jackie to give expression to this self-(Sun) assertive (Mars) energy. This dialogue enabled Jackie to find out the positive intent of the gnome and what the purpose of the headache was. The gnome could then be an ally rather than an adversary in her process.

# DIALOGUE WITH ARCHETYPAL ENERGIES

A dialogue process is especially important with archetypal energies since, when they first appear to help you heal and evolve, they are often contaminated with complexes and seen through the filters of your own emotional issues. In addition to representing an aspect of your own soul essence, archetypal energies can reflect subpersonality dynamics and carry collective psychic elements that are not directly a part of you as an individual. They sometimes present themselves in a very powerful or intense fashion. For this reason, it is absolutely imperative that you participate in a conscious way with these energies. Also, each archetypal energy represents only one aspect of your total Self. This whole core Self is the guiding mechanism that must discern the internal and external information we receive and determine what is true for us. It would be just as wrong to let a single archetype have total control as it would be to ignore it altogether. The Embodiment Dialogue process can help you participate with all the parts of yourself in a balanced way, to help you determine what is useful for you and what is not.

As you interact with archetypal energies, use your journal to write down both sides of the communication. Be sure to ask the archetypal presence who or what it is, what its message is, and let the archetypal energy know your concerns, needs, and feelings about the issue concerned. Once again, use discernment. If you have any questions or doubts about what you're hearing, notice how you experience the communication in your body and bring your awareness to the feelings involved, then express your feelings in the dialogue.

The conscious choices that you make with regard to the information that you receive in a dialogue should be life affirming and for your highest good. If anything that you hear makes you feel uncomfortable or fearful, it may be beneficial to have assistance from a therapist in working with the dialogue process. You can also call on the presence of your Higher Self to assist you in knowing what is for your highest good.

The following session illustrates how a communication with archetypal energies can emerge when working with body issues. It developed from my client Karen's concern about an increase in body weight. Her body had been slender, angular, and straight, and it now looked much softer with her hip area and breasts appearing rounder and fuller. The first archetype that came forth in her session was an image of the Virgin Mary, an expression of archetypal Mother. Then a snake appeared as part of Karen's process. This is an interesting and not so unlikely pairing considering the often depicted image of the Virgin Mary with the defeated serpent underfoot.

Karen had indeed tapped into some powerful archetypal forces, the sacred and sexual aspects of the Feminine that are often polarized in our culture. As you will see, at first Karen simply talked and listened to the archetype, but then she actually became the snake in the dialogue. After discussing her body concerns, I asked Karen to follow the movement of her breath for a moment to help her relax and center inside, and then continued.

Pam:      Karen, I'd like you to be aware of what you're experiencing in your body right now, just allowing any sensations, feelings, or images to present themselves.

Karen:    I see an image of the Virgin Mary upside down.

Pam:      Just notice, now, where in your body you feel this image.

Karen:    In my solar plexus area.

Pam:      Yes, is the Virgin Mary communicating anything to you, here?

Karen:    It's about how tired I am of the Mother energy being so mixed up inside of me and in our culture . . . I just had a memory of sitting there helplessly as my mother was physically abused by my dad . . . I see a snake there now, just a snake. (*For a fleeting moment Karen has a memory of some of the abuse she endured as a child. As is sometimes the case, things are moving and changing rapidly.*)

Pam:      I wonder if this snake has a message for you?

Karen:    It's come to awaken me to something that is not of my mind, but connected with my body in some way. The snake is like a guide helping me to become aware of my body and my identity as a woman. The weight gain is part of this in some way.

Pam:      And the memory that came right before the snake appeared, perhaps this memory is a part of you reclaiming your feminine nature too?

Karen:    Yes, the weight and snake are bringing my attention to it.

As the session continued, Karen was guided in assisting the helpless Child part of her in order to heal this emerging painful experience from childhood. By internally removing her Child within from this traumatic situation of the past, Karen was not only able to comfort and love this vulnerable part of herself, but was also able to evoke healthy, nurturing Mother qualities within herself to change the previous "upside down" pattern.

The snake appeared once again in a later session when Karen was working on childhood issues regarding her parents.

Karen:    I can hear my mom say I'm evil . . . The snake is here. I like the snake, but I'm afraid because everyone has told me it's evil and bad. I want to feel it. (*At this point, Karen automatically began to feel the energy of the snake. There was an immediate shift in her body and mannerisms as she amplified the experience through snake-like movements. This was not an intellectual concept, but rather a somatic experience of being a snake.)* This snake energy feels very natural in some way . . . I remember this feeling as a child. This feeling, it was like a playmate except it was not separate from me. It's so nice and peaceful. I want to share this with my mom and dad, to bring them to this place, so they'll understand. My mom is afraid . . .

Pam:      What about your mom? What do you have to say to her?

Karen:    I don't want to be like you, unable to move or change because of fear.

Pam:      I wonder if the snake would be willing to assist you in becoming aware of your true identity as a woman, to replace your mother's negative legacy of fear?

Karen:    Yes, I can connect with the natural, peaceful feeling of the snake.

Karen's experience with the serpent is a clear example of how these archetypes are with us in childhood. The snake represented Karen's life force and sexual energy. As a child she was naturally in touch with her body, instincts, and sensuality. Her mother was afraid of these things in herself and so projected this fear on to Karen, seeing her as a threat and evil. Karen, as was mentioned earlier, was also sexually abused by her father and, in such cases, the mother is often jealous or threatened by the daughter, blaming and punishing her for what is happening. Karen's mother was afraid of Karen's life force and sexual energy. Her father abused her, using her life force to fulfill his own needs. In order to survive, this essential part of Karen that the snake represented had to be repressed and denied. The dissociation and separation from her body and the feelings that Karen experienced as a result is common in survivors of sexual abuse. To fully reclaim her feminine and sexual self, this incest wound had to be healed.

In these sessions, the snake presence returned to Karen to act as a guide in this process. It came to bring Karen's awareness to her body and the painful issues that were held there concerning her sexuality and womanhood. At the same time, it brought the wonderfully natural and peaceful sensation that Karen had known in childhood before the abuse; she was able to reconnect with a part of her that she had lost a long time ago. The snake reminded her of this disowned part, bringing union once again with her body, life force, and sexual energy. The serpent represents these things as well as the kundalini and the transformational aspect of the Birth/Death archetype, relating to Pluto, which is also a dominant natal planet for Karen.

## THE HEALING CAVE

The Healing Cave is an exercise that provides a method for amplifying body experience and also facilitates a dialogue process with subpersonalities or archetypal energies related to your body concern. It is based on an inner visualization technique that involves exploring a body symptom by means of a journey through a cave. To do this process, you simply imagine that your body condition is a cave that you are exploring. Jane, the woman mentioned in chapter 5, used this method to explore her stomach problems further. She experienced her tight abdomen as a big, huge cavern that looked lumpy—like a toad's back—on the outside. There was a secret entrance, which had barely noticeable hinges and a handle, leading into the cavernous space inside.

One of the first things Jane noticed when entering the cave was a blue and gold medicine bottle with a squeeze-dropper top and an prescription label. It was high up on a ledge, and after noticing how it felt, Jane sensed that it wasn't for her right now. She described it as, "Something my parents said I had to take."

When Jane looked around for her true medicine object, she saw a red heart sitting on a very shiny gold box which had lots of positive energy emanating from it. In dialoguing with the symbolic heart, it told her, "I give you energy to heal. You don't have to use the anger energy anymore. I will help you fill the hole. Go slow . . . it's very powerful. Use it as you need it."

At times when Jane was feeling the emptiness within her, she could tap into this energy and fill the void she felt inside. Jane described it this way, "I picked up the heart and put it in my heart slowly . . . I felt taller, more alive, straighter. I can remember to access it when I need it . . . It feels like it's changing the energy in my body. It [the energy] is being pulled into my heart instead of my stomach."

Jane was abused and neglected as a child. Externally, she passively endured this, while inside of her was a very angry child. About the age of four, she realized that she was on her own and would have to take care of herself. Fighting for her existence, she decided that despite everything, she was going to endure. Her anger was her motivator. In essence, it kept her life force vibrating enough for her to survive. As an adult, however, it no longer served her. She was exhausted and was venting her anger on others. The anger imprint was a part of her body. Her nervous system ran on it. Astrologically, Jane had Mars rising opposite Jupiter setting on the horizon, with Saturn conjunct Venus near the Ascendant, as well. Both Mars and Jupiter formed a challenging ninety degree square to Chiron at the Nadir. For Jane, an important path to growth and a connection with her spiritual Inner Teacher was in healing the shadow elements, the righteous (Jupiter) anger (Mars), of her archetypal Warrior.

The heart energy that emerged as part of Jane's work came to assist this. It carried the archetypal presence of Love (Venus). This healing energy of the heart seemed to infuse her nervous system and revitalize her entire body. After the session, Jane reported that her whole nervous system felt energized in a new way that seemed calmer and smoother. She could feel it through her whole body, and she felt somehow bigger. Jane was experiencing more of her energy field, thus experiencing her body as bigger. She reported, "It feels better than anything." This is the type of expansion and growth that Jupiter is known for.

The shift that she experienced as energy being pulled into her heart instead of her stomach was the heart energy coming in to balance the lower chakra centers. The heart brought healing energy that she could feel, instead of stuffing herself with food. This energy would provide the love and emotional nourishment that Jane needed, the nurturing care that her parents never gave her. After this session, Jane's food cravings lessened dramatically. She continued to feel a smoother, calmer energy even in the midst of chaos.

The blue bottle that Jane first came upon in the cave represented the old patterns from childhood and all the abuse that she had to endure from her parents. Jane eventually had to deal with this element and release the bound-up energy—the anger and other feelings relating to these issues—in order to heal her childhood pain. However, in this session, it was important for her to have her own boundaries and just say no to everything her parents had made her swallow. This brings up a significant point: it was important for Jane to be both listening to her subconscious mind and be interacting with it. The blue bottle showed up as a message from the unconscious. It represented something that needed to be addressed. At the same time, Jane's feelings provided her with further information about what the medicine bottle represented, thus helping her decide how and when she wanted to deal with it.

*[handwritten margin note: heart energy is the love & compassion that will give a chakra & help to heal some aspect of our life.]*

This work is often done in layers. This means that you may end up doing pieces of the work, one step at a time, over a certain period. Be sure to respect your unfolding process as you integrate each part of your work in this way. If you are working with a facilitator, it is also important for that individual to be sensitive to this progressive unlayering. Remember, you don't have to do anything that doesn't feel right to you, whether it is something an internal character tells you or something that comes from an external therapist. Something may not feel right in a dialogue if it is a negative, internalized message—perhaps from Mom or Dad, or some other shadow aspect. If you feel resistance to what you're experiencing, center into your body and notice what the feelings are connected to it. The feelings that emerge may be important for you to consider in your dialogue process. You may also find that you need more support or certain resources in order to feel safe. The resources you established in chapter 3 may then be useful.

To make the Healing Cave process easier for you, I have included the following guided meditation for your internal journey. First, choose a physical issue or somatic experience to work with. Then, read through the exercise fully and familiarize yourself with it so that you can go through each step of the process in a relaxed state. You can also record this meditation on audio tape. Have your journal close at hand, so that you can record any dialogue or other experiences.

## *A Guided Meditation: The Healing Cave*

Take a relaxed comfortable position, allowing your breath to take you deeper inside. Have a sense that with each exhalation you can sink a little deeper inside into your body and into a more internal place within you. Close your eyes and see, sense, or imagine a soft healing light all around you. It may be radiant white or have a particular color such as pink, blue, or gold.

State your intention. This could be to heal, explore a body sensation, or to find out what is creating your physical illness.

When you're ready, imagine yourself walking along a pathway in nature. Take time to notice the place that you've come to in your mind's eye. It may be a forest, garden, beach, or mountain scene. Bring your consciousness as fully as you can to the possible colors, sounds, and smells of nature all around you in this place. Feel the warmth of the sun on your skin. Enjoy the distant sound of birds and the tranquil blue sky. Feel the gentle breeze as it softly touches your cheek.

As you walk along this path, you come to a cave, which represents the body experience or illness which you have chosen. As you enter, be aware of what you experience and what the cave looks like inside. If you need more light to see into the cave, you will find a torch or lantern at the cave entrance. There may also be openings in the cave ceiling at certain points that can let in more light.

Notice how you feel, here, in the cave, and how the quality of this cave may relate to your body sensation or symptom. As you proceed through the cave, you may find certain objects that draw your attention. Notice if anything you find here has meaning for you in some way.

Perhaps there is a person or animal present in the cave, someone who has some information for you. *(Often, archetypal guides or the symbolic presence of a body symptom will show up in the cave.)* You may find that this person or thing has a message for you or has some information that can give you new understandings about your condition. Notice how it feels to be with this figure and what your response is to what is being said or done. You may also have questions for this figure regarding what you're presently experiencing or about your body concern. *(If you desire, this communication can be done as a journal dialogue.)*

Continue to explore the cave. Somewhere in the cave is a symbol of your healing process, a medicine object for your process of healing and transformation. If an archetypal guide or other figure is present, it may have information that can provide you with some insights about the meaning of this medicine object and how you are meant to use it to assist your healing.

When your process feels complete, exit the cave and bring your journey to a close. Take a moment to come back to external awareness and then when you're ready, open your eyes.

Write your experiences in your journal along with any guidance you received with regard to the issue you chose. How do the things you experienced relate to your body concern, and how will you now use these new understandings in your daily life to assist your healing process?

# RECLAIMING FRAGMENTED ENERGY

When you are working with subpersonalities and archetypal energies, you are reclaiming energetically lost and disowned parts of yourself to once again become whole. In the process, as in Karen's case with the snake, the memories and feelings from the original fragmenting experience or core wounding can come flooding forth. Although sometimes difficult, these feelings are the healing pathway to discovering your true spiritual nature.

In Shamanic traditions, this type of fragmentation is believed to come from a loss of soul. The soul, or part of it, leaves the person and lives a parallel existence in another dimension. The soul, then, has to be retrieved by the shaman from places in these other dimensions known as the Upper, Middle, and Lower Worlds.[2] In her book, *Soul Retrieval*, Sandra Ingerman describes her experience of these worlds. The Upper World is often ethereal with bright light and sometimes crystalline structures. The Lower World is reached through a tunnel down into the earth. It has more earthly landscapes such as caves, dense jungles, and oceans. In the Middle World, the shaman can travel back through history to past moments in time where souls may be residing.

I am struck by how these non-ordinary dimensions correspond to the qualities associated with the energy planes. For example, it is through the higher energy planes that we experience the divine spiritual worlds of light. The Lower World relates to the physical earth of our bodies and the first etheric plane. I feel the two are connected, our own energy bodies being a reflection of, as well as doorways to, these non-ordinary dimensions of the shaman's world. The energy planes represent states of consciousness, and are indicative of the different dimensions of our own being to which we must return in order to reclaim these lost parts of ourselves.

Just as shamans see into these other worlds to retrieve lost souls, I often psychically see the lost or disowned parts of individuals present on some level of their energy body system. Sometimes when I see these denied parts of individuals, it is like a freeze frame of a film. Instead of seeing the person as they normally appear, I see them as a particular aspect of themselves. This can involve an essential archetypal quality. For example, I might see a Wise Crone, a Tibetan Sage, an ancient Warrior, or Queen. Other times, I see shadow aspects or subpersonalities such as an arrogant narcissus, Child, or an addictive personality. I have even, at times, received this type of psychic impression from photographs.

According to Shamanic belief, souls can also be psychically stolen by another.[3] I feel that we are only vulnerable to such a thing when we deny ourselves and our own needs in favor of another. In such a case, we give away our power to another and betray ourselves. What commonly happens is that in an unconscious process, parts of ourselves leave and are held in the energy field of another. For example, you may have felt like your heart or soul was stolen away after ending an intimate relationship. This often happens because there is an actual mingling of the two partners' energy fields in the act of lovemaking. There are energetic connections that form between the chakras of two people. When the relationship ends, the ties are still there and some of one person's energy may still reside in the energy field of the other. If things are left incomplete or unresolved in some way, this energy can continue to be held by the other person.

This is especially true if the original emotional attraction involved an unconscious need to reclaim a lost part of yourself that you see reflected in the other person. For example, during a meditation eight years after my divorce, I became aware that I had a part of my ex-husband's soul. He had much of his own feminine soul quality projected on to me during the marriage, and when I left, that part of him went with me. Through an inner dialogue, I was able to return this essence to him. This illustrates that not only can we have parts of ourselves split off, we can also have other people's energies residing in our energy fields.

Some psychics recommend actually cutting and severing the energetic connecting cords that can remain after a relationship ends. However, I have found that this technique is too great of a shock to the energy system and is usually very traumatic for the people involved. It is much more benign and just as effective to gently dissolve the ties with light, after releasing any energy of the other person that you are holding, and calling back all of your own energy from the other individual.

*[handwritten margin note: auric cleaving?]*

Mara was able to use this process after ending a relationship with a man she deeply cared about. She realized that even though the relationship could no longer continue because this man was involved with someone else, he had treated her with respect as a woman and had let her know that she was special. Because of this, she now felt like she deserved that respect from a man and didn't want to lose it. Mara had also given him a lot of love that he couldn't really receive fully because of his fear of intimacy. She now had to go on and bring that love back into her life in other ways. Mara had to let go so that she could make a loving connection with someone else.

After surrounding herself in a protective orb of light, I had Mara send back this man's energy to him with her intention, breath, and words. This released energy was composed of his fear, which had kept them from further intimacy. She then called back from this individual the part of her that knew she was worthy of respect, so that she could internalize it and not have it remain projected outside of herself on to him any longer. Mara continued by visualizing and feeling the energetic ties between them dissolved in a radiant white light. After doing this, Mara did not feel tied to this man any more and was able to move on in her life.

In any type of relationship, people who have poor personal boundaries, without the ego strength to distinguish their own feelings and needs from those of other's, remain vulnerable to this type of energetic contamination. Empathically sensitive individuals, as well, are very susceptible, often acting as psychic sponges for other people's energy.

Children are particularly vulnerable to other people's energy because their auric fields are very open and receptive, without the protective defense barriers of adults. For instance, even in more covert types of sexual abuse where actual physical touching does not take place, the abused child is in the energy field of the perpetrator. The perpetrator's negative energy overwhelms and contaminates the child's own and can continue to be held in the energy bodies long after the abuse has stopped. One of my clients said she experienced the shame of her incest in her body as a poison with tentacles spreading throughout her whole body, reaching down to her very cells. This shows how pervasive and intrusive this contaminating energy can be. Needless to say, the chance of fragmentation is great for sensitive children who are exposed to enmeshed family dynamics or for any child exposed to abuse. Dialogue and emotional clearing, followed by cleansing the body and energy system with healing light, can help release this type of toxic energy from the body-mind system.

I have found that what a shaman calls soul loss actually takes four main forms related to the chakras and aspects of our own being. This type of wounding can involve loss of spirit, heart, will, or physical vitality. The precipitating trauma and fragmentation can involve any one or several of these parts of us. The resulting effects are similar to dysfunction in the corresponding chakra centers.

With a loss of spirit essence, you lose a sense of who you are to some degree. You may not have a sense of your spiritual nature and may feel disconnected from a Divine Source or higher consciousness. You may feel your life lacks meaning or any type of higher purpose. Loss of heart can result in a lack of feeling, compassion, or understanding for yourself or others. You may tend to be unloving toward yourself, lack intimacy with others, or feel like there is a big needy hole in you that can't be filled.

Loss of will can leave you passive with a lack of personal power or without a sense of your personal needs and wants. There may be a tendency to abdicate your own power and will to others. You may be cut off from your instincts or discount the gut-level feelings that you do have through denial. Depression can result and the desire to live can be affected.

Loss of physical vitality can happen through surgeries, accidents, stress, or chronic illness and the immune system is often affected. In the process of surgery, a part of the physical body is often actually lost as an organ or substance is cut out and removed. No matter how necessary the surgery is, a part of the physical body is diminished and lost. The physical vitality is also greatly affected by loss of spirit, heart, and will. With all these types of loss, you can experience a lack of energy or feel dissociated, like a part of you is somewhere else.

It's important to listen and respond to all the parts of your being—spirit, heart, will, and body. Communication between all of these aspects is essential and the dialogue process can be used to assist you with this. My session with Chris, which was discussed in the last chapter (page 187), is an example of this. These different parts of you may each have their own concerns, suggestions, and opinions. By listening to these different points of view with consciousness, you can discover new options and problems can be resolved. This, then, helps you develop a more unified state of consciousness. As part of this process, deeper emotional clearing concerning certain issues may need to take place.

The following session, again with Jane, illustrates how body-centered processes can be used in healing the loss of spirit, heart, will, or body. At the time of this session, Jane was beginning to realize that the core of her anger related to the emotional and physical abuse by her parents. She was ready to face the things symbolized by the blue medicine bottle in her Healing Cave process. Jane came into the session talking about how familiar, and almost comfortable, the feelings of unhappiness and anger had become in her life. It was all she had known for so long. I had her close her eyes, relax, and center inside by allowing her breath to take her deeper into her body self. The session continued with the following dialogue.

Jane:     I feel this swirling, spinning energy all around me.

Pam:     Does this swirling energy have a color?

Jane:     Yes. It's red and yellow. It's a very agitated feeling.

| | |
|---|---|
| Pam: | Just notice where in your body you feel this agitated energy. |
| Jane: | In my midsection, from my shoulders down to my hips. |
| Pam: | What words or sounds might this red/yellow energy in your midsection like to make? |
| Jane: | Get out of here. Get out. |
| Pam: | Who do you want to get out, Jane? |
| Jane: | My father. |
| Pam: | Do you have a sense of your father here with you now? |
| Jane: | Yes. |
| Pam: | Tell him how you feel. |
| Jane: | Get out and leave me alone. Get your energy out of me. I can't carry it anymore. (*Jane starts crying, deeply.*) You hurt me so much, all that you did. I gave and gave, and it was never enough. I feel like I've had my heart ripped out. There's a deep hole there, all bloody where my heart should be. |
| Pam: | Tell him the things he's done. |
| Jane: | All of it. (*Jane starts crying again. I sense that this is all she can say about the past for now.*) |
| Pam: | Yes, you needed him and he hurt and abused you. You lost your heart. Are you ready to bring your heart energy back into yourself now? |
| Jane: | Yes. |
| Pam: | Tell your father. |

| | |
|---|---|
| Jane: | You can't have my heart anymore. It won't do you any good, and I need it now. You have to be responsible for your own heart . . . It's like I handed him a silver platter with all of myself on it . . . How could you do that? How could you expect me to do that? How could you take my heart? |
| Pam: | What's your father's response? |
| Jane: | He doesn't have one. He just looks sorry for himself. |
| Pam: | Call back your heart energy that you gave away to your father. Breathe it back into the heart area of your body. Welcome your heart back. Receive it in. I'll help you as you do this. (*I put my hand above her body, over the area of her heart chakra. At one point, there was a vibrating surge of energy that shook my whole arm. I sensed her heart energy had returned to her at this point and this was confirmed by my Higher Self. I then checked it out with Jane.*) |
| Pam: | Jane, what's happening now? |
| Jane: | I feel like I've never been in my body before and now I am, like I was somehow turned inside out and now I'm right side in again. It feels so new and different. (*Jane starts to cry and then crosses her hands over her heart area.*) I have to protect it now. |
| Pam: | I wonder if you would like to provide something like a sanctuary to hold and protect this new heart energy. |
| Jane: | Yes. It's like a golden globe of light around my heart. |
| Pam: | The globe protects it, and yet the heart energy can still shine through. Now just the right amount of |

|       |                                                                                                                                                                                                                                 |
|-------|---------------------------------------------------------------------------------------------------------------------------------------------------------------------------------------------------------------------------------|
|       | this heart energy can permeate the rest of your body, just the right amount for you at this time.                                                                                                                                 |
| Jane: | I'm aware of my body being out of synch somehow, like disjointed pieces. I just want to feel it a while . . . I have more of me I need to get back, other parts, when I'm ready.                                                   |
| Pam:  | Yes, parts of yourself that have been fragmented. I'd like you, Jane, to notice if there are any places in your body where your father's energy still seems to reside.                                                             |
| Jane: | Yes, in my abdomen, fingertips, and my left foot.                                                                                                                                                                                |
| Pam:  | Just have a sense of sending this energy back now, noticing if it has any particular quality or form to it.                                                                                                                       |
| Jane: | It's heavy, like lead.                                                                                                                                                                                                           |
| Pam:  | Tell your father how it's going to be now as this energy goes back.                                                                                                                                                              |
| Jane: | I need respect, for you to tell the truth and to stop criticizing me or I won't be with you.                                                                                                                                      |
| Pam:  | So, in order to have a relationship with you, he's going to have to respect you and who you are, to be honest, and to stop criticizing you.                                                                                        |
| Jane: | Yes. Dad, I can't take care of you anymore. I need my energy for my own healing. I want to get me back, all of me back as I'm ready.                                                                                              |
| Pam:  | Jane, allow your whole body, especially those places where you may have been feeling your father's energy, to be filled with a soft healing light . . . just noticing now if that disjointed feeling in your body has changed in any way. |

Jane:      Yes. It's aligned now . . . It's time for my father to go now . . . He's leaving. I want to return another time to get the rest of me, all of myself back.

Pam:       Yes, you can continue to experience your heart energy and reclaim all the lost parts of yourself.

This session gives more information on how Jane's archetypal energies, relating to the planetary configurations at birth, were all working together in her soul's evolution. Jane's critical Father (Saturn) overshadowed her Venus compassion, keeping her from the authority and wisdom (Saturn) of her own heart (Venus) and from having the courage (Mars) to respond from the Teacher (Jupiter) within her. She could now reclaim that courage, wisdom, and love of her essence Self.

As sometimes happens in this type of heart healing, childhood memories of pain emerged. Prior to this, Jane had difficulty connecting emotionally with the Child within her. However, that changed after this session. Getting her heart back created a shift that opened the door to Jane's Child of Light and the essential Self that it represents.

In the week following this session, Jane reported that she had more of a sense of herself as an individual, in her own energy, and not as easily influenced by the energy of others. As was discussed earlier, this type of individuation experience is an attribute of the heart chakra. The heart energy brought Jane back a sense of self that provided a foundational strength to deal with more emotionally overwhelming issues. In Jane's case, this heart healing had to take place before any deeper emotional clearing could be done concerning childhood issues.

When the heart energy started permeating the rest of her body, Jane started feeling her body like disjointed pieces. As the higher vibration of this energy moved through her body, it started pushing out any energy that wasn't aligned with it. The places in her body that held the energy of her father's abuse were experienced as out of alignment. As this held energy was released, the disjointed feeling disappeared. To fully clear all of this somatically held energy, Jane did further work concerning specific traumatic childhood events.

It is best if this particular type of work is done by a trained healer because of the intense feelings that often surface. The chakra meditation at the end of chapter 1 can also be used to facilitate the healing of such issues. After completing this chapter, you may now be able to return to the chakra meditation with a new awareness of what specific parts of yourself you need to call back, leading to enhanced results with the process.

## Notes

1. Robert Johnson, *Inner Work: Using Dreams and Active Imagination For Personal Growth* (San Francisco: Harper San Francisco, 1986).

2. Sandra Ingerman, *Soul Retrieval: Mending the Fragmented Self* (San Francisco: Harper San Francisco, 1991).

3. Ibid.

# 7

# DREAMS

*Bridge to the Soul*

DREAMS ARE AN INVALUABLE SOURCE OF guidance and wisdom that can help you connect with deeper subconscious feelings. This is because dreams act as a bridge between the conscious mind and subconscious elements of the psyche, revealing what your rational thinking mind is not yet able to acknowledge. Since dreams often mirror the symbolic messages that we receive from the body, working consciously with your dreams will also enhance any somatic awareness work that you do, opening yet another doorway to your feeling self and your true spiritual nature.

Dreams speak to us in the language of symbols. A symbol is an object, image, physical phenomenon, or event representative of something else. It operates as an outwardly visible sign of an inner unseen reality and conveys a certain message to our conscious mind from deeper subconscious levels. The symbol thus acts as a catalyst that brings about a response or realization. Whether symbols appear as dream content, synchronistic events, or as meaningful images in our lives, they are powerful carriers of psychic energy that can impact us at a soul level.

Everyone has probably experienced being touched by an image that seemed to have an emotional or spiritual impact on them. When we resonate with a symbolic image, it activates a core element within us and illuminates our consciousness while a deeper realization of its essential meaning unfolds for us. This dynamic is seen in the symbolic forms and images that are used as part of religious ceremony. Such symbols awaken deeper levels of our consciousness because they activate the subconscious memories carried on our soul. As we experience a symbolic image, deep feelings and soul memories are aroused. The soul recognizes the symbol and can transmit its energy and truth to the conscious mind. This is like selecting an on-screen computer software application icon (the recognized symbol), which brings up a program from the hard drive (subconscious soul level), and starts running the program so that we can use it (conscious awareness).

The symbol also focuses our conscious mind so that we stop, listen, and experience the message that our essence Self is seeking to communicate. Dreams and other symbolic phenomena can thus be a powerful form of guidance and connection with Spirit as they motivate us in our process of growth and spiritual unfoldment.

One day, I had a wonderfully symbolic event happen that was very significant for me. I was walking on a hill near my home, when suddenly a hawk flew by with a snake in its mouth right in front of me at eye level. The moment it flew by there was a booming clap of thunder. I stood motionless as all my senses reeled and my conscious mind attempted to absorb the experience. When I continued walking, I looked down and saw a snakeskin on the ground. These events were made all the more incredible by the fact that the area was not a remote wilderness area by any means. It was just a normal suburban neighborhood.

In Yogic philosophy, the ultimate transformation of matter into spirit, which relates to the seventh chakra, is symbolized by a snake (the kundalini, sexuality, and the body), being carried off by an eagle. I knew that this was a powerful message of transformation for me. In fact, it happened just prior to a very ecstatic kundalini experience and during a relationship in which I was able to unite the sexual and spiritual energies for myself for the first time. During this period, a whole way of being, an old layer of defensive protection, was falling away just like the skin that I saw which was shed by the snake. This synchronistic event, complete with a Cecil B. De Mille-type thunderclap, certainly got my attention. It also enabled me to be more conscious of the transformation that I was experiencing. To assist myself with this, I took the snakeskin home and placed it on my altar, so I could continue to be attentive to my process of letting go.

## DREAM CATEGORIES

I find it useful to look at dreams in terms of several different categories, although many dreams will have significant meaning on more than one level. Most dreams are reflections of unresolved material from one's personal subconscious mind; if you have frustrations going on at your job, you may have a dream in which you angrily strangle your boss. Such dreams often involve repressed feelings or shadow elements, and the dream allows you to channel feelings that might be inappropriate in your external world. However, the dream also informs you of feelings that you may not have been consciously aware of so that you can take steps to resolve the inner conflict. A female client of mine once had a dream that I was late for her appointment, was distracted, and very rude to her during our time together. While working with the dream during her therapy session, she discovered that the dream related to her mother's detached unavailability and the fear of intimacy that she had as a result of this emotional abandonment. Prior to this session, the dream had dominated her consciousness. It had really bothered her because she felt that she had a good therapeutic relationship with me. However, it is because the dream had this kind of effect that the repressed subconscious feelings of abandonment could be recognized and healed.

Other dreams involve larger, collective issues containing psychic material from the collective unconscious, the vast recorded storehouse of information from all humanity. Thus, this type of dream is often about archetypal issues that affect humanity as a whole. For example, people sometimes access events that have taken place on the planet in the past, or dream of the Earth being affected by some natural disaster that dramatically changes the world as we now know it.

Collective-level dreams can also be those that contain ancient archetypal images that are not a part of our everyday culture. For instance, my client Mara dreamed of a large snake-like worm that was just beneath the surface of her skin. The worm was curled in a circle and eating its tail, much like the symbolic ouroborus. The ouroborus serpent eating its tail, often depicted encircling the Earth, is an ancient religious symbol found in the mythology of many cultures. It signifies, among other things, the totality of the universe and the oneness of all creation. Mara had no conscious knowledge of this symbol and its meaning, yet it appeared in her dream and was significant of her process of individuation. Just as the worm was surfacing from beneath her skin, Mara was emerging as a psychologically separate human being out of the enmeshed collective oneness that she had known. At this time, there were unresolved emotional issues surfacing for Mara that were a part of this process. She was also acknowledging her feelings and accepting her physical self for the first time in her life. This was reflected in the fact that, in the dream, the worm was actually embedded in her body beneath the skin.

Even though collective dreams deal with elements beyond the purely personal realm, it is important to derive personal meaning from them and apply the learnings to your own life. It would have been of little use to Mara to become inflated with the larger significance of her dream—the mystical oneness of all creation—and not directly apply it to her own process of personal growth.

Many dreams are what I call sacred dreams or Higher Self dreams. These are dreams containing direct guidance of an expansive or spiritual nature. You will recognize a sacred dream because it has a very significant impact on you at a very deep level. These dreams feel powerful and transformative even when you have no idea what they mean. Such dreams often come when you are at a transition point in your life and need direction, although you may sometimes be unaware of this fact until you have the dream.

I had this type of dream at a time in my life when I was part of a spiritual group centered around an emotionally unbalanced teacher. I needed to leave the group—I was getting increasingly unhealthy due to the teacher's dysfunction and my own dependence on her. I had a dream that the group was meeting in an outdoor camp setting. As I walked along the road, I was guided away from the place where the group was sitting and was told that I needed to leave the group and take another path. As I stood at the fork in the road and looked down at the ground, I saw that in one direction the path was covered with sparkling gold flecks. I had a feeling that this was the way I was supposed to go. I asked someone passing by if they knew what was down that road but the person couldn't tell me anything.

Although, I didn't immediately respond to what the dream was instructing me to do, it did provide me with confirmation when I did finally sever my ties with the organization. It also reflected my feelings of uncertainty, having to take a path— even a golden one—into the unknown. There were many times when I referred back to this dream to strengthen my faith and remind myself to trust in the spiritual force that was guiding me. Sacred dreams can definitely provide this kind of reassurance and encouragement to strengthen your connection with Spirit during difficult times.

One's Higher Self often takes the form of an archetypal figure in a sacred dream. The archetypal soul essence that you were guided in meeting with in chapter 2 could easily show up in some way in your dreamworld as well. A client, Susan, had a dream about a Native American man and woman. In the dream, the man spoke to Susan about the "Great Mystery" of creation. He then instructed the other Native American woman to dance and sing, saying, "There is something in this movement which brings spiritual vitality." A wolf, bear, and mountain lion also appeared in the dream. These medicine animals were all very meaningful to Susan and represented aspects of her spiritual nature. The archetypal Native American guide was instructing Susan to not only bring more joy into her life, but also more physical movement, exercise, and play, things she had been neglecting at the time. This physical component provided her with the necessary balance for further spiritual expansion and growth.

This guidance from the Higher Self can also take the form of people you actually know, especially individuals that have a spiritual significance to you. I once had a dream in which a former spiritual teacher of mine came and told me that I needed a specific homeopathic remedy. I didn't tell my homeopathic doctor about the dream until after he ended up prescribing the exact remedy my teacher had mentioned in the dream!

Occasionally, dreams are not what I would call dreams at all, but rather communication on subtle astral levels. Perhaps, you have had a talk with someone during dreamtime that seemed very real, as if you were actually with them. This was probably an astral-level communication. It was real, it was just happening on an energetic plane other than the physical. People often describe such an experience after a loved one has died. The communication allows them to express their grief and to resolve any other issues as part of saying goodbye. In such a communication, the deceased can also assure the person that they are peaceful and happy.

Since dreams contain elements from the subconscious mind, repressed memories will often surface in this way. In our daytime world, the conscious mind often works to keep memories and other fears at bay. However, at night, the unconscious rules and these feelings and memories can surface. In working with individuals with a history of sexual abuse, I found that they often relive aspects of the abuse in their dreams. This might involve such things as seeing a shadowy figure at the foot of their bed, a dream scene from the room where the abuse took place, or feeling a suffocating weight on them during the dream. This type of dream can be a terrifying experience and is similar to the dreams of other individuals with Post-traumatic Stress Disorder who continue to relive painful life events in this way until the issue is healed.

In these instances, dreams can be taken quite literally. These are actual events that have already happened and are either being denied or are still unresolved. Thus, the subconscious mind continues to replay them. A word of warning here: if you have an incestuous dream, it does not necessarily mean that you have a history of sexual abuse. This type of dream can be symbolic of other things. The feeling quality of the dream will help you determine its true meaning. If you have this type of dream and it brings forth a sense of fear, shame, or other uncomfortable feelings, then please seek some assistance from a professional therapist in determining what the meaning of the dream may be for you.

Caution should always be exercised in taking dreams literally since they speak to us in the often illogical symbolic language of the subconscious mind. Just because you have a dream in which you have an affair, it doesn't mean that you should go right out and do it because your dream told you to. It is true our dreams can guide and instruct us. However, one of the ways they do this is by revealing the often distorted contents of our personal subconscious mind. What happens in the dream world is not always appropriate in the external world. It is better to explore the meaning of our dreams in an inner way than it is to unconsciously act them out in the external world.

Another concern people have in regard to sexual dream content involves the expression of intimacy with someone of the same gender if they're heterosexual, or of the opposite gender if they are gay or lesbian. If you have a dream of this nature, it doesn't necessarily mean that you have repressed sexual feelings. Many times, this type of dream speaks to seeking union with an inner masculine or feminine aspect of your own being. In any case, don't make any rash interpretations about your sexual dreams. The true significance of any dream is often quite different from what the conscious mind thinks it is. This is why mentally analyzing a dream does not necessarily reveal its full meaning.

The final type of dream I have worked with is one that is psychically precognizant—a dream revealing a possible future event. Many people who don't necessarily consider themselves psychic have precognizant dreams. One such case involves a woman who, over a period of several years, had a reoccurring dream about being in a plane crash. Finally, one day she actually was involved in a plane disaster during a flight to Hawaii. She attributed her survival to the fact that she insisted on having an aisle seat just like the one she had in all of her dreams.

People often find precognizant dreams unnerving because they aren't sure if the information is meant to be taken literally or symbolically. Even if individuals have a strong feeling that the dream is true, they don't always know what to do with the information they have received. I once had a very powerful and upsetting dream about a big nuclear explosion. It felt as though it had a greater impact than a personal dream, and I remember wondering if something like a volcanic eruption was going to happen somewhere, since the chances of a nuclear bomb going off seemed slim. Several days later, the nuclear disaster at Chernobyl occurred. It is one of those times that I wish I had further explored the dream to more fully understand its meaning for me. I don't know if it would have made any difference, but I did feel an awesome responsibility in channeling this type of information. This precognizant dream also had personal meaning for me relating to the chaotic upheaval in my life at the time, and obviously had collective-level significance as well since it involved an event that affected the world.

I'm often asked if some dreams are just nighttime mind chatter and not significant of anything. I think it's quite possible that, for example, upsetting movies or television programs can show up as nightmares. These dreams may simply be the subconscious mind's way of throwing off the garbage it has had to ingest. Remember, only the conscious mind rests at night. The subconscious elements of the psyche are still active and processing the events of the day. However, this doesn't mean that you should ignore certain dreams and simply label them as video backlash. Every dream contains useful information and can be used as a doorway to transformation.

A note about nightmares. The language of the subconscious mind is often violent and disturbing. Sometimes such violent dreams are meant to affect us in a way that gets our attention. By conveying information in this powerful way, the subconscious mind can get its message across. This type of dream indicates that highly charged psychic information is being conveyed regarding a particular issue. It means that the issue that the adversarial or violent dream energy represents may need to be confronted in order to be resolved. I have also found that when individuals initially enter drug and alcohol recovery, they will often have intense dreams and nightmares. This happens because addictions can have the effect of anesthetizing the psyche, repressing feelings and often dreams as well. During the recovery process, these elements from the subconscious can come forth with great intensity, like a wild animal that has previously been caged.

# HOW TO WORK
# WITH YOUR DREAMS

You may be wondering how you can know what your dreams mean if you don't know how to interpret the symbols in them. Well, the fact is, you don't have to intellectually interpret the symbols. All you have to do is feel them.

In his book, *The Jungian-Senoi Dreamwork Manual*, Strephon Kaplan Williams talks about a term I'd like to borrow here. Instead of encouraging dream interpretation, he talks about dream actualization. This means that rather than mentally analyzing the dream, you re-experience the dream in a way that naturally reveals its meaning on a feeling level. In this way, you can receive the guidance it has for you and manifest the fullest potential of the dream for your own development. The methods given here—Dream Symbol Meditation, Dream Symbol Dialogue, and Dream Repatterning—all involve this type of feeling-level process and can be used with dream imagery as well as synchronistic events. This is not to say that using various forms of symbolic and mythic interpretation is not useful. In fact, referencing such material is often very helpful in amplifying and enhancing the dream experience. However, it should never be used as an intellectual substitute for the direct experience of the dream itself.

In working with a dream, it is important to connect with the inner dynamics of its content and to recognize how the specific elements demonstrated in the dream are currently functioning in your life. One way to do this is by noticing whether the feelings or issues in the dream are a familiar theme in your life or remind you of one that is. It is also useful to identify a dream symbol or a part of the dream with an aspect of yourself. To assist with this, ask yourself if there is a part of yourself that at any time feels or behaves as your dream character does. Compared to the exaggerated actions taking place in the larger-than-life dreamworld, these similarities may sometimes seem quite subtle. Perhaps a negative dream figure relates to a critical aspect in yourself, a helpless character represents a more vulnerable part of you, or a healing quality in the dream is an aspect of your Higher Self. It is also possible that the dream figure represents a part of you that you deny or behaviors and feelings that you tend to avoid.

In addition to these internal dynamics, dream figures can represent other people in your external world. However, such external relationships with others often act as a mirror reflecting your own denied aspects, both positive and negative. Be careful of dream interpretations that judge or blame others without addressing any personal inner dynamics of your own.

In keeping a dream journal, be aware of recurring themes, symbols, or settings in your dreams. Relate any connections between these themes, outer events in your life, and inner feelings. Notice if these patterns seem to shift and change at certain points. For example, you may have an inner feeling of needing changes in your life. You have several dreams that you have moved into a new house, but each time it is a horrible situation, much worse than your former living space. This might indicate a fear of these needed changes. If you later had a dream in which you moved into a lovely house that was really pleasing and comfortable, it might indicate that an inner shift had taken place with regard to this issue, or that at least you were being encouraged to open yourself to a different experience.

Since a central part of healing and spiritual growth involves reclaiming the creative Child of Light within us, the child symbol is a common reoccurring theme in dreams. For example, a dream may initially contain the image of an uncared-for, weak, abandoned child or a child in danger. Later, as more emotional healing takes place, the child symbol may reappear in a healthier, happier form. Likewise, those with a history of sexual abuse often experience dreams of being chased, threatened, or victimized by an overpowering pursuer such as a shadowy figure, giant, or gunman. As these individuals progress through their recovery process, these dream images change to empowered ones in which they confront the menacing force or seek aid in defeating it. Being conscious of patterns of this type can help you track your process and make you aware of the encouraging support that is coming to you through your dreams.

The way you appear in your own dream can be important. If you are lost, running away, or taken over by other forces, it can indicate a similar dynamic operating in your life. For example, it may represent an overwhelming issue that you're confused about or afraid to confront. Sometimes you may notice that you appear as more of an objective observer in a dream. You can see, feel, and observe what is happening with an unattached presence without being overwhelmed by the unconscious elements of the dream. This often means that, at least with this particular issue, you have the ability to observe your personal process without being submerged in subconscious elements. It often indicates a strong positive ego relationship to the particular issue involved. This omniscient observer role in a dream can thus represent the ability to be an objective observer in your life; that is, being able to consciously see, in an objective way, the different polarities and roles you're involved in without being overidentified with any of them.

Sometimes you will also notice a sequential movement in a dream that forms a beginning, middle, and conclusion. These dream sequences often move from more superficial aspects of the dream to a deeper level of material that may be more sensitive or meaningful. Working with these dreams can be much like peeling an onion as you uncover deeper layers of the dream and the deeper levels of meaning within it. Remain open and receptive to further insights regarding the meaning of any of your dreams. A truly significant dream can continue to be worked with over a period of time with information emerging even years later.

## Remembering Your Dreams

If you would like to begin to work with your dreams, but have difficulty remembering them, here are some things that you can do to achieve greater recall.

1. Before going to bed at night, verbally declare your intention to have a dream and also have total memory of it when you awake. Do this every night. This will plant a seed in your subconscious mind so that it can manifest. If you desire, you can also ask your Higher Self to provide some insight about a particular issue through a dream.

2. Keep your journal, a pen, and lamp or penlight by your bed. If you wake up from a dream in the middle of the night, record it in your journal immediately, while your memory is fresh, rather than risk waiting until the morning. Some people find it easier to keep a tape recorder by

the bed that they can simply turn on and speak into, in order to record their dreams at night.

3. Record your dream experience first thing in the morning when you wake up. The information will be more available to your consciousness at that time and unclouded by the activities and thoughts of your day. However, you may also find that further information regarding your dream comes to you sometime during the day when you are not thinking about it. Record your dreams every morning, even if all you remember is a feeling, an image, or the fragmented pieces of a dream. If you don't remember anything, then write down your first impressions or feelings upon waking. As you do this and establish a pattern, it will prime the pump of your subconscious mind and allow you to consciously remember your dreams. Also, by acknowledging any information that the Higher Self and your own subconscious mind has for you in this way, it demonstrates your receptivity and desire to know more. This intention opens a pathway for further information and assistance to come to you through the dreamstate.

## Discovering Your Dream's Meaning

To discover the meaning of your dream, work with the following techniques.

1. First, get a sense of the overall feeling in the dream. Are you or the dream figures sad, confused, angry, frustrated, anxious, happy, empowered, or scared?

2. To make it easier for you to work with your dream, break it down into its component parts. Make a list of the dream scene(s), symbols, and characters. First write down the dream scene or surroundings. Your dream, for instance, may take place on a desert, in a house, or on a crowded

city street. Then, list the dream characters in your dream, which would include you and any other persons or figures in the dream. Also, include their relationship to one another. Some dream figures may be adversaries or confrontational, while others operate as a supportive ally or guide. Two opposing dream figures often indicate polarized forces at war within your psyche regarding a particular issue. Next, list the significant dream symbols. This would be any other objects in your dream.

3. After identifying the scene, characters, and symbols, note the primary action in the dream and what issue is being confronted, avoided, or left unresolved. Sometimes, rather than action or confrontation in the dream, there is something that is being noticeably avoided. This could be important information regarding some issue in your life that is not being addressed. Also identify any wounding—emotional or physical—that happens as part of the dream action.

4. Finally, list any healing factor present in the dream or any guidance that is given. If you should become anxious or uncomfortable at any time when working with negative dream issues, remember to access these healing elements from the dream as a positive internal resource.

Organizing your dream in this way will make it easier for you to understand and work with. To illustrate, let's take the following dream of a fifty-year-old woman and break it down into its component parts. In the dream, the woman is walking through a maze of big white rooms to a group of upstairs bedrooms. In the first bedroom is her eldest son. The bed is neatly made but there are no windows. In another cavernous room is one of her daughters. There is a small table in this room and a window beside the bed looking out on beautiful lush greenery. In a third room, her other daughter is on the floor. This room feels very messy, is cheaply done, and the window looks out on a busy street with people going to work.

In the next dream scene, the woman is standing before a large, dark garage door. People are waiting for the door to open. There is also the dark figure of a maintenance man and a black woman at the door who thinks the dreamer is an intruder and won't open the door. The maintenance man says, "I can remember when there was a security system here." A sick-looking black dog and a golden retriever then show up, and there are also beetles there, which have a hard outer shell. Suddenly, the dreamer's ex-husband appears as an exterminator, but she doesn't want him to spray the insect poison. However, he ends up painting the lenses of her eyeglasses pink.

**Feelings:** Frustration over daughter's messy room, lack of control over garage door and exterminator.

**Dream Scenes:** Maze of white rooms, bedrooms of the three children, garage door area.

**Dream Figures:** The dreamer, son, daughters one and two, maintenance man, black woman, ex-husband/exterminator, black dog, and golden retriever.

**Other Symbols:** Two windows with views, black garage door, beetles, eyeglasses, pink paint.

**Action or Conflict:** Journey through the house, conflict with black woman over opening the garage door, and conflict with the exterminator regarding spraying.

**Healing Factor:** Lush green beauty out of first daughter's bedroom window feels pleasant; golden retriever's energy feels comforting.

Dreams are sometimes short and to the point, but often, as this dream shows, they are drawn out much like a three-act play. This can often seem quite overwhelming if you are just beginning to do dreamwork. If this is the case, work with just one symbol or segment of the dream. In deciding what specific part to work with, choose a section of the dream that evokes feelings and makes an emotional impact on you in some way, or pick a dream symbol that you are curious about.

## Dream Symbol Meditation

One very simple but effective way to work with a dream symbol on your own is to meditate on it as you would if you were using an object or mantra. Allow yourself to enter a relaxed meditative state and bring the symbolic object clearly into focus. Notice its qualities and characteristics, its color, shape, and form. Let your mind be still, yet receptive to the impressions from the symbol. Be aware of your feeling connection to the symbol, especially your feelings related to it from the dream. Many people confuse the feelings they experience in a dream with the thoughts they have about the dream after it is over. Although both may be significant, they are really two different things. I find that the actual feelings from the dreamstate itself contain the psychic energy that ultimately reveal the dream's meaning. What you feel within the dream may be more important than what you consciously think or feel later about the dream content in the waking state.

As you meditate on the symbol, you may see it change in some way. This may represent how its energy is meant to transform or evolve and can represent an inner aspect in yourself that is seeking transformation. For example, during a meditation process, the garage door in the previous dream might begin to open, representing an inner openness that needs to take place. Let yourself flow with the feelings, images, and sensations that emerge for you as you meditate on the symbol. You can learn more about the purpose of the symbol and your relationship to it through this type of process.

The woman who had the dream mentioned above chose to do the meditation process with the symbolic image of the two dogs. She discovered that the golden retriever felt warm, loving, and was a protective element within her. The sick black dog was the part of her that feared the unknown and was scared of the changes that she needed to make in her life. This fear had caused her to have a hard shell of protection like the beetles and the black garage door. She then realized that protection didn't need to be like that. It could be soft and loving like the golden retriever. This type of loving protection could be used as a positive resource to protect her more vulnerable aspects.

## Dream Symbol Dialogue

To gain more insight and clarity about specific dream figures and symbols, you can use the dialogue process. A dialogue with symbols and dream figures can be a very natural extension to dream symbol meditation. In fact, this type of relaxed, inwardly focused state is excellent for dialogue because it quiets the conscious thinking mind so that feelings and the subconscious elements of the psyche can emerge. Unlike symbol meditation, however, which is a purely a receptive process, Dream Symbol Dialogue involves an interaction between your conscious mind and subconscious elements of your psyche as you communicate with the symbol. You express your feelings and then focus your consciousness on the symbol in a meditatively relaxed state to receive its information. An active state of contemplation is involved, much like you might experience in a guided visualization process. As with the Embodiment Dialogue process, it may help you to have a sense of shifting your consciousness over to speak as the dream symbol or figure. Once again, dialogue is like a type of roleplay where you become the symbol as you speak, yet keep your consciously aware ego as an objective observer or witness to the process. As you do this, be aware of what the quality of the symbol is and how it feels in your body to be the dream symbol.

When working independently with the dialogue process and your dreams, record both parts of the communication in your journal as you go along. As before, because dialogue is more effective if done in a relaxed meditative state, it may be helpful before beginning to center yourself by taking a few relaxing breaths. Also remember to make sure that you have some quiet time to yourself in order to complete the dialogue without interruptions. If your environment feels safe and secure in this way, it will be easier for you to go deeper into your process.

To gain information, here are some questions that you may want to ask while dialoguing with dream symbols or figures.

- Who or what are you?

- What is your purpose here? (If the response to this question seems extremely negative ask, "Is there a higher purpose or positive intent to your presence in this dream?")

- What is the purpose of (a specific action, conflict, or wounding)?

- What do you want of me?

- What is your guidance, meaning, or dream message for me?

Allow yourself to be spontaneous and ask what you want to know. Then shift your consciousness and let yourself feel the qualities and characteristics of the symbol. In this way, find out what the symbol is about and how it feels. Remember, in addition to words, you may receive information in the form of images, feelings, or body sensations. After you record the answer that you receive from the symbol regarding your initial questioning, you can then respond to what is said and continue until the journal dialogue feels complete.

The information revealed in a dream dialogue often requires self-evaluation and change when a very clear and direct message is given that needs to be paid attention to for continued emotional health and spiritual well-being. However, it is very important to stay connected with your feelings during this process. How does the symbol's information feel? Does it bring forth any responses or sensations in your body? Do you feel peaceful, angry, or feel a knot in your stomach? Are you uncomfortable with what is being said or disagree with it entirely? It is important to express these feelings in the dialogue, such responses are a necessary part of the process.

As you stay present with your own experience, notice if the contents of the dialogue or your emerging feelings remind you of any dynamics in your own life. Is it familiar to you in any way? These feelings can connect you with the deeper subconscious elements that are seeking healing and will help you to more effectively integrate the positive intent of the dream into your life.

To illustrate Dream Symbol Dialogue, let's continue working with the dream of the fifty-year-old woman. Here is an excerpt from the dream dialogue that she did with the pink spray-painted glasses.

Woman:    Who or what are you?

Woman:    *(Speaking as glasses)* I am the part of you that is always seeing things in an unreal way. No more rose-colored glasses!

Woman:    What do mean?

Glasses:   You take care of other people but not yourself.

Woman:    What do you want of me, then?

Glasses:    Protect the Child part of you by being soft and warm, more gentle towards yourself, let this gentleness in.

Woman:    Yes, like the golden retriever.

Through this dialogue, the women realized that she was often dealing with life situations in an unreal, childlike way. Consequently, she would get hurt and then put up a hard shell of defensiveness. The dream symbol was telling her to deal with these external situations in a practical and realistic way, yet be soft and gentle in dealing with herself. This short working on this one dream symbol contains much of the essential message of the entire dream. In the dream, the rooms of the three children all represent a different aspect of the dreamer. The son's room, which had no window and was neat with everything in its place, symbolizes a more rational, austere, and perfectionistic part of her that lacks self-love and joy. The first daughter's room represents a more feminine quality as symbolized by the cavernous space and pleasurable lush nature scene out the window. The second daughter's messy room symbolizes the shadowy chaos of the dreamer's subconscious mind, filled with the confusion, fear, and pain that were creating codependent behaviors. This particular daughter, although loving, was also very needy, often negative, and always in crisis. Her mother would get sucked in to trying to take care of this daughter's problems without expressing her own needs and feelings.

The second part of the dream continued with symbols that represent this woman's system of psychological controls (the security system) that were creating a need to hide her true needs and feelings behind a hard shell of protection. These defense mechanisms and inner controls were based on old feelings of abandonment. However, the old behaviors were now having a toxic effect (the poison) and making her sick, like the black dog.

She now needed to have healthier boundaries while being more loving toward herself, as the pink glasses suggested.

If you have difficulty with a symbol dialogue and don't feel like you receive any information, feel free to move your body to imitate the symbol's form and movement. This will amplify the experience and make it easier to connect with the energy of the dream symbol or character. It can sometimes be fun to actually get up and act out the dream scene in a type of personal psychodrama. The following dialogue, taken from a client session, is an example of how powerful and effective this can be.

My client Karen had a dream about a man in luminous, shell-like armor who had a sword in his right hand and ghostlike mist where his face should be. She began the dialogue as herself and then switched over to play the role of the dream figure by taking on the exact body stance and manner of this armored man.

Karen:     Who are you?

Karen:     *(as dream figure)* I am a fighter who has been protecting you and yet I can't show myself to you because you hate me.

Karen:     I want to see you . . . *(A real sadness and frustration come forth in Karen at this point.)* . . . I want you to be there to love me. *(Karen starts to cry.)*

Pam:       Who do you want to be there, Karen?

Karen:     My dad.

Pam:       Tell him.

Karen:     *(to her dad)* I need you. I needed you as a child and you were never there . . . My dad is just a floating head in the air.

Pam:       How does this feel to you?

Karen:    The feeling is disconnected, ungrounded, like my dad can't pull together all the pieces of himself. I feel I've been the same way, detached and unconnected with my body and feelings. I've been so scattered and unable to accomplish my goals.

Pam:      I wonder if the dream figure can help you in some way?

Karen:    *(With her eyes closed in an internal state.)* Yes, I can see his face now. *(Karen then speaks directly to the dream character who now appears to her as a positive figure who can assist her.)* . . . I want to accept you and let you be a part of me so I can go after what I want and accomplish things.

Karen     *(as dream figure)* Yes, I can help you with that.

Karen:    Yes, I need patience but I want to feel you penetrate me, to be a part of me.

Pam:      Just take a moment then, right now, to feel this new pattern of wholeness, strength, assertiveness. Drink it in and allow this feeling to sink into the very cells of your body.

In this session, the Warrior dream figure represented the masculine part of Karen's own being. She could not fully accept it because of the distortion created by her father's abuse and the lack of healthy masculine role-modeling. The dream figure helped her discover the male wounding by her father that needed to be transformed, and brought in a new pattern that represented a positive masculine element that she could internalize. In this way, she could replace the scattered lack of confidence that she learned as a child with assertiveness and a courage to step out and accomplish things in her life. This session also illustrates how the dialogue process can be used with archetypal energies, dream characters, and external figures. In fact, as this session shows, dialogue can easily move from one to another in a single session.

Sometimes, when people work consciously with their dreams, they begin to see a connection between dream symbols and physical conditions.[1] Usually the body symptom and the dream symbol are expressing the same message from the sub-conscious mind, each in their own way bringing it to the individual's conscious awareness. Another session with Karen illustrates this point and shows how body-centered work can mirror the symbolic meaning found in a dream.

Karen came in talking about a dream in which there was some excrement in a container. At the bottom of this container were some diamonds. In the dream, she was trying to get around the excrement with tweezers to get the diamonds. Karen said her life felt like that. There was all this ugliness that she had to deal with and she felt overwhelmed. She began to talk about some of her problems in an analyzing way that seemed to be taking her away from her experience and the feelings that she came in with. To bring her awareness back to her body and feelings, I had her center inside for a moment and do a body scan. In noticing what she was feeling in her body, she became aware of her feet. I asked her to describe what her feet felt like to her. Karen described her bunions and a feeling of deformity. Her feet were like a handicapped, deformed part of her that was untouchable, something that she was ashamed of and didn't want anyone to see. As I had her exaggerate this, she twisted her feet in a way that amplified the deformed, untouch-able feeling. Soon, she had a sense of herself as a little girl in a corner, feeling too ugly to touch. She was afraid because of the domestic violence in her home and had internalized a lot of the ugliness of the situation, taking it into her body and sense of self. Her feet had embodied her childhood shame.

The message held within Karen's feet was similar to that of the symbols in her dream. The abusive environment that she had endured in childhood contaminated her sense of self just like the excrement in her dream had covered the beauty of the diamonds within the container. The diamond itself, concealed as it is in the heart of black carbon, represents this dynamic and symbolizes the light of the spiritual Self within us. Karen was overwhelmed because of her life difficulties at the time and was feeling disconnected from her spiritual essence. The dream was reminding her of who she really was, even in the midst of all the surrounding darkness, showing Karen where her healing journey was leading her. Through the body-centered session, Karen was able to release the ugliness that she had internalized and could then realize more of her essential Self—the diamond to which her Child of Light was leading her. She was able to remove the diamond from the excrement that she had experienced in her dream.

## *A Guided Meditation: Dream Symbols and the Body*

Here is a guided exercise designed to help you make a conscious connection between dream content and symptoms that are an expression of your body's wisdom. When doing this body-centered exercise, people often experience some type of relationship between the dream symbol and a physical condition or problem. I find this exercise can be especially useful when first starting to use the Dream Symbol Dialogue process.

Before beginning, pick an image or dream symbol for your process. This can be an object in the dream, a dream figure, or even the setting in which the dream takes place. This may be from a dream that you have had recently or one from the past that seems to stand out.

Take a few full relaxing breaths and let yourself sink a little deeper inside into your body and your own internal world. Close your eyes and have a sense that with each exhalation of your breath, you release any tensions right out of your body.

With each exhalation, any unwanted thoughts are just cleared away so that your mind becomes like a still pool of water. It is from this place of stillness that your body and subconscious mind will impart its wisdom to you here today.

Take a moment to bring your consciousness to the image or symbol from your dream. Bring that symbolic object clearly into focus with your inner eyes. Be aware of its qualities and characteristics, its color, shape, form, and so on. What feelings does this symbol bring forth in you?

Notice, then, how you experience this dream symbol in your body, where it seems to reside physically, or the location of any feelings or body sensations that seem to be associated with the dream symbol in some way. Breathe into this area and be aware of how the symbol feels from this body place, or how it feels to experience the dream image in your body in this way. Perhaps it is a familiar sensation or reminds you of something. Be attentive to any impressions that you receive. Ask your body and the symbol to communicate the purpose, meaning, or message that they have for you. This is nothing you have to work at. Just allow any sensations, feelings, words, or further images to emerge.

Perhaps you have a response, something that you also would like to say to the symbol. Continue to allow this communication to flow until it seems complete. Then, as you are ready, come back to external awareness and open your eyes.

When you are finished, write about your experience in your journal. Record the feelings and sensations that emerged for you and how they relate to the message that you received from your body and the dream symbol. Was there a correlation between the content of your dream and any synchronistic body symptom that you may have been experiencing? Name one thing that you could do in your life this week to help you act upon the healing intent of this dream and/or body symptom in order to integrate what you received.

## Dream Repatterning

Dream Repatterning is the name I give to the process of reentering a dream so that it can be continued or reworked in some way. Repatterning a dream is useful in order to more fully understand and integrate its meaning, to complete a dream that you woke up from before it was finished, and to resolve or rework psychic elements of a dream for your own process of transformation. Repatterning can allow you to confront issues and make conscious choices that were not made in the original dream. You can also call forth the assistance of positive archetypal forces, such as a Warrior for protection or a Healer for comforting, as well as any spirit helpers, in a way that was not available in the initial dreamstate. (See chapter 8 for further information on connecting with your personal spirit guide.) This process can change a traumatic, unresolved dream into a positive and empowering experience that can act as an inner resource for you.

Although dream repatterning can be done working on your own, it can sometimes be useful to have a facilitator for the process. Many therapists specializing in dreamwork, using shamanic techniques, or certain methods of hypnotherapy can facilitate this type of dream reentry. It is especially helpful to have someone assist you when you feel stuck or are dealing with dream material that is very charged and difficult to work with by yourself. Having a facilitator will enable you to feel safe in going into the deeper elements of the dream.

Another dream that Susan had will illustrate how dream repatterning works. The dream is rich with symbolic imagery and Susan said it felt like a past-life experience to her. In the dream, Susan is in a large cave that is dark, cold, and damp. She needs a torch to see and there are primitive markings on the rock face. There is an opening in the rock that an older caveman takes her through, into another chamber. It is a sacred place with petroglyphs on the wall of animals and people. One primitive picture is of an animal with red horns. In the dream experience, Susan is aware that there is an initiation that she did not finish, possibly in a past life. She is then alone in the dark cave and is drawing the pictures on the wall. The old man guide appears and points to the middle of the room where there is a fire. There is an animal heart that is supposed to be by the fire, but it is missing. A deer comes forward and she realizes that she is meant to sacrifice the deer for its heart as part of a sacred ritual of initiation. However, she is unable to do it because she doesn't want to sacrifice the animal. The deer wants to make the sacrifice and needs to in order to fulfill its purpose. The deer is offering itself with love but she cannot accept it. A woman dressed all in blue, who calls herself Blue Spirit Woman, tells her to spend time preparing for the ritual by talking to the deer and learning to take in the love that it offers.

Susan felt that she wanted to reenter the dream with the intention of completing the ritual that she had not been able to finish. She chose to return to the scene at the beginning of her dream. However there are slight differences in how things appear this time. Her dream repatterning process was described by her in this way:

> As I return to the dream I am in a dark tunnel. The ground is wet, cold stone. The tunnel is small and I have to crouch down and crawl through the entrance to the ritual place. As I enter the ritual place, I can then stand up. The light from the fire shows the pictures on the wall. The cave man is there and I can also see the blueness of Blue Spirit Woman. The cave man points to the stone ledge which has a knife on it. He asks, "What do you offer this life?" (*Meaning the deer's life.*) I reply, "My fears and doubts." He says, "Receive this love and grace fully and have an open heart." I now feel cleansed and worthy of what I will receive as I enter the ritual. The

deer is here standing by a tree which Blue Spirit
Woman is a part of or one with in some way. I take the
knife to the deer's heart and build a pyre for it. I draw
the symbol of the deer with antlers on it on the cave
wall with the deer's blood. I then pull the deer into the
fire and leave the knife laying next to the heart. I take
part of the tree which now appears crystal-like. It is my
gift from Blue Spirit Woman.

After doing this dream process, Susan said she experienced
the knife as a penetrating active force, which represented an
assertive aspect that she wanted to integrate. She felt that she
especially needed to be more assertive in expressing feelings of
anger. The deer heart burning in the fire felt alchemically transformative to her and symbolized the courage that she would
need to accomplish this. Through the deer's surrender, she was
able to feel a connection to an unconditional source of love. The
deer's death represented her letting go of the fears and doubts
that had been blocking her in the dream and in her external life.
By being willing to surrender this, she was able to open up more
fully to the love that she wanted to experience. After this dreamwork, Susan continued to work with the Blue Spirit Woman
guide to assist her in opening her heart up to this love.

This Dream Repatterning illustrates that it is important not
to have any concepts about certain dream content. Death, for
example, is often significant of transformation and renewal in
the symbolic world of dreams. It can, as it does in this case, represent letting go of lower aspects of the ego in order to experience greater life; indeed, this dream repatterning was a powerful
initiatory experience for Susan. It is also possible that Susan
accessed past-life material through this dream, since the ceremony that she experienced was similar to the rites of tribal soci-
eties who believed that totem objects could transmit power and
enable them to acquire certain qualities or abilities; for example,
that by eating the heart of a lion, one could assimilate courage.

The following steps will enable you to do the Dream Repatterning process working by yourself. As with symbol dialogue, the dialogue in Dream Repatterning can be done as a journal process, which is very helpful when working alone.

1.  Write your dream in your journal exactly as it happened. Be as specific as you can.

2.  Note any areas that are disturbing, unresolved, or that in some way have an impact on you. What issues does it bring forth for you? What would you choose to do differently now? What would you need to do this? For example, different skills or tools; a change in attitude; or assistance from a spirit helper, archetypal guide, dream ally, or any other healing element from the dream.

3.  Choose the scene of the dream that you want to work with, the part that you need further resolution of or understanding about, then formulate and state your intention for the dream repatterning. For example, an intention might be to have the courage and strength to resolve a personal issue reflected in a dream conflict or to heal a part of yourself through helping a wounded dream figure.

4.  Take a few moments to enter a relaxed, meditative state. As with other processes we have used, it may be helpful to take a few cleansing breaths, sensing that with each exhalation, you can just sink a little deeper inside into your internal world. Allow your mind to be clear and quiet like a still pool of water. Feel, sense, or imagine an orb of soft protective light and love all around you. Breathe in this unconditional light and love as you affirm that everything that transpires in this dream process will be for your highest good. Declare your intention for the Dream Repatterning and, if desired, call on your Higher Self or

any archetypal guides that you need if they aren't already a part of the dream scene which you are working with.

5. Bring the dream scene you have chosen into your consciousness. It may be helpful to imagine seeing the scene on a movie screen before you with the film on *Pause*, so that none of the action of the dream starts until you are ready. You can also choose a code word for your dream repatterning, such as *Pause* or *Freeze Frame*, which will stop the action of the dream at any time. Take a moment to visualize the details of the dream event clearly.

6. When you are ready, imagine yourself in the dream place you have chosen and let the dream action begin. Proceeding much like a self-guided visualization, dialogue with dream figures and, if need be, redo the action of the dream in order to obtain resolution and repattern the psychic energy of the dream in a way that is for your highest good. This may mean confronting a dream figure that you were running away from, renegotiating a particular situation, or nurturing a wounded dream figure. Stay connected with your feelings and remember that you don't have to do anything that doesn't feel right to you or that you are not ready for. You can also freeze the dream action again at any time by saying the code word you have chosen.

7. When you are finished, record your feelings and any further insights about the dream experience in your journal. Notice how this new dream working feels and how you now feel about the issues involved in it. Write down how it relates to other aspects of your personal growth process. Note any further actions that you will need to take or changes you will need to make in your life in order to complete the intention of this dreamwork. For

example, an extension of a confrontational dream experience may mean that you finally tell your mate exactly how you really feel about the issues involved in your relationship. A healing dream situation may require that you be more conscious of self-care and have specific relaxation time in your life. These external actions will assist you in fully integrating or actualizing the positive intent of the dream.

---

## Notes

1. For further study of the relationship between dream symbols and body symptoms, see Arnold Mindel, *Dreambody: The Body's Role In Revealing the Self* (Portland, OR: Lao Tse Press, 1997).

# PART IV

## EMBODYING SPIRIT

# 8

# THE TRANSFORMATIVE POWER OF LIGHT AND LOVE

*Utilizing Healing Energy*

LIGHT IS AN ALIVE, CONSCIOUS, AND love-infused substance you can use for healing and spiritual growth. When you work with it, you are essentially accessing the creative substance and matrix of energy that composes all things. This glue of the universe can be seen or visualized as light, and felt as love. Light waves actually carry new levels of information to us, while the compassionate love aspect brings in the understanding that we need to access it. Consciously using light and love for this purpose can create a tangible shift in your experience mentally, emotionally, physically, and spiritually. You may have already begun to tap into the possibilities of using light and love in this way through your experiences with the processes presented so far.

Besides using the transformative power of light and love after emotional release as part of the reorganization process, you can use it for healing any time that you are having difficult feelings or experiencing discomfort in your body. At such times, breathe light and love into these feelings, sensations, or the affected area of your body. If this is difficult for you to do, you can call on the presence of Divine Love for assistance. Ask this spiritual consciousness to help you experience the love and feel it fill you according to your need. It may help you to imagine being enfolded by this conscious presence of light and love as you allow it to fill your whole body. You can have a sense of immersing yourself in it as you breathe the love and soft healing light into the uncomfortable feelings or sensations.

If you want to expand on this, you can consciously let the light flow through every part of you. Feel it infuse your mind, emotions, and body as it permeates your entire energy system. Allow this love and light to bathe and soothe every physical system, organ, bone, muscle, tissue, even the very cells of your body. Your cells have an intelligence and can receive in this energy. Affirm that the healing intelligence within you is allowing this energy to be used for your highest good.

In addition to the feeling sense of being enfolded in a soft healing light, it may be helpful to visualize yourself surrounded by a column of light or infused by a radiant sunbeam. Some people prefer imagining themselves in a pool, stream, or waterfall of liquid light, letting it flow all around and through them. These images can be particularly useful in cleansing any negative feeling energy, or any energy that is not your own, from your body and auric field. It can assist in the process of healing from any type of trauma or fragmentation.

For example, my client Adrian used this cleansing process after being very affected by her father's death. His passing occurred after a long illness and Adrian was pleased that she had lots of time to spend with her father in the weeks before his death. She was also able to be with him at his bedside in his final hours. However, at the moment of his death when his heart stopped, her heart had started racing furiously. It was a very strange energetic sensation for Adrian that hadn't seemed connected with an adrenaline rush or other physical cause. Since his death, she had continued to have uncomfortable sensations in her throat and chest along with images of him struggling near death with labored breathing.

I had Adrian feel and visualize a cleansing stream of golden white light flow through her whole body from head to toe, especially in the area of her throat and chest, in order to release and clear this internalized residual energy of her father's pain. She let her father know that she could not hold this pain anymore as she felt the flowing liquid light cleanse it right out of her body and energy system. She verbally set him—and also herself—free to move on, each in their own ways. After this cleansing process, she no longer felt the throat and chest sensations or the emotional burden of her father's death. As mentioned in chapter 5, when working with this type of process, through intention and visualization the released energy can be returned to the universe to be transmuted by Spirit or dissolved in a flame of violet light (see violet light, page 275).

This process can also be useful for people with a history of sexual abuse in order to cleanse the feeling of the perpetrator's energy out of their bodies. This allows such individuals to make their bodies their own again, feeling a sense of their own energy for perhaps the first time in their life. Sometimes, an individual with a history of trauma will only be able to let a little bit of light in at first. If pain has been a way of life, it may be too difficult to let go of it all at once. Focusing on the comforting, soothing, and nurturing sensations of the loving, radiant energy, rather than the intensity of the light, may be helpful in such cases. As more healing and clearing are done, the person will be able to allow more of the light energy in.

You may find that as you work more with the light, your experience of it will grow. Initially, you may have to visualize it or see it in your mind's eye. Then, you may feel the presence and energy of it in your body, or have it automatically appear in your inner vision. For example, in my body dialogue with my uterus, light spontaneously became present. If it is easier for you to visualize light than to feel its loving presence, the guided meditations in chapter 4 for week three (on the quality of love), week seven, and week eight will assist you in sensing and feeling this love infused nature of the light.

When you envision light, it may have a shimmery white quality or have a particular color that you're drawn to. Different colors, relating to the various chakras associated with them, can be used to bring in specific healing qualities.

**Red** is warming, energizing, and increases your overall vitality. It can strengthen your connection with the Earth and the creative life force in your body.

**Orange** is revitalizing if you feel tired or fatigued and can be stimulating for the respiratory system as well. This color supports your immune system and increases your sexual energy, creativity, and drive while assisting the other areas of your body which are related to the sacral chakra.

**Yellow** is stimulating to the nervous system and metabolism, brings mental clarity, and can improve weakened kidneys, adrenals, and organs of the abdominal region. It is also good for unclogging the lymph system.

**Green** has a harmonizing quality bringing balance, renewal, and general healing. It is good for high blood pressure, cleansing infection, and for repairing damaged or diseased tissue, especially of the heart and lungs.

**Pink** brings in a healing presence of unconditional love and is good for healing the emotional and spiritual components of heart and lung problems.

**Blue** is soothing, calming, cooling, and sedating, bringing a serene stillness and quiet. It is helpful for high blood pressure, fever, inflammation, and certain infections, and is also good for throat and thyroid problems, assisting you in speaking forth your own truth.

**Indigo** can enhance your intuitive perception and assist you in seeing past the mundane appearance of things into their deeper meaning and spiritual purpose. It also has a sedative pain-relieving effect.

**Purple** relates to a sense of royalty, rulership, and spiritual authority. It can help you connect with the energy of the spiritual planes and to respond from that place of consciousness.

**Magenta** combines the qualities of red and violet, helping you to integrate the energies of the physical and spiritual realms. It can also be used to improve circulation and strengthen the heart.

**Violet** light, which I sometimes experience as a neon radiant violet, can be used for clearing negative energy and psychic contamination as well as physical parasites, microorganisms, and other toxins. I have found that this color can be very potent and deeply cleansing. For this reason, you may want to start out using it in small doses for five minutes or less in order to determine the specific affect that it will have on you. If you are using violet light for physical detoxification, alternate it with green light which will help to cleanse and remove wastes from your system, or use yellow afterward to facilitate the cleansing process by stimulating your lymph system.

**White** light is purifying and can lessen pain while bringing expansion, connection to the unity of all being, and a connection with the compassionate spirit within others, as well. Because of its purifying qualities, white light can be visualized infusing your food or water in order to raise its energetic vibration before consuming it.

**Gold** light strengthens the whole organism, imparting a sense of empowerment to your entire being. It enhances your higher mind connection to the Source of all. Gold and white hues both work with you on a soul level, enhancing your spiritual body. They are good to use alone or together for the column of light and the cleansing pool, stream, or waterfall of liquid light.

Within each color there are also various shadings that may be the exact color that is appropriate for your healing process. For example, the orange that you are working with may have strong red tones to increase your connection to the Earth, or be more dominantly yellow to help impart mental clarity. The green you envision may be a turquoise shade, blending the calming peacefulness of blue with the overall healing quality of green. You may also sense more than one color present as you do clearing, reorganizing, or healing work. Be open to the guidance of Spirit and your own Higher Self in this process. When you use any of the colors listed above, remember to feel-sense them as much as possible. It will help you if you recall the feeling response that these colors have for you when you experience them in your everyday life.

# GUIDES AND SPIRIT HELPERS

Consciously creating a connection with your guides and spirit helpers can help you attune to Spirit and your own Higher Self in order to be receptive to this type of healing, spiritual guidance. Since spirit guides bring direction and understanding, your relationship with them is an important resource for your process of personal growth and spiritual awakening.

As was mentioned in chapter 2, you may see spirit helpers internally during a visualization process, in meditation, or dreams. It is also possible to experience a spirit guide as an inner voice or intuitively sense one as a presence accompanied by an inner knowing. Sometimes, such guides represent a wise part of ourselves, an aspect of our own Higher Self. They may come in a variety of forms including human figures, animal allies, nature spirits, and mythical beings. However, there are also guides and helpers that work with us who are actually beings from the spiritual realms. They may be angel messengers, ascended masters, or other beings of light who support and encourage us in the way of our own spirit essence. Working with either type of spirit helper can assist you in trusting your intuition and developing a relationship with your own higher wisdom and inner guidance. You can consciously call on their presence when you want support or need assistance in some way.

We all have times when problems seem overwhelming and we feel out of touch with our expansive spirit essence. At these, or other times, inner guides or spirit helpers can bring reassurance and act as a doorway to your own inner wisdom and knowledge.

## *A Guided Meditation:*
## *Journey to Your Evolutionary Soul Guide*

Each being may have several helpers from the world of light that bring assistance and guidance for that person. However, each of us has a particular guide who works directly with our soul and its evolutionary process of growth in this lifetime, helping us to fulfill our soul purpose here on Earth and in other dimensions, as well. I call this particular spirit helper your evolutionary soul guide. The following guided meditation will help you connect with this specific spirit guide that has been overseeing your soul's evolution in this lifetime. It will also assist you in developing a safe place where you can go to emotionally and spiritually nourish yourself with light and love. Before beginning, you will first want to go through this guided imagery process and thoroughly familiarize yourself with it. You can also audio-tape it or have someone read it aloud to you as you proceed.

Find a relaxed, comfortable position, either sitting or lying down, somewhere where you won't be disturbed. Take time to focus your mind and heart inward. Close your eyes and take a few full, slow breaths, allowing your breath to become soft and easy as you settle inside, into a deeper part of yourself. Then, surround yourself with a soft, healing light and, as you breathe it in, feel it circulate throughout your whole body, letting your whole body relax with the soft, melty feeling of this healing light.

Now, imagine yourself in a beautiful place in nature. This can be a place that you have never seen before or one that you have actually been to as long as it instills only feelings of comfort and safety. You have nothing else to do right now and have plenty of time to just rest in the peaceful serenity and loving energy present in this place. You can feel the earth beneath your feet, here, and smell the sweet fragrances that fill the air as a gentle breeze caresses your cheek.

You joyfully savor the deep blue of the sky, the lush green of the plants, and the rich tones of the earth. All the colors here are very vibrant and alive. The Sun gently warms you as its light sparkles and glistens everywhere. The plants and trees are almost luminous with radiant health and vitality. Swirling streams and cascading waterfalls revitalize the air with their dynamic energy. As you listen carefully, you can almost hear the nature spirits in the sound of rustling grass and singing birds. The soothing sounds of nature are deeply relaxing here. It's easy to feel nourished, safe, and comforted in this place, like you've been here in nature for a long time, just resting and relaxing with nothing else to do.

Resting here in this healing space, you begin to see, sense, or imagine a shimmering rosy gold light all around you. As it gently enfolds you, becoming brighter, you notice that you feel lighter and more expansive, filled with a sense of loving acceptance and peace. This compassionate energy softly pulsates in spiraling waves of light and color all around you. You seem to be lifted upward along this spiraling energy, increasing the amount of love you feel as you expand into higher levels of the world of light. As you receive in this love and serenity, continue to sense your energy lifting and expanding, in some way, with this harmonious vibration of light and love.

Reach forth, now, to your highest sense of spiritual consciousness and being. As you do, affirm your intention to connect with your spiritual helper, the one who has been with you since the beginning, guiding your soul's journey on Earth. Then, begin to sense the presence, in some way, of this special being of light who has only your highest good at heart. You may feel certain feelings, sense a subtle presence, hear specific words, or see a particular image in your mind's eye. Notice what you see, sense, or experience within you.

The presence of your soul guide is radiant, and you now realize that it is this one who is emanating the pulsating waves of light and love to you. Feel this loving energy from your soul guide and allow it to permeate your entire being, infusing every muscle, organ, and system of your body, down to the very core of your cells. Feel this loving substance gently comforting, healing, and revitalizing your entire being. Deeply and completely, now, breathe this radiant energy and love right into your heart, and into your very soul. In whatever way you experience it, allow this loving energy to flow into every part of you and completely infuse your body, mind, and emotions.

Then ask for guidance from your soul guide regarding some aspect of your personal growth and notice what you experience. This could involve information on your spiritual development, a physical or emotional concern, or some other life issue. Remain open to impressions, receiving guidance in whatever form it may come to you. You may have insights, see images, hear words, either your own unspoken voice or one quite different, or have a strong sense of something being true for you.

The answer you receive may be clear and strong, or may come through very subtle feelings and sensations, perhaps even in symbolic form as a gift that your guide has for you. The guidance that you receive may be immediate or come to you gradually over the next few days, through a dream or other synchronistic experience. However it comes, this wisdom will always be expressed to you with love and compassion.

Take a few moments to receive any guidance that your soul guide has for you, now. Spend as much time as you like being here and communicating with your soul guide.

Complete your time here with your soul guide in whatever way seems appropriate, knowing that you can return to this special place in nature to be with this spirit helper whenever you need to or want to. Be sure and thank your soul guide for what you have received. Then, gently feel yourself move back down through the realms of light, bringing your time within to completion.

Come back more fully to external awareness in the room, perhaps stretching and moving your body as you do, and when you're ready, open your eyes.

Take a few moments to write your experience down in your journal and record the information that you received.

When working with light and color or before doing the other processes in this book, you can call on your evolutionary soul guide to provide assistance. You will find that as you continue to work with your soul guide, your experience of this spiritual resource and your own intuition will strengthen and grow. You may also want to use the inner spiritual workplace that you created in the meditation for week five (page 138) for meeting with your evolutionary soul guide.

# 9

# INITIATION AND THE
# BODY OF LIGHT

*Your Path of Spiritual Awakening*

As YOU CONTINUE ON YOUR PATH of healing and personal growth, you may begin to have specific experiences of an expansive or spiritual nature. This may manifest in many ways, such as an ecstatic feeling of oneness with all things, a meaningful vision, a profound shift in perception, or a sustained feeling of unconditional love. You may also go through experiences that feel as if you are being tested or strengthened in some way in developing a greater level of consciousness. Such experiences are often part of a specific process of spiritual development known as initiation.

Initiations are certain steps on the path of spiritual growth that are part of the evolution of the soul. They are universal in nature, each one containing certain components and involving certain processes. Initiation means beginning, and it is the beginning or entering into a new level of consciousness and energetic vibration. Higher vibrational energies are received into the person, changing the individual's energetic frequency and the consciousness with which he or she functions. Since all people do not develop in the same way or at the same rate, the experience of each initiation may vary from person to person.

A basic foundational level of initiation, which has to do with our primary human development, is actually experienced in the process of growing up. However, another whole series of initiations take place when one consciously puts a foot on the spiritual path. Often there is a yearning at this time, a feeling that something is missing. There is an awakening to something more than the material world, a search for meaning in life and a desire to both know one's self and feel a connection with Spirit. At this point, people often seek out a teacher, guide, or particular spiritual practice to help them give birth to this spiritual awakening within them. Meditation or other methods of quieting the thinking mind are often initiated in order to bring the physical, mental, and emotional faculties into alignment with the soul's true intention. In this way, the desires of the outer persona or false self of the individual identity no longer have such a strong control.

As the spirit consciousness grows, one's physical form and etheric body are prepared to receive a higher vibrational frequency of energy from the upper planes. This preparation involves a purification or cleansing of the mental, emotional, and physical aspects of being as the kundalini life force ascends the spine through the energetic chakras. This process of kundalini awakening is sometimes accompanied by physical and psychological manifestations called *kriyas*. These changes, which occur due to the accelerated evolutionary process of the rising kundalini, can come about gradually as part of an ongoing spiritual discipline or altruistic focus in life and can be practically unnoticed. However, they can also occur with sudden overwhelming intensity, opening you to a reality not known before.

Kriyas can include sensations of heat and energy either in specific chakras or streaming up the spine, or may be experienced as tremors, spasms, shaking, or other spontaneous movements. When the kundalini is activated, an individual may see visions and radiant lights, emit vocal noises, or experience a variety of sounds such as buzzing, humming, tinkling bells, rushing water, musical tones, or even singing voices.[1] Intense pain can sometimes be felt as the kundalini reaches areas of stress in the body. These physical sensations may be indicative of specific blocks to the newly awakening consciousness and one's true soul intention. As the stressful blockage is purged from the system by the kundalini, the discomfort or pain goes away.[2] This process can be greatly assisted by working consciously with such physical symptoms through the methods provided throughout this text.

During a period of kundalini awakening, individuals may have uplifting transcendent experiences or enter expansive altered states of consciousness. However, it can also be a time of great change, life transitions, or even crisis.[3] Emotional patterns may intensify as they are brought to the surface to be transformed. This can result in feelings that seem overwhelming and states of depression, anxiety, confusion, anger, and the like. Memories from the past can also be triggered as elements of the subconscious mind are activated. For these reasons, methods providing for emotional clearing and healing are particularly helpful at this time.

If the accelerated process of spiritual awakening is happening too rapidly, these psychological and physical kriyas may even, in some cases, be aggravated by certain types of intense meditation practice. When this occurs, the spiritual practice may need to be temporarily discontinued to allow a more gradual integration of the expansion experience. Additionally, proper diet, exercise, and rest are important for the physical body.

I have also found that cranial-sacral adjustments made to the cranial bones, which affect the movement of cerebrospinal fluid around the brain and along the spinal cord, can be immensely helpful in assisting the physical body adjust to expansion experiences of this type. There is an actual breathing, a flexion and extension, of the cranial plates with the cerebrospinal pulse. When higher vibrational energies impact the etheric body, the physical nervous system can be overwhelmed as the organism tries to integrate these new experiences. The cranial system can then get jammed up or misaligned and stop its normal pattern of movement, resulting in headaches and other physical or emotional difficulties. As you come into alignment with higher frequency energies, your cranial system may have to adjust in order to move within a more expanded range. Cranial-sacral work—done by many osteopaths, bodyworkers, and chiropractors—can assist you in this process. Chiropractic spinal adjustments, bodywork, acupuncture treatments, homeopathic remedies, and flower essences can also be beneficial during this time to assist the physical body in adapting to the changes taking place.

As the purification process continues and the ego consciousness begins to be transformed, the being becomes ready for the energy of the soul body to permeate the physical vehicle. An initiation takes place in which the body is infused with light. This initiatory process, known by different names in various spiritual disciplines, may occur spontaneously as part of spiritual awakening or be facilitated by a spiritual teacher as part of an ongoing spiritual practice.

When this illuminative initiation occurs, the faculties are imbued with light emanating from the soul body and the Cosmic/Solar force. As this radiant energy descends, all the chakras and auric bodies are vivified. The chakra centers are more fully awakened to the inflowing Cosmic energies by the kundalini ascending up the spine in a column of light. Through this process, the individual's etheric light body is activated as this light from above is sealed in the physical body. The actual vibratory frequency of the body accelerates as the soul energy pours into the physical vehicle and is anchored in Earth. The individual, then guided by the soul, walks as a conduit of energy, a transmitter of light and love aligned with Heaven and Earth.

Eventually, as the light continues to transform the ego consciousness and the individual's life is directed more fully by Spirit, the next level of initiation is reached when the soul veil to the radiant Self is parted. At this point, the individual realizes and knows the divine Self as his or her true being and is now able to function from that state of consciousness, rather than from the ego persona. Continuing spiritual development then involves greater and greater levels of Self-mastery with total and complete functioning from the God Self.

I went through this first initiation, known to me as illumination, when I was studying with an esoteric community in the spring of 1972. At the time, I was several months pregnant. Interestingly, years later, my daughter, twenty-two at the time, was regressed to her in-utero period during a hypnotherapy session. She reported that she experienced an infusion of light in the womb during the exact month when I went though this initiation.

Although I felt and saw the radiant energy as my teacher sealed the light in my body, it was really only the beginning of a process that continued for some time. As I was able to heal emotionally and integrate more of this consciousness into my daily life, my experience of my true essence Self deepened. Also, I feel that initially in 1972, because certain changes in the planetary consciousness had not taken place yet,[4] and because of my own lack of connection with my physical form, the energy of my soul body could not be fully anchored into the Earth at that time. Subsequently, when working with another teacher in 1991, I was able to experience my soul energies anchored into the planetary body and thus more fully align the different dimensions of my being with Cosmic and Earth forces.

This experience of being connected to the planetary body of Earth involves another chakra, called the Earth chakra, which is located about six to eighteen inches below the feet.[5] This operates in conjunction with the root chakra at the coccyx where the life force of the kundalini is stored. Fully activating the consciousness of the Earth chakra, sometimes referred to as the Earth Star, takes us beyond just using the creative life force of the Earth—available through the root chakra—to actually being anchored into Earth and interrelating with the living consciousness of the planet. Through this connection, we feel the breathing pulsations of the planet's magnetic field (between 7.8 and 8 hertz or about eight times per second),[6] and sense the energies at sacred vortexes where the these Earth forces are particularly powerful.

The sacred knowledge that the Earth is indeed a conscious and evolving entity has been lost in our modern technological society with tragic results. Most individuals have no awareness of this consciousness and therefore do not feel these wonderful magnetic energies flow into their body from the Earth Mother. People remain cut off from the powerful healing energies that the Earth has to give. It is known, for example, that during healing sessions, the brain waves of healers will become synchronized at 7.8–8 hertz alpha rhythms with the Earth's magnetic field fluctuations. Through resonating with the Earth's magnetic field pulsations, the healer is able to tap into a powerful healing energy and channel it to others.[7] Yet, this energy is also available to all of us at any time.

Our connection with the Earth is particularly important at this time because of the many changes that are now taking place on the planet. These changes are due to a transformation in consciousness that is taking place for all of humanity. In relating these changes to the chakras, Brugh Joy states:

> We are preparing for a transformation of consciousness
> that supersedes the past, moving from the more power-
> controlled areas, the areas of mastery of the material
> plane, into a blend with the higher awareness that is asso-
> ciated with the upper chakras . . . This shift of the center
> upward will imbue humanity with a sense of relationship,
> the deeper aspects of which rest on spiritual values rather
> than on power and control over others.[8]

Other sources, such as Hopi and Mayan legends, also speak
of this time as a period of transition leading into a new age of
greater spiritual consciousness.

Study of the Mayan Calendar and Mayan astrology reveals
that December 21, 2012 will mark the end of a Great Cycle
that began in 3114 B.C.E.[9] Based on his investigations, Jose
Arguelles believes that the next several years will be ones of significant changes leading to a quantum leap in planetary consciousness. In his book, *The Mayan Factor*, he describes a syn-
chronization with galactic consciousness through the Earth's
alignment with a radiant beam of energy emanating from the
core of the galaxy. (In modern astrophysics, such beams or density waves are believed to sweep through space and influence
galactic evolution. It is thought, for example, that the igniting
of our own Sun resulted from such a wave.)[10]

According to Arguelles, the continuous signals from galactic
center, identified as radio emissions, are actually intelligent
waves of information impulsing the planet to align with a higher
level of galactic consciousness. This radiant code of light information from galactic core will result in the evolutionary quickening of our DNA and an activation of the planetary etheric
light body. The Earth itself is going through a great initiation
and it will be felt in the hearts and minds of all who live here.

The Earth is a living being seeking to come into harmony
with its own soul essence. Cosmic pulsations of energy from
galactic center are now streaming forth to the planet via the Sun

of our solar system. As it resonates with these emanations from the heart of the galaxy, the Earth is quickly evolving toward a point of conscious radiance. The planetary body will soon be infused with light, creating a dimensional shift in consciousness for all of us. The initiation of light, mentioned previously, is what the Earth is going through now on a planetary level.

As part of this illuminative process, the vibratory frequency of the planet is accelerating. You may have felt that your life has been increasingly accelerated and intense during the last few years. This is because the final stage of this Mayan Great Cycle has already begun, ushering in a new increased level of vibration. Remember that these accelerated energies are also affecting the physical substance of our bodies. The vibratory rate of our bodies' atoms increases as they harmonize with this influx of Cosmic energies. I had a sense of this happening in my own body while doing some work with the light during a healing session. I experienced a vision of what appeared to be strands of DNA molecules breaking up and reorganizing in the light. This was a microscopic front row seat to the molecular changes that are now taking place as part of this planetary transmutation.

Right now, the Earth is going through a process of preparation and cleansing. Just as there are certain mental, emotional, and physical kriyas in the individual, so too is the Earth experiencing changes as it comes into this initiation. We continually see the effects of this in the form of earthquakes, destructive storms, volcanoes, and other Earth changes. The years ahead will indeed be times of great change. A new consciousness and higher vibrational frequency of light and love is coming. We must all prepare ourselves for this transformation and what it will require both individually and globally. It will mean letting go of certain concepts of our thinking minds that we so tenaciously hold on to, as well as outmoded ways of relating to the Earth and one another.

As this transition continues into the new millennium, many people look for dramatic changes to occur. Everything from Armageddon and destructive meteor showers to extraterrestrial visitations and a great golden age have been predicted. It is even believed by some that there may be an alteration in the Earth's axis, leading to a polar shift and other cataclysmic Earth changes. Indeed, psychics and astrologers throughout the ages, including Nostradamus and Edgar Cayce, have seen this period as a time of great upheaval. It is important to remember, however, that the Earth changes are not something separate from us. They are intricately connected with our own consciousness and process of spiritual development. Quantum theory has shown us this, that consciousness and matter are inextricably interwoven. We live in a holographic matrix of consciousness, a universal energy field in which consciousness determines what will be seen, experienced and made manifest. Therefore, as we raise our own consciousness, we in turn help the Earth through its process of spiritual unfoldment.

There may indeed be dramatic changes on the Earth. However, we have the ability as a conscious collective of human beings, dedicated to the healing of the Earth, to bring powerful forces into manifestation. This kind of synchronized intention can have a stabilizing effect on the Earth, thus averting a cataclysmic end and opening the door to magnificent possibilities. Whatever the Earth changes may be, they are not something to fear, but rather something for us to be aware of so we can participate consciously in this process of planetary evolution.

We can all assist the planet through these changes in several ways. First, by making a conscious commitment to our own healing on every level. Each person who heals themselves in turn helps heal the Earth. Unhealed elements held in the body and subconscious mind create a certain density or heaviness in the cells so that the atoms vibrate at a slower rate. When this dross in the physical body is released through healing and emotional clearing, people can embody a higher frequency of energy. As this happens, individuals become carriers of this higher frequency of light, acting as transmitters sending light not only to the Earth, but to others.

Secondly, get to know the Earth. Spend time in nature, preferably away from populated areas. Sit on a rock, by a stream, near a tree, or lie face down on the ground to increase your connection to the Earth's emanations. While in the vibrant stillness, commune with the Earth Mother's energy. As you let go and allow yourself to be touched by Gaia's pulsations, let your energy flow into her also. Notice how this experience feels in your body, so that you can access it and reconnect with this feeling even when you are in the city.

In addition, individually or in groups, we can consciously put forth an intention or prayer for light and love to fill the Earth. See, sense, or imagine the energetic grid of the Earth as a shimmering matrix of light enfolding the planet. Feel yourself and millions of others around the world as luminous connecting points along this energetic grid, accepting Cosmic light into the Earth. Then, let go and allow the Earth to use this energy in the way that is most needed. We must remember, also, to love and respect the Earth and its resources in all that we do.

The Native American cultures have always understood living in harmony with the Earth Mother. They ask and give thanks when using the fruits of the Earth, partaking of its gifts in a wise and balanced way. There is a great need to return to this consciousness of honoring the Earth as the living being that it is. We can no longer afford to deny the truth that we are one with the Earth. What we do affects the Earth, and what happens to the planet directly affects us. This is especially true now, during this time of great transition, as the Earth goes through its process of initiation.

# THE RHYTHMS OF NATURE

You can also strengthen your connection to the Earth by honoring the lunar phases and other cycles of nature, specifically the New and Full Moons as well as the seasonal solstice and equinox times. You can greatly accelerate your spiritual growth through ceremony or meditation at these times because these cycles represent patterns that are a part of our own conscious development. The Sun, Earth, and Moon are constantly enacting a sacred journey, taking us from darkness into greater light and understanding.

At the New Moon, the disc of the Moon is invisible to us since it is directly between the Earth and Sun. The Sun and Moon are together at this phase and so both forces, conscious and subconscious, act as one fused energy. There is therefore, at the New Moon, an opportunity to break down the separation between conscious and subconscious mind and bring masculine and feminine polarities within us into alignment. Since, in this way, the intellectual/assertive function can work in harmony with the instinctual/intuitive nature, it is a good time to start new projects.

New realizations and information can also be brought to consciousness at this time from the fertile darkness of the subconscious mind. The waxing or increasing of the Moon's light is symbolic of this new energy growing, expanding, and manifesting in some way. Be aware of how the feelings and issues concerning any new realization brought forth at the New Moon grow in intensity as the moon increases in light over the next two weeks.

At the Full Moon, the Moon and Sun oppose one another in the sky and so the face of the Moon is fully illuminated. At this phase, the subconscious Moon forces are separate or polarized from the Sun's energy and so the unconscious rules, unchecked by the normally vigilant conscious persona. This can produce the so-called craziness of a Full Moon. However, this dynamic allows us to be more fully aware of how both conscious and subconscious elements operate in our lives. We can, then, more objectively see the various polarities within us, such as masculine/feminine, adult/child, and spirit/body, so that greater integration can take place as a result. A strong funneling effect also occurs at the Full Moon, so that both the Solar forces and the magnetic Moon energies are received by the Earth in a magnified way.

As the Moon begins to wane and show less light, it is a time for completing projects as well as purifying yourself in preparation for a new cycle. At this time of the month, you can release the false patterns of the persona, which may have surfaced from the subconscious mind at the Full Moon, so that more of your essence Self can manifest. For this reason, the balsamic or dark Moon period, in the hours just prior to the next New Moon, is a time of stillness that lends itself to quiet introspection, meditation, and rest. In this way, you become a clear, receptive vessel, ready once again to receive the illuminations of the Moon's reflective consciousness at the next New Moon.

The solstice and equinox points represent the four quarters or seasons of the year, and also relate to the four directions of the Earth which are honored in Native American traditions. In order to understand these cycles more fully, it may be useful to imagine a circle divided into four quarters representing the four seasons of the year and the four directions: north, south, east, and west.

The Winter Solstice occurs on about December 21 or 22, when the Sun enters the astrological sign of Capricorn. It is associated with the north direction, which represents the inspiration of Spirit wisdom. During this time, a divine seed of greater consciousness is sparked within us as we conceive the light of Spirit within. At this time of year, we are naturally drawn within (and inside by colder weather), as all of nature rests in the dark stillness. Although the Northern Hemisphere is tilted away from the Sun's rays at this time and therefore days are shorter, the Earth is also closest to the Sun in its orbit. In this time of greatest darkness, the presence of the light is nearest as we are taken into the deep dark womb of Winter to conceive. This is also a time to celebrate the rebirth of the light because after the Winter Solstice, the shortest day of the year, the time of light will increase as days get longer. This is the significance of the traditional Yule log burning. What a fitting time of the year to celebrate the Christ's birth as this gift of Light into the world.

At the Winter Solstice, the seed of light is enfolded in the Earth Mother's womb as an abundance of Cosmic energy pours forth to the heart of the planet. During this sacred time, celestial forces are very present here on Earth and each individual has an opportunity to receive of this abundance and experience the light of his or her true divine Self. It is especially important to spend quiet time apart from the hustle and bustle of this season in order to be receptive to these celestial energies.

The Spring Equinox occurs around March 20 or 21, when the Sun enters Aries and crosses the celestial equator. It is associated with the east direction, which relates to illumination. At this time, the seed of spirit wisdom conceived during the Winter Solstice bursts forth into the light of consciousness and is given birth into form. As this greater awareness emerges, it manifests more consciously, much like the young seedlings that are beginning to sprout through the earth in response to the Sun's warmth at this time of year. We awaken and realize more consciously, in some way, the seed of wisdom that was gifted in the winter. All of nature jubilantly responds to this birth as new life springs forth everywhere in budding flowers and trees. After the dark stillness of winter, nature comes to life once again and growth begins. However, just as a vulnerable young plant needs careful tending, our awakening consciousness also needs nurturing attention and assertive energy at this time so that the life force within us can continue to grow and develop.

At the Spring Equinox, the Sun and Earth are in alignment with the day and nighttime periods being of equal length. Solar and Earth forces, both active and receptive energies, are thus in balance and we can readily access both of these aspects for our spiritual growth.

The Summer Solstice occurs about June 21 or 22, when the Sun enters Cancer. It is associated with the south direction and the spontaneity, innocence, and playfulness of the child. The summer is a time for play and the fullness of nature's growth. At the Summer Solstice, the childlike seed of consciousness within us continues to grow and mature into fullness as it is nurtured by the light. This is an energizing time of nurturance, expansion, and prosperity. It is a period of celebration as we rejoice in what we have gained and also continue the healing that sustained spiritual growth and maturity require.

The Autumn Equinox occurs around September 22 or 23, when the Sun enters the astrological sign of Libra. It is associated with the west direction, the "goes within place." At this time of year, we give thanks for what has been accomplished in our self-development of the past year and celebrate our spiritual harvest as the fruits of our labors are revealed. However, as the days grow shorter and the weather cooler, we also draw within to begin a time of reflection and introspection. We celebrate the things enhancing our spiritual development and also have an opportunity to look at those things that are no longer useful in our new state of consciousness. The Autumn Equinox begins a time of cleansing and purification during which to prepare for the new seed of consciousness, which will again be conceived at the Winter Solstice.

As in the spring, the Sun and Earth are aligned and in balance at this time. In the fall, we align and balance aspects of ourselves to begin a period of inner preparation and rest, as nature does the same. We must also balance the time devoted to the outer world and our inner spiritual life.

# SACRED CEREMONY: SPIRITUAL FOOD

Setting aside a special time to acknowledge Spirit in your life through sacred ceremony is a way to strengthen your connection with your own divine essence. It provides an opportunity to tap into the Great Mystery of creation and bring Heaven down to Earth. At times when our mundane lives are keeping us bound to the limited view of our thinking minds and third-dimensional reality, sacred ritual can remind us of our true spiritual beingness. The spiritual nourishment this can provide is reflected in the actual communion rituals of several religions.

Sacred ceremony can also be a time to gather with others in spiritual community. This not only provides group support for the participants, but also amplifies the expansive energy that can be created. The New and Full Moons, as well as solstice and equinox points, provide an excellent time for this type of sacred ritual, helping you attune to the rhythms of nature, as well.

## *Preparing Your Ritual*

To create a ritual for yourself, begin by preparing a space for this purpose. Use your meditation spot or another suitable quiet place and include any objects that are sacred or meaningful to you in the space. A candle, representative of the light and spiritual illumination, is always a wonderful addition. You may also want to acknowledge the four directions in some way by marking them with crystals, candles, or other meaningful objects. If you wish, this can also be done verbally as part of your ceremony.

Further prepare the area by purifying it with incense. Sage, frankincense, and sandalwood all work well for this purpose and are available at most metaphysical shops or bookstores. Each of these substances carry their own particular vibration.

**Sage** is a denser, more earthy substance that can stabilize the energy while providing purification. It clears away negative forces while creating a strengthening foundation for the ritual. In Native American traditions, individuals themselves are also smudged with sage smoke in preparation for sacred ceremony. The addition of cedar sprigs to the sage also brings in positive helping spirits.

**Frankincense,** which represents the element of fire, brings in a higher vibrational energy to your space. It will invoke very positive purifying energies which help you connect with a deep spirituality. It can provide energetic protection around your auric field while bringing in assistance from the higher spiritual realms.

**Sandalwood** is cleansing, produces a feeling of peace, and also brings in the presence of the masters from the spiritual realm.

Experiment for yourself with the various types of incense and notice what you experience. Use the one which appeals to you or combine the ones that you like.

As you begin your ritual, take a few moments to quiet your mind and align yourself with the intention of your ceremony. Visualize yourself surrounded in light and, if you wish, call on the presence of your evolutionary soul guide, your Higher Self, or any of your spirit helpers to assist you. You may want to include a short meditation on the significance of the Earth or Moon cycle that you are celebrating, as well as any affirmation, prayer, song, or reading that you would like.

The following meditation can also be used at any of these times to embody more of your own spirit essence and to increase your connection with the Earth and the influx of Cosmic energies. As with other processes in this book, you may want to tape-record this meditation for yourself, or have a participant read it aloud if you are gathered as a group for your ritual.

## A Guided Meditation: Light Embodiment Process

Sit comfortably. Adjusting your body so that your spine is straight and your head and neck are relaxed. This will allow energy to flow smoothly.

As you sit quietly, take a few full breaths, letting your breath touch deeply into the bottom of your belly. Feel yourself sink down inside with each exhalation as waves of deep relaxation gently flow through every part of you.

Your heart and soul have been waiting to take you into this deeper place inside your own being, to let your true essence Self emerge. See, sense, or experience, in some way, a soft, healing light all around you. Put forth an intention that everything you experience will be for your highest good, and that you will open to receive just the right amount of light and energy for you at this time.

Breathe fully and consciously, now, into each of your seven main chakra centers, one at a time, from the root chakra up to your crown. Then, bring your consciousness to a radiant orb located above your head which looks and feels like a large, shimmering matrix of energy and light. Reach up to experience this, your own divine essence and highest spiritual consciousness. Feel the expansive unconditional love, acceptance, and peace of your spiritual being. As part of this, connect with the positive attributes of your archetypal soul essence and those soul qualities which you are seeking to give expression to at this time.

When you are ready, feel this matrix of energy and light flow down through your entire energy system and auric bodies, permeating your mind, emotions, and physical form. Let the streams of light and love enter through your crown and infuse your entire body via the chakra centers all along your spine. Feel it as liquid light pouring into the container of your body vessel. It will be just the right amount for you at this time. Drink this energy in as it infuses every part of your body, permeating even the DNA at the very core of your cells.

Breathe in this radiant spirit light fully and feel the expansion as this patterned language of light and love speaks to your whole being. Receive this love in as it bathes and infuses every part of you, easily allowing you to release the mask of the false self that you sometimes present to the world, letting this false image of yourself just gently and lovingly fall away, so that your true essence Self can emerge. Feel the loving qualities of your true spirit essence deepening within you as every cell in your body welcomes in this nourishing energy.

As this light energy of your own spiritual essence continues to move down along your spine, feel it flow through your root chakra, into your legs and feet, and then extend into the earth. Just like the trees, with roots that extend deep into the ground, you also are rooted in Earth through your Earth chakra.

Bring your consciousness, now, to this place about twelve inches below your feet, and feel your connection to the planetary body through this chakra vortex. Allow the energy and light of your spirit essence to flow down through your legs and feet and continue into the ground through your Earth chakra. Then, let this light energy curl around to hook into the Earth like a tree root, anchoring you and grounding you here.

Let yourself be touched deeply and completely by the Earth Mother's gentle strength as she supports and nourishes your spirit. Feel the solidity of deep power that moves within her and within you, also, through your Earth chakra.

Let your consciousness continue to travel down through the layers of the Earth beneath you. See, sense, or imagine the layers of dirt, minerals, crystals, and molten rock as you descend through the layers of the Earth's mantle. When you reach the magnetic iron core, send your love into the heart of the planet and feel the waves of light and love that are returned to you.

Gradually bring your consciousness back to your heart chakra, the heart center of your own earth body. Take a moment to feel the balance of Spirit and Earth forces within you, feeling very whole and centered in your own being. Notice how you feel in your body at this point. You may want to stop here to allow integration of what you have already experienced. Don't push yourself if you are feeling uncomfortable in any way. An agitated feeling or headache, for example, may be signs that your body has had enough for now. Continue if you wish to do further work for the Earth.

As you're ready, reach up once again to the radiant orb of light just above your head. Now, imagine that a doorway opens through this orb of light that allows you to expand out into space, beyond our Sun and the various planets, to the vortex of energy at the core of the Milky Way. Feel the streams of light and love flowing forth out of this galactic heart; and then, follow them back into our solar system through the focal point of our Sun.

Allow yourself to gently float through space with these radiant emanations to a place just above the Earth. Feel these wave-like pulsations of love and light bathe the entire planetary body. Take a moment to enjoy this beautiful blue-green jewel in space as you bring your consciousness to a shimmering grid-like web of light that surrounds the planet, Mother Earth's raiment of light.

Let yourself be guided to a particular place on the Earth, along this grid, to act as a connecting point, and allow your consciousness to be added to those of the other workers of light all along this grid. Feel this collective light and energy channeled into the planet. Put forth an intention that these energies will be used by the Earth in a way that is most needed for the planet at this time. Ask that divine order be restored in all ways on Earth and give thanks to Spirit and our Mother Gaia for what you have received.

As you complete your process, begin to bring yourself back to external awareness and when you are ready, open your eyes. Be gentle with yourself afterwards, letting the experience settle within you.

Recording your process in your journal will also help you ground and integrate your time within. Be sure to note the feelings or bodily sensations that you experienced and any shifts or insights which you may have had. Make sure that you don't overdo it with this meditation, as it can powerfully accelerate your process. Pay attention to how you feel over the next few days. Old mental patterns or emotional issues may surface to be healed in order to bring you into alignment with this higher frequency of energy. You may also need more physical exercise or rest to allow the energy to move through your physical body.

In addition, make sure that you drink plenty of pure water to assist your body in clearing away any energy that needs to be released. It is important that the water you use for this purpose be filtered, bottled, or fresh from a clean source, since water holds the vibration and energy of the place from which it comes. If you are drinking city tap water that has been through the water treatment system, then it is contaminated with this vibration and that frequency is carried into your body, along with any actual chemicals that have been added to the water for purification purposes. At any time, but especially when you are going through any type of cleansing or detoxification process, it is preferable to drink water from a pure source.

The light embodiment guided meditation can help you more fully embody your own spirit essence and open you energetically to receive the light and love from a Cosmic source seeking to inform and transform each one of us. As you continue to participate in this transformation involving both individual and planetary processes of initiation, the vibratory rate of your physical body can increase to take on the "body of light" of the etheric vehicle. As the physical cells of your body continue to expand into a higher frequency with this process, it enhances your ability to experience a more expansive state of consciousness and fully align with the intentions of your essence Self. Ultimately, the vibration of the physical vehicle accelerates so that it is radiantly transfigured in light as one ascends into other dimensions of being.

With our light bodies fully activated, we will then have the choice to either leave the body at the transition known as death, or to take it with us in the form of light. This is exactly what the great ascended masters have done and as Jesus has said, "All these things and greater shall you do." This ultimate embodiment of spirit is what can await us, then, in our evolutionary process of spiritual awakening.

## Notes

1. Stanislav Grof, M.D. and Christina Grof, editors, *Spiritual Emergency* (New York: Jeremy P. Tarcher/Putnam, 1989); and Lee Sanella, M.D. *The Kundalini Experience: Psychosis or Transcendence?* (Lower Lake, CA: Integral Publishing, 1987).

2. Itzhak Bentov, *Stalking the Wild Pendulum: On the Mechanics of Consciousness* (Rochester, VT: Destiny Books, 1988).

3. Christina Grof and Stanislav Grof, M.D., *The Stormy Search For The Self: A Guide To Personal Growth Through Transformational Crisis* (New York: Jeremy P. Tarcher/Putnam, 1990). Stanislav Grof, M.D. and Christina Grof, editors, *Spiritual Emergency* (New York: Jeremy P. Tarcher/Putnam, 1989).

4. This refers to changes, mentioned by Jose Arguelles in *The Mayan Factor*, which opened the planetary body of Earth to Cosmic energies pouring into the planet since the Harmonic Convergence in August of 1987.

5. Barbara Hand Clow, *The Liquid Light of Sex: Understanding Your Key Life Passages* (Santa Fe, NM: Bear and Company, 1991); and Katrina Raphaell, *The Crystalline Transmission: A Synthesis of Light* (Santa Fe, NM: Aurora Press, 1990).

6. Barbara Ann Brennan, *Light Emerging* (New York: Bantam Books, 1993).

7. Ibid.

8. Brugh Joy, *Joy's Way: A Map for the Transformational Journey: An Introduction to the Potentials for Healing With Body Energies* (New York: Jeremy P. Tarcher/Putnam, 1979), p. 194.

9. John Major Jenkins, *Maya Cosmogenesis 2012: The True Meaning of the Maya Calendar End-Date* (Santa Fe, NM: Bear and Company, 1998).

10. Jose Arguelles, *The Mayan Factor* (Santa Fe, NM: Bear and Company, 1987).

# APPENDIX

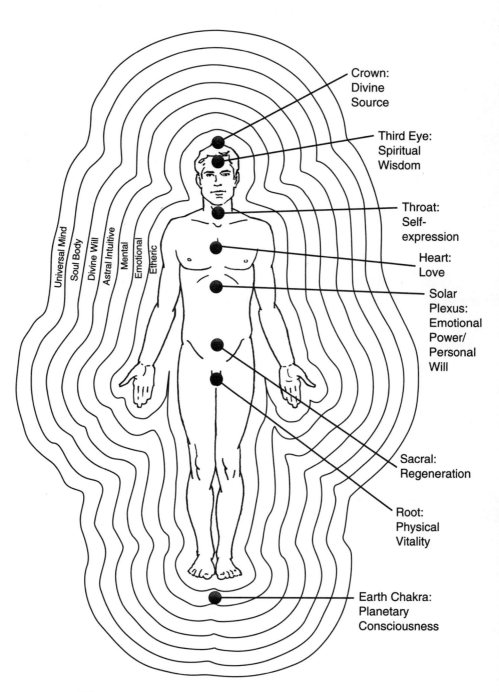

Crown:
Divine
Source

Third Eye:
Spiritual
Wisdom

Throat:
Self-
expression

Heart:
Love

Solar
Plexus:
Emotional
Power/
Personal
Will

Sacral:
Regeneration

Root:
Physical
Vitality

Earth Chakra:
Planetary
Consciousness

Universal Mind
Soul Body
Divine Will
Astral Intuitive
Mental
Emotional
Etheric

*The Energy System: The Energy Planes and Chakras*

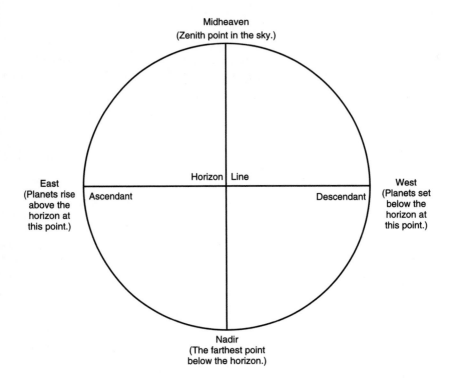

## *The Zodiac Points of Significant Planetary Influence*

Because, in the Northern Hemisphere, the Sun is due south at the peak of its daily arc, the top part of a natal chart is south, rather than north. To adjust for this, charts are drawn up reversed with east on the left and west on the right. Southern Hemisphere charts look the same but use different calculations.

# GLOSSARY

**Amplification/Magnification:** A Gestalt method used in a state of attentive awareness to exaggerate a particular experience so that its meaning can emerge. Amplification allows the energy connected with a body-mind dynamic to be concentrated and magnified so that the experience is fuller and more obvious. The issues and feelings relating to it can then be explored.

**Archetypes:** The universal principles of life or patterns of consciousness that act as a common blueprint for the human experience. These fundamental guiding themes of life function as the core focus around which emotionally charged groups of ideas, memories, feelings, or experiences are formed in the psyche, and influence our psychological and spiritual development.

**Armor:** A pattern of fixed muscular tension and holding in the body developing from physical trauma, psychological states, and habitual styles of behavior.

**Ascended Masters:** Spiritual beings who have lived in a body on Earth, reached enlightenment and self-mastery, and then ascended into the spiritual realms of light either through the transition of death or full ascension of the body. Such beings are then available to provide guidance and spiritual assistance to those souls still residing on the Earth plane.

**Aspect:** In astrology, an aspect is an angular relationship between two or more planets. The nature of the connection between the two planets depends on the specific geometric angle which is formed, such as a 60 or 90-degree angle, and the particular energy which that aspect expresses. For example, a square is a 90-degree angle, which can involve discord or friction. An opposition is a 180-degree aspect, which represents a polarization and tension between two planets. A conjunction occurs when two planets are close together and operate as one fused energy.

**Aura/Auric bodies:** The electromagnetic field of energy surrounding the physical body that shows a person's physical, mental, emotional, and spiritual health through the degree of radiance and the colors that are emitted in the various layers. See also Energy bodies.

**Awareness:** Being totally present and fully conscious of your experience in each moment, perceiving how you feel mentally, emotionally, physically, and energetically. It involves a conscious feeling, sensing, and seeing, rather than a mental focusing. See also Presence.

**Body-Centered Therapy:** A therapeutic approach that seeks to heal the body-mind split by using the body as a doorway into other dimensions of the psyche. The body's innate wisdom and one's somatic experience are used to gather information and increase self-awareness by working with such things as breath, sensation, muscular patterns, and movement.

**Body-Mind:** The connection between the physical body and the conscious and subconscious elements of the psyche. This includes both personal subconscious forces and the deeper universal components of the mind, which all humans share, referred to as the collective unconscious.

**Boundaries:** The self-awareness of one's personal experience, thoughts, feelings, and desires as distinguished from those of others. Clear, yet flexible boundaries allow us to maintain a sense of our own energy while being able to interrelate with others in a harmonious way. We can screen out those things from the world that aren't beneficial to us and can still assimilate those things that are useful or needed. Vague or weak personal boundaries can lead to enmeshment with others, an unhealthy emotional merging, and an inability to discern our own feelings and needs in relationship. Rigid boundaries, on the other hand, can separate us from others in defensive and isolating ways.

**Chakras:** The chakras are dynamic energy centers located along the spine that distribute energy throughout the body. Their main function is to take in the primary energy from the universal field all around us and break it down to be used by the body. Each of the seven major chakras is related to a particular area of the body and is associated with and affects a major nerve plexus and endocrine gland, influencing our physiological and psychological well-being.

**Collective Unconscious:** The deeper universal structures of the collective psyche that all humanity shares. Archetypal images and other psychic material can emerge through dreams, meditation, or body-centered work from this vast recorded storehouse of information for all humanity.

**Complex:** An emotionally charged group of ideas, memories, feelings, or experiences that form in the psyche and constellate around a central archetypal theme or element such as Mother or Father.

**Dissociation:** The disconnection and separation from one's environment, body experience, or feelings as a protective defense mechanism, usually to avoid a painful situation or uncomfortable feelings. The pattern of splitting off in this way is often learned early in life because of some trauma and continues into adulthood as a way to manage the unresolved feelings that resulted.

**Ego Self:** The part of the psyche that provides the basic framework of self-identity and consciousness by which we experience and interact with the world. Although a strong, positive sense of self is a necessary element for a healthy psyche, the false ideas of the ego personality and thinking mind must be transformed in order for our lives to be directed by our true divine nature.

**EM Fields:** The electromagnetic fields of energy that radiate into the environment from electrical sources such as television, computers, and microwaves. The term ELF (Extremely Low Frequency) is also used to refer to the radiation emitted by such things as the electrical wiring in our homes and the high-tension power lines used for the transmission of electricity.

**Embodiment:** The process of realizing one's spiritual essence, the divine Self within, and fully manifesting it in physical form. Embodiment involves allowing one's true spirit nature to be fused with and expressed through physical matter.

**Energy Bodies, Fields, or Planes:** The concentric interpenetrating planes of energy that surround the physical body, with each successive layer being less dense and of an increasingly higher vibrational frequency. Along with the chakras, the energy bodies (etheric, emotional, mental, astral-intuitive, divine will, soul, and universal mind), form the human energy system.

**False Persona:** The false concept of ourselves based on erroneous information as the ego develops from interaction with the external world. This mask, as it is sometimes called, can dominate the soul personality, rather than allowing the true expression of the essence Self to guide one's life.

**Fragmentation:** The process by which a person's identity and cohesive sense of wholeness is damaged, usually through an emotional injury or physical trauma. Through such painful experiences in this lifetime or past lives, certain parts of us become unacceptable and actually split off in an energetic sense. Healing and wholeness can be restored by reclaiming these denied parts of ourselves and returning this lost energy to us once again. In extreme cases, fragmentation can manifest in a lack of personal identity and regression to an undifferentiated state or result in a severe splitting of the ego personality in what is known as Multiple Personality Disorder.

**Frequency:** The rate at which something such as an electromagnetic wave or sound wave vibrates. This oscillation is measured in cycles per second or hertz (hz). If a violin string is plucked and vibrates back and forth 256 times per second, it will create a sound wave with a measured frequency of 256 hz.

**Galactic Core/Galactic Center:** The black hole vortex of energy which is the center of our galaxy; the central axis around which the entire galaxy rotates.

**Geomagnetic Field:** The magnetic field of the Earth.

**Grounded:** In terms of the body-mind, being grounded refers to the state of being fully and consciously present in one's physical body in the "here and now." In its most exalted form, grounding involves bringing the higher consciousness of one's divine being fully into matter in the present moment.

**Guide, Spirit Helper:** Guides are wise beings representing inner aspects of our Higher Self, or actual beings from the spiritual realms such as angels or other messengers of light, who bring direction, understanding, and guidance. Guides can be experienced as an inner knowing, sensed as a presence, heard as an inner voice, or take form through a vision, meditation, or dream.

**Higher Self:** The spiritual aspect of your being as opposed to the ego persona or false self; the center of your highest spiritual consciousness, wisdom, creativity, peace, joy, and love; the soul or the spark of the Divine Presence contained within it.

**Hologram/Holographic:** This refers to something that has all the components of the whole contained within each of its separate parts. It has its origins in holographic photography, which produces a three-dimensional image in space.

If you divide the photographic plate used to create a holographic image and focus a light beam to illuminate only a small portion of the remaining film, it will still produce the whole three-dimensional object in space. Each section of the hologram contains all the information which constitutes the whole image.

**Holomovement:** A term used by Dr. David Bohm to describe the basic nature of reality. It means that all things are part of whole unbroken flow of movement, with each part of this dynamic flux affecting and affected by the other and containing within it the nature of the whole.

**Homeopathy:** A system of medicine established by Samuel Hahnemann that uses minute doses of natural potentized substances, which in a healthy person produce the symptoms of the illness being treated. Homeopathy looks at health in relationship to the whole person and examines the physical, mental, emotional, spiritual, and environmental factors of the patient.

**Horizon:** The apparent meeting of the sky with the earth or sea; the great circle of the celestial sphere whose plane cuts the Earth midway between the Zenith and Nadir. In astrology, the horizon is the horizontal axis line in a birth chart that connects the Ascendant, where planets rise and the Descendant, where they set. Specific natal planets located at the Ascendant and Descendant horizon points have been shown by Gauquelin to have a relationship to certain essential qualities and characteristics found in particular individuals.

**Illumination:** An initiation in which the physical body is infused with light emanating from the soul body and the Cosmic/Solar force. As this radiant energy descends, the faculties are imbued with light and all the chakras and auric bodies are vivified. The individual's etheric light body is activated as this light from above is sealed in the physical body.

**Individuation:** The process by which one becomes a psychologically separate and autonomous individual, thereby giving expression to the essential Self.

**Initiation:** 1. A step on the path of spiritual growth in which you are tested or strengthened in some way in developing a greater level of consciousness. 2. A specific initiatory process or ritual in which you receive higher vibrational energies, changing your energetic frequency and the consciousness with which you function.

**Karma:** In Hindu and Buddhist philosophy, karma is the doctrine of responsibility for one's actions in all incarnations which explains and justifies one's experiences in this present life. Many people misunderstand karma as a type of punishment and judgment when, in actuality, it is concerned with learning, gaining new soul experience, and evolving as a spiritual being.

**Kriyas:** The psychological and physical symptoms, sometimes dramatic, which manifest as a result of kundalini awakening.

**Kundalini:** The primordial life-giving substance, the vital creative force that we draw forth from the essence of the Earth as an integral part of our human energy system. This powerful life force energy lies coiled at the base of the spine in a more dormant state until it is aroused as part of spiritual awakening. It then begins to ascend up the spine, energizing and activating the chakra centers, more fully awakening them to inflowing Cosmic energies.

**Light Body:** This refers to the radiant body which is activated when the etheric vehicle and the physical cells of the body are permeated and illuminated by the Cosmic/Solar force and the light essence of one's own divine Self.

**Magnetosphere:** An upper level of the atmosphere extending to a height of about 40,000 miles that contains a band of ionized particles trapped by the Earth's magnetic field.

**Mantra:** A specific word or sound which is meditated on or repeated as a chant. The actual sounds or words of a mantra carry a certain vibrational frequency. By repeating the mantra, you can attune yourself to its particular energy or the state of consciousness associated with it.

**Mass Mind:** The collective consciousness of the planet as a whole or any specific area of it, such as a city, which contains the combined thought patterns of all who live there. The more densely populated an area is, the greater the influence of this local mind field. This is one reason why less populated or remote areas feel more peaceful than large cities.

**Midheaven:** In astrology, the highest point of the natal chart which is the approximate position of the Sun at noon. Specific natal planets located here have been shown by Gauquelin to have an important relationship to certain essential qualities and characteristics found in particular individuals. See also Zenith.

**Nadir:** The point of the celestial sphere located directly beneath the position of an observer on the local horizon and opposite the Zenith. The astrological Nadir, which is opposite the Midheaven, is where the Sun is found at about midnight. Planets located here at the time of birth can represent those shadow elements of which we are not as consciously aware. Along with the Ascendant and Descendant horizon points and the Midheaven, the Nadir is considered a significant position for natal planetary placement.

**OM:** In Hindu philosophy believed to be the primordial sound from which all creation originated. It is often chanted repeatedly in order to connect with this consciousness of the One.

**Presence/Present-Centered:** The state of consciousness characterized by being mindfully aware and attentive in the "here and now" moment; being free to observe one's experience and fully participate with the environment without the mental interference of projections and reactions based on the past. See also Awareness.

**Psychodrama:** A method used in certain forms of psychotherapy in which a person acts out, sometimes before a group, the dynamics of a particular problem or psychological issue.

**Psychosomic:** Refers to patterns expressed both psychologically and physiologically through the body.

**Quantum Field:** In quantum physics, the continuous medium present everywhere in space with the potential to manifest as particles or waves, as material substance or its surrounding field. Particles of matter exist where there is a local concentration of this quantum energy field.

**Resonant Amplification:** The principle by which any vibratory system responds with maximum amplitude (wave height) to the force of a frequency similar or nearly equal to its own. When one wave frequency is in resonance or like another, it can exert an effect on the vibratory rate of the other frequency, which increases its amplitude. This dynamic allows a singer to sound a note that can match the resonant frequency of a glass, thereby affecting its vibratory rate to the point that it can shatter.

**Shadow:** The denied, distorted, unexpressed, or rejected parts of the self that may be perceived as undesirable elements which need to be suppressed or avoided.

**Shamanic:** Relating to the practices used by shamans, the native healers/priests found in many indigenous cultures, who may enter altered states or travel into other dimensional realms in order to deal with the spiritual aspect of an illness.

**Somatic:** Of or pertaining to the physical body. Somatic awareness involves sensing, feeling, and experiencing through the body, an awareness of the body's structure, processes, and energy.

**Soul:** The immortal part of us that records experiences and learning as it evolves through each lifetime. The soul acts as a sheath or protection for the divine God Self and contains the memory of all our experience. It is the intelligence of the soul that keeps the body functioning.

**Subpersonalities:** The semi-autonomous parts of the personality that are generally expressions of complexes that develop as distortions of an essential archetypal energy. Some common subpersonalities are the Critic, Child, Skeptic, Perfectionist, Caretaker, and Controller.

**Sufi Dancing:** A type of ritual dancing involving a spinning motion practiced by the whirling Dervishes, followers of Moslem mysticism, in order to bring about ecstatic states.

**Symbol:** An object, image, physical phenomenon, or event representative of something else; an outwardly visible sign of an inner unseen reality that conveys a certain message to our conscious mind from deeper subconscious levels.

**Synchronicity:** The meaningful connection between two or more events that have no apparent causal relation. These events are linked by a similar meaning or archetypal theme being expressed, acting as significant guiding messages in our process of healing and growth.

**T'ai Chi:** An ancient Chinese movement meditation practice consisting of continuous postures executed through the rhythm of relaxed, flowing movement and slow, deep breathing.

**Transpersonal:** Therapeutic approaches acknowledging the spiritual dimension and recognizing the potential for experiencing states of consciousness that extend beyond the usual limits of ego and personality.

**Universal Energy Field:** The ocean of energy that connects all things and of which all matter is composed. This universal energy field surrounds the physical vehicle in the form of energy bodies or planes. See also Quantum field.

**(Earth) Vortex:** Vortexes are locations along the electromagnetic grid of the Earth where the naturally flowing electric currents are particularly concentrated or powerful. These places act as doorways into other dimensions of consciousness and are often where ancient temples or sacred sites are located. The energy at such sacred power places in nature can help you align with a greater spiritual consciousness.

**Witness State:** A technique of Buddhist meditation in which the flowing river of feelings, sensations, and thoughts are simply watched, noted, and let go of without judgment. This type of unattached reference point, also known as the objective observer, allows one to just experience what is, without mental or emotional reaction and interference.

**Zenith:** The point of the celestial sphere located directly overhead and opposite to the Nadir. See also Midheaven.

# BIBLIOGRAPHY

Arguelles, J. *The Mayan Factor.* Santa Fe, NM: Bear and Company, 1987.

Arroyo, S. *Astrology, Karma and Transformation: The Inner Dimensions of the Birth Chart* (2nd ed., Rev.) Sebastopol, CA: CRCS Publications, 1992.

Assagioli, R. *Psychosynthesis.* New York: Viking Penguin, 1971.

Bandler, R. and J. Grinder. *Frogs Into Princes.* Moab, UT: Real People Press, 1979.

Becker, R. O., M.D. *Cross Currents: The Perils of Electropollution, The Promise of Electromedicine.* New York: Jeremy P. Tarcher/Putnam, 1990.

Bentov, I. *Stalking the Wild Pendulum: On the Mechanics of Consciousness* (Rpt.) Rochester, VT: Destiny Books, 1988.

Bohm, D. *Wholeness and the Implicate Order.* New York: Routledge, 1980.

———. *The Undivided Universe.* New York: Routledge, 1995.

Bradshaw, J. *Homecoming: Reclaiming and Championing Your Inner Child.* New York: Bantam Books, 1990.

Brennan, Barbara. *Hands Of Light.* New York: Bantam Books, 1988.

———. *Light Emerging.* New York: Bantam Books, 1993.

Brooks, C. V. W. *Sensory Awareness: Rediscovery of Experiencing Through the Workshops and Classes of Charlotte Selver* (Rpt.) Great Neck, NY: Felix Morrow Publisher, 1986.

Burr, H. S. *The Fields Of Life: Our Links With the Universe.* New York: Ballentine, 1972.

Burt, K. *Archetypes Of The Zodiac.* St. Paul, MN: Llewellyn Publications, 1988.

Cameron, J. *The Artist's Way: A Spiritual Path To Higher Creativity.* New York: Jeremy P. Tarcher / Putnam, 1992.

Capacchione, L. *Recovery Of Your Inner Child.* New York: Simon and Schuster, Fireside, 1991.

Capra, F. *The Turning Point.* New York: Bantam Books, 1983.

———. *The Tao Of Physics: An Exploration of the Parallels Between Modern Physics and Eastern Mysticism* (3rd ed., Rev.) Boston: Shambhala Publications, 1991.

Chopra, D., M.D. *Quantum Healing: Exploring the Frontiers of Mind/Body Medicine.* New York: Bantam Books, 1989.

Clow, B. H. *Liquid Light of Sex: Understanding Your Key Life Passages.* Santa Fe: Bear and Company, 1991.

————. *Chiron: Rainbow Bridge Between the Inner and Outer Planets.* St. Paul, MN: Llewellyn Publications, 1987.

Coward, H. *Jung and Eastern Thought.* Albany, NY: State University of New York Press, 1985.

Dychtwald, K. *Body-Mind* (Rev. ed.) New York: Jeremy P. Tarcher/Putnam, 1986.

Edinger, E. F. *Ego and Archetype: Individuation and the Religious Function of the Psyche* (Rpt.) Boston: Shambhala Publications, 1992.

Epstein, G., M.D. *Healing Visualizations: Creating Health Through Imagery.* New York: Bantam Books, 1989.

Feldenkrais, M. *Awareness Through Movement* (Rpt.) San Francisco: Harper San Francisco, 1991.

Forrest, S. *The Inner Sky: The Dynamic New Astrology for Everyone* (Rpt.) San Diego: ACS Publications, 1989.

Gauquelin, M. *Neo-Astrology: A Copernican Revolution.* London: Arkana, 1991.

Gendlin, E. *Focusing.* New York: Bantam Books, 1981.

Goldman, J. *Healing Sounds: The Power of Harmonics* (2nd ed., Rev.) Rockport, MA: Element Books, Ltd., 1996.

Grinder, J. and R. Bandler. *Trance-Formations.* Moab, UT: Real People Press, 1981.

Grof, C. and S. Grof, M.D. *The Stormy Search For The Self: A Guide To Personal Growth Through Transformational Crisis.* New York: Jeremy P. Tarcher/Putnam, 1990.

Grof, S., M.D. *The Adventure of Self-Discovery: Dimensions of Consciousness and New Perspectives in Psychotherapy and Inner Exploration.* Albany, NY: State University of New York Press, 1988.

————. *Beyond the Brain: Birth, Death, and Transcendence in Psychotherapy.* Albany, NY: State University of New York Press, 1985.

————. *Realms of the Human Unconscious.* New York: Viking, 1975.

Grof, S., M.D. and C. Grof. (Ed.) *Spiritual Emergency.* New York: Jeremy P. Tarcher/Putnam,1989.

Gunther, B. *Energy, Ecstasy, and Your Seven Vital Chakras.* North Hollywood, CA: Newcastle Publishing, Co., 1978.

Hendricks, G., Ph.D. and K. Hendricks, Ph.D. *At the Speed of Life: A New Approach to Personal Change Through Body-Centered Therapy.* New York: Bantam Books, 1994.

Hewitt, William W. *Astrology For Beginners: An Easy Guide to Understanding and Interpreting Your Chart.* St. Paul, MN: Llewellyn, 1997.

Hill, Ann. (Ed.) *A Visual Encyclopedia of Unconventional Medicine.* New York: Crown Publishers, Inc., 1979.

Huffines, LaUna. *Healing Yourself With Light: How to Connect With the Angelic Healers.* Tiburon, CA: H J Kramer, Inc., 1995.

Ingerman, S. *Soul Retrieval: Mending the Fragmented Self.* San Francisco, CA: Harper San Francisco, 1991.

Janov, A. *Imprints: The Lifelong Effects of the Birth Experience.* New York: Coward-McCann, Inc., 1983.

Jenkins, John Major. *Maya Cosmogenesis 2012: The True Meaning of the Maya Calendar End-Date.* Santa Fe: Bear and Company, 1998.

Johnson, R. A. *Inner Work: Using Dreams and Active Imagination For Personal Growth.* San Francisco, CA: Harper San Francisco, 1986.

Joy, B., M.D. *Joy's Way: A Map for the Transformational Journey: An Introduction to the Potentials for Healing With Body Energies.* New York: Jeremy P. Tarcher/Putnam, 1979.

Jung, C. G. *Memories, Dreams, Reflections.* New York: Random House, Inc., 1961.

———. *Synchronicity: An Acausal Connecting Principle.* (Princeton/Bollingen paperback ed.) Princeton, NJ: Princeton University Press, 1973.

Jung, C. G., M. L. Von Franz, J. L. Henderson, J. Jacobi, and A. Jaffe. *Man and His Symbols.* New York: Dell Publishing, 1964.

Kapit, W. and L. M. Elson. *The Anatomy Coloring Book.* (2nd ed., Rev.) New York: Harper Collins, 1993.

Keepin, W., Ph.D. "Astrology and the New Physics: Integrating Sacred and Secular Sciences." *The Mountain Astrologer,* August/September, 1995.

Keleman, S. *Your Body Speaks Its Mind.* Berkeley, CA: Center Press, 1981.

_____. *Somatic Reality: Bodily Experience and Emotional Truth.* Berkeley, CA: Center Press, 1982.

Kurtz, R. *Body-Centered Psychotherapy: The Hakomi Method.* Mendocino, CA: LifeRhythm, 1990.

Kurtz, R. and H. Prestera. *The Body Reveals: How to Read Your Own Body.* San Francisco: Harper San Francisco, 1984.

Larson, David E., M.D. *Mayo Clinic Family Health Book.* New York: William Morrow Co., 1990.

Leadbeater, C. W. *The Chakras* (7th Quest Book Rpt.) Wheaton, IL: The Theosophical Publishing House, 1994.

Lowen, A. *Bioenergetics.* New York: Penguin Books, 1975.

MacIvor, V. and S. LaForest. *Vibrations: Healing Through Color, Homeopathy, and Radionics.* York Beach, ME: Samuel Weiser, 1979.

Mindell, A. *Working With the Dreaming Body.* New York: Viking Penguin, 1989.

———. *Dreambody: The Body's Role In Revealing the Self* (Rpt.). Portland, OR: Lao Tse Press, 1997.

Mindell, A. and A. Mindell. *Riding the Horse Backwards: Process Work in Theory and Practice.* New York: Penguin Books, 1992.

Missildine, W. H. *Your Inner Child of the Past* (Rpt.). New York: Simon and Schuster, 1991.

Orr, L. *The Healing Power of Birth and Rebirth.* Stanton, CA: Inspiration University, 1994.

Orr, L. and S. Ray. *Rebirthing in the New Age* (Rev. ed.). Berkeley, CA: Celestial Arts, 1983.

Pelletier, K. R. *Mind As Healer, Mind As Slayer: A Holistic Approach to Preventing Stress Disorders.* New York: Dell Publishing Co., 1977.

Perls, F., M.D., Ph.D. *The Gestalt Approach and Eye Witness to Therapy.* Palo Alto, CA: Science and Behavior Books, Inc., 1973.

Perls, F. S., M.D., Ph.D., R. F. Hefferline, Ph.D., and P. Goodman, Ph.D. *Gestalt Therapy: Excitement and Growth in the Human Personality* (Rev. ed.). Highland, NY: Gestalt Journal Press, 1994.

Pert, C. B., Ph.D. *Molecules of Emotion: Why You Feel The Way You Feel.* New York: Scribner, 1997.

Polster, E. and M. Polster. *Gestalt Therapy Integrated: Contours of Theory and Practice.* New York: Random House, Inc., 1982.

Raphaell, K. *The Crystalline Transmission: A Synthesis of Light.* Santa Fe: Aurora Press, 1990.

Reich, W. *Character Analysis* (Rev. ed.). New York: Farrar, Straus, and Giroux, Inc., 1980.

Rogers, C. R. *On Becoming A Person.* Boston, MA: Houghton Mifflin Co., 1961.

Rolf, I. P. *Rolfing: The Integration of Human Structures* (2nd ed.). Santa Monica, CA: Dennis-Landman Publishers, 1977.

Rosenberg, J. L., M. Rand, and D. Asay. *Body, Self, and Soul: Sustaining Integration.* Atlanta: Humanics, Ltd., 1985.

Sannella, L., M.D. *The Kundalini Experience: Psychosis or Transcendence?* (Rev. ed.) Lower Lake, CA: Integral Publishing, 1987.

Scheffer, M. *Bach Flower Therapy in Theory and Practice.* Rochester, VT: Healing Arts Press, 1988.

Schwarz, J. *Voluntary Controls.* New York: NAL/Dutton, 1978.

———. *Human Energy Systems.* New York: NAL/Dutton, 1979.

Seymour, Percy. *The Scientific Basis of Astrology: Tuning to the Music of the Planets.* New York: St. Martin's Press, 1992.

Sheldrake, R. A. *New Science of Life: The Hypothesis of Morphic Resonance* (Rpt.). Rochester, VT: Park Street Press, 1995.

Stapleton, R. C. *The Experience of Inner Healing.* New York: Bantam Books, 1979.

Stone, H. and S. Winkelman. *Embracing Ourselves: The Voice Dialogue Manual* (Rpt.). Novato, CA: Nataraj Publishing, 1993.

Thibodeau, G. A., Ph.D. and K. T. Patton, Ph.D. *The Human Body in Health and Disease* (2nd ed.). St. Louis: Mosby-Year Book, Inc., 1997.

Ulman, D. (Ed.) *Discovering Homeopathy: Your Introduction to the Science and Art of Homeopathic Medicine* (2nd ed., Rev.). Berkeley, CA: North Atlantic Books, 1991.

Vaughan, F., Ph.D. *The Inward Arc: Healing in Psychotherapy and Spirituality* (2nd ed.). Nevada City, CA: Blue Dolphin Publishing, Inc., 1995.

Vithoulkas, G. *The Science of Homeopathy.* New York: Grove/Atlantic, 1980.

Walker, B. G. *The Woman's Encyclopedia of Myths and Secrets.* San Francisco: Harper San Francisco, 1983.

Walsh, R., M.D., Ph.D. and F. Vaughan, Ph.D. (Ed.) *Paths Beyond Ego: The Transpersonal Vision.* New York: Jeremy P. Tarcher/Putnam, 1993.

Weiner, M. and K. Goss. *The Complete Book of Homeopathy* (Rpt.). Garden City Park, NY: Avery Publishing Group, Inc., 1989.

White, J. (Ed.) *Kundalini: Evolution and Enlightenment* (Rev. ed.). New York: Paragon House Publishers, 1990.

Whitfield, C. *Healing the Child Within: Discovery and Recovery For Adult Children of Dysfunctional Families.* Deerfield Beach, FL: Health Communications, 1987.

Whitmont, E. C. *Psyche and Substance: Essays on Homeopathy in Light of Jungian Psychology.* Berkeley, CA: North Atlantic Books, 1980.

Williams, S. K. *The Jungian-Senoi Dreamwork Manual* (Rev. ed.). Berkeley, CA: Journey Press, 1985.

Wolf, F. A. *The Body Quantum: The New Physics of Body, Mind, and Health.* New York: MacMillan Publishing Co., 1986.

————. *The Spiritual Universe: How Quantum Physics Proves the Existence of the Soul.* New York: Simon and Schuster, 1996.

Woodrofe, Sir J. (pseudonym Arthur Avalon). *The Serpent Power: The Secrets of Tantric and Shaktic Yoga.* New York: Dover Publications, 1974.

Woolger, R. J. *Other Lives, Other Selves: A Jungian Psychotherapist Discovers Past Lives.* New York: Bantam Books, 1988.

Wright, M. S. *MAP: The Co-Creative White Brotherhood Medical Assistance Program* (2nd. ed.). Warrenton, VA: Perelandra, Ltd., 1994.

# INDEX

# ☽ REACH FOR THE MOON

*Llewellyn publishes hundreds of books on your favorite subjects!
To get these exciting books, including the ones on the following pages,
check your local bookstore or order them directly from Llewellyn.*

## Order by Phone
- Call toll-free within the U.S. and Canada, 1-800-THE MOON
- In Minnesota, call (651) 291-1970
- We accept VISA, MasterCard, and American Express

## Order by Mail
- Send the full price of your order (MN residents add 7% sales tax) in U.S. funds, plus postage & handling to:

**Llewellyn Worldwide
P.O. Box 64383, Dept. K819-2
St. Paul, MN 55164–0383, U.S.A.**

## Postage & Handling
(For the U.S., Canada, and Mexico)
- $4.00 for orders $15.00 and under
- $5.00 for orders over $15.00
- No charge for orders over $100.00

We ship UPS in the continental United States. We ship standard mail to P. O. boxes. Orders shipped to Alaska, Hawaii, the Virgin Islands, and Puerto Rico are sent first-class mail. Orders shipped to Canada and Mexico are sent surface mail.

**International orders:** Airmail—add freight equal to price of each book to the total price of order, plus $5.00 for each non-book item (audio tapes, etc.).

**Surface mail**—Add $1.00 per item.

*Allow 2 weeks for delivery on all orders.
Postage and handling rates subject to change.*

## Discounts
We offer a 20% discount to group leaders or agents. You must order a minimum of 5 copies of the same book to get our special quantity price.

### Free Catalog
Get a free copy of our color catalog, *New Worlds of Mind and Spirit*. Subscribe for just $10.00 in the United States and Canada ($30.00 overseas, airmail). Many bookstores carry *New Worlds*—ask for it!

**Visit our website at www.llewellyn.com for more information.**

# Energy Focused Meditation
## *Body, Mind, Spirit*

## GENEVIEVE LEWIS PAULSON

Formerly titled *Meditation and Human Growth*.

Meditation has many purposes: healing, past life awareness, balance, mental clarity, and relaxation. It is a way of opening into areas that are beyond your normal thinking patterns. In fact, what we now call "altered states" and "peak experiences"—tremendous experiences of transcendental states—can become normal occurrences when you know how to contact the higher energy vibrations.

Most people think that peak experiences happen, at best, only a few times in life. Through meditation, however, it is possible to develop your higher awareness so you can bring more peak happenings about by concentrated effort. *Energy Focused Meditation* is full of techniques for those who wish to claim those higher vibrations and expanded awareness for their lives today.

**1-56718-512-6, 6 x 9, 224 pp., 17 illus.**                    **$12.95**